ON YOUR OWN IN
EL SALVADOR

ON YOUR OWN IN
EL SALVADOR

by Jeff Brauer, Julian Smith
and Veronica Wiles

with Tim Freilich

illustrated by
Jennifer Sorensen
and
Lorena Aguilar

ON YOUR OWN
PUBLICATIONS

On Your Own in El Salvador
Copyright © 1995 by On Your Own Publications, Ltd.
All rights reserved under International and Pan-American Copyright Conventions.
No maps, illustrations or other portions of this book may be reproduced in any
form without written permission from the publisher.

Published by
> On Your Own Publications
> Head Office: PO Box 5411, Charlottesville, VA 22905, USA

Printed by
> SNP Printing Pte Ltd

Photographs
> Front cover: Sulema Antonia Soriano, San Juan Opico (Jeff Brauer)
> All others by the authors.

Distributed to the book trade by
> National Book Network

First Published in November 1995

ISBN: 0-9643789-0-6

First edition
10 9 8 7 6 5 4 3 2 1

With six months of intensive language study under his belt, **Jeff Brauer** left Taiwan for the Chinese mainland and spent the next two years exploring Asia. Along the way he wrote articles for some newspapers, observed the crackdown on the 1989 Chinese democracy movement and quietly slipped into the Central Asian states of the former USSR. With these adventures behind him, Jeff returned to law school in the US at the University of Virginia, founded OYO and began planning out new adventures. Without OYO or law school on his mind, Jeff finds peace in a 16" pizza and a big bowl of salad.

Julian Smith has published numerous accounts of his adventures around the world, from freezing atop Kilimanjaro to jumping out of a plane back home in the United States. In between, he has somehow found time to enjoy (and write about) his experiences traveling in the Brazilian Amazon, fleeing from pygmies in Uganda and studying the cloud forests of Costa Rica. When he's not on the road or in the office, Julian enjoys a good book, snowboarding and all the warm smells of home.

Veronica Wiles is the bubbling product of a Peace Corps dad and an Ecuadorian mom. She spent most of her childhood in Bolivia, where she learned new languages, met a continent of friends and had an all-around good time. Veronica has travelled from one end of South America to the other and has explored most of Eastern Europe and the Middle East, picking up even more friends along the way. Back in the US, Veronica studies law at the American University in Washington, DC. When Veronica has time to herself, she bikes with her dad, daydreams about roads in the French Alps, talks with her mom and hangs out with her brothers, Benjita and Tewee.

**Special thanks to
our sponsor:**

El Salvador, like much of Latin America, is in the middle of an historic period of transition. Prices will go up, restaurants and hotels will close and others will open. Bus schedules, government regulations and street names will change.

When you discover something newer, better, worse or just plain different from what we have reported, please write us and tell us about it. Your letters will be used to help us update the next edition of *On Your Own in El Salvador*.

We read every letter we receive, and especially appreciate those with practical information, travel tips, opinions and entertaining stories. The best correspondence will earn a free copy of one of our books. Drop us a line at PO Box 5411, Charlottesville, VA, 22905, or email us at jjb9e@uva.pcmail.virginia.edu.

Also, we always welcome inquiries from young, experienced writers interested in helping to compile a book to another destination. It's hard work, but we'd love to hear from you.

Muchas Gracias

Sergio Acevedos, Carlos Alfaro (TACA), Geofredo Amaya, Guadalupe Ayala (Hotel El Salvador), Miriam Bass (National Book Network), Josef Beery, Michael Blackmore, Herbert Braun, Rick Brockett (Crown Books), Silvia de Castro (ISTU), Patrick Chung (Singapore National Printers), Helen Guardado de Del Cid (El Salvador National Library), Heidi Cotler (Tower Books), Blanca de Cruz (ISTU), Mary Anne Deany (Crown Books), Ingrid Escapini, Robert Fader (Posman Books), Marcela Figueroa (AT&T), Peter Fusco (Barnes and Noble), Spencer Gayle (Walden Books), CLO office at the US embassy in El Salvador, especially Gail, Glenn Griffin (US State Department), Robert Hatch (Hatch's Inc.), Vanessa Interiano (American Airlines), Ion Itescu (Seven Hills), Ben Jones, Catesby Jones (Peace Frogs), Vilma de Kalil (Hotel Sahara), Michael and Faye Koons, Richard Koontz, Alicia de Landaverde (Tesoro Beach Hotel), Everette Larsen (Library of Congress), Christine Larson, Stephen Lim (Singapore National Printers), Rosa López, Roxana López, Silvia López, the López family (Clásicos Roxsil), Bryan Lovits, Jared Lowenstein, John Lyons, Ernesto Magaña (Banco Agricola), Stewart Malone, Map and Geography division of US Library of Congress, Malena Mayorga, Ricardo Mayorga, Román Mayorga, Fred and Pat Messick, Christopher Midura (US Embassy in El Salvador), Kaki Mitchell, Rod Mitchell (Smithbooks), Eduardo Mixco (Hotel El Salvador), Donna Oakley (The Surf Report), Jorge Palomo (Embassy of El Salvador), Kent Peterson (Brentano's), Jeanie Quinn (Encore Books), Sandra Patricia de Rojas (Hotel El Salvador), Joel Rosen, Rosemary and Pati (Hotel El Mandarin), Ben Sargant, Karla Simmons (Publishers Group West), Christie Stephenson, Denise Stephens, Stephen Strickland, Brigitte Suhr, Floyd Sykes (Grand Central Books), Ellen Traupman, Luisa Valle (ISTU), César Velasco, John Wheeler, James Yenckell (Washington Post), Thomas Zeisal (Hotel El Salvador).

Muchísimas Gracias

The Brauers (Robert, Linda, Leslie and Sandy), the Smiths (Jim and Jane) and the Wiles (Papi, Matilda, Tewee and Benjita). From Julian: *la brujita—para tu paciencia, apoyo y el amor sin fin.* From Jeff: to my *amorcita* for your encouragement, cooperation and patience.

Contents

Introduction 1

Background 3

Basics 49

San Salvador 91

To the West 127

Culture Boxes

Timelines

Charts and Graphs

Map Key

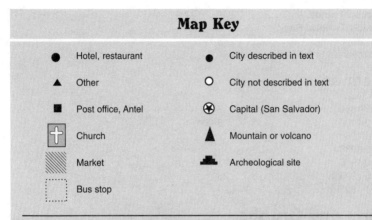

- ● Hotel, restaurant
- ▲ Other
- ■ Post office, Antel
- ✠ Church
- ▨ Market
- ⬚ Bus stop

- ● City described in text
- ○ City not described in text
- ✪ Capital (San Salvador)
- ▲ Mountain or volcano
- ⛰ Archeological site

Avenidas: Even numbers increase to east
Odd numbers increase to west

Calles: Even numbers increase to south
Odd numbers increase to north

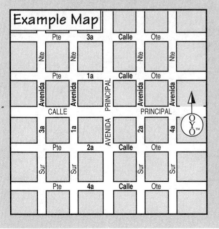

Map Abbreviations

Av   Avenida (avenue)
C   Calle (street)
Nte   Norte (north)
Sur   (south)
Ote   Oriente (east)
Pte   Poniente (west)
Col   Colonia (suburb)
Bo   Barrio (neighborhood)

Other General Notes

- ● Hotels and restaurants not reviewed in text are italicized on maps.
- ● City population figures refer to entire municipalities, so actual city populations may be smaller.
- ● All prices are in US dollars ($).
- ● Festival dates in parentheses are main day(s) of festival.

Introduction

It's ten o'clock on a rainy Monday morning and the museum is closed. Here we are in Perquín, Morazán department—the end of the road, even as far as El Salvador is concerned—and the only person at the guerrilla museum is a solemn young guard who's telling us, "No, sorry, you'll have to come back later...." The rutted road back to San Miguel suddenly looks a lot longer. With one last effort, we prevail upon the guard and beg him to help us find someone in town who can open up the museum. The guard is resolute—he takes his job seriously—but eventually starts to give in to our entreaties. Finally, he concedes and takes us to find the museum's creator. Soon Señor Vigil is walking up the path. He proceeds to give us a once-in-a-lifetime tour of his museum and the war, from the perspective of an ex-guerrilla.

The preconceptions most Westerners have about El Salvador are based on sound bites and snatches of newspaper articles: "There was a war there, right?" There was a war, but El Salvador has a larger story to tell. Like the guerrilla museum, El Salvador shows signs of its violent past at almost every turn, and it can be a frustrating place to travel. But, with a little effort, it's easy to uncover a different side of the country that makes the potholes, unpredictable bureaucracy and everything else worthwhile.

Traveling in El Salvador used to be a questionable proposition. Scattered gunfire, suspicious soldiers asking what you were doing in the country and an atmosphere of tension almost thick enough to bump into made traveling there unforgettable but nerve-racking. Today, things aren't perfect—crime is a problem, many bridges are still out and the potholes are just as large—but all in all life is more normal than it has been in over a decade.

The political situation has cooled down, and many things about El Salvador make it a fascinating and enjoyable place to explore. The food is tasty and cheap, and hotels are inexpensive. The tropical climate makes travel possible year-round, and you can get just about anywhere in the country in a few hours by bus. Whichever direction you choose, you're bound to run into an ancient volcano, a deserted beach, a beautiful mountain village or a serene colonial city. El Salvador has it all—you just have to know where to look.

That's where this book comes in. *On Your Own in El Salvador*, the first travel guide devoted exclusively to the country, has a twofold purpose. First, by providing extensive background information on the country, *On Your Own in El Salvador* enables you to fully experience El Salvador by helping you understand the country's history and culture. Our **Background** sections cover El Salvador from its pre-Columbian roots to the results of its latest elections and beyond, touching on topics such as its people, traditions, food and politics along the way. Historical information is provided on almost every city, and **culture boxes** throughout the book offer interesting glimpses into many aspects of Salvadoran life.

Second, *On Your Own in El Salvador* gives you practical travel information to let you devise your own itinerary to explore the country. Our **Basics** sections tell you all you need to know to prepare for your trip and to make it as enjoyable and hassle-free as possible once you're there. Our **detailed maps** show you where to go, and we provide specific travel information on each city and sight, from hotel prices and restaurant hours to hiking distances and bus schedules. After all, background without practical information is only a history book, and a Must-See list without a historical framework is just a travel brochure. *On Your Own in El Salvador* gives you both, and we know it's enough to make a trip to El Salvador easy and rewarding.

El Salvador's Best	El Salvador's Worst
(In no particular order)	
• **La Pema** (Santa Rosa de Lima)	• **Crazy bus drivers**
• **Beautiful children**	• **Starving stray dogs**
• **Playa El Espino** (Usulután department)	• **Potholes**
• **Bosque Montecristo** (Santa Ana department)	• ***Manteca*** (lard)
• **Sergio Acevedos' boots** (Santa Ana)	• **Pollution**
• **Delicious fruit**	• **Tinted car windows**
• **Mountain villages** (Apaneca, Juayúa)	• **Petty crime**
• **FMLN museum** (Perquín)	• **Mid-day drunks**
• **Volcano climbing**	• **Car accidents**

Background

El Salvador Yesterday

Pre-Columbian History

Nearly 40,000 years after the first nomadic tribes crossed into the Americas, the cultures of North and South America met in the lowlands of Central America and gave rise to the flourishing civilizations of Meso-America. The most advanced of these cultures were the Aztec and the Maya, both of which had reached their peak long before the "New" World was discovered by the "Old."

■ **The Maya.** Of the two, the Maya were the most successful and had the greatest impact on the early peoples of what would become El Salvador. The Mayan world spread from central Mexico to Nicaragua, flourished while Europe endured the Dark Ages and survived six times as long as the Roman Empire. El Salvador sits on the southern fringe of this vast territory but bears traces of its influence even today.

The **Formative Period** of the Maya (1800 BC to 100 AD) saw the gradual development of many large, competitive city-states that were tied to cultures from Mexico to Panama by extensive trade and communication networks. Most of the Mayan accomplishments, though, came during the **Classic Period** (200 to 900 AD). During that era, complex agricultural bureaucracies supported large populations and Mayan thinkers predicted eclipses, "discovered" the zero in mathematics and developed a highly effective system of hieroglyphics. Their incredibly accurate "Long Count" calendar tracked the days while Mayan architects constructed the huge ceremonial centers that still stand throughout Latin America.

Cuscatlán's "Children"

The Pipil spoke Nahuat, a dialect of the Nahuatl language spoken by the Aztecs of Mexico. When the Spanish arrived in El Salvador, the Aztecs that accompanied them recognized that the indigenous language was similar to their own, although the intonation was completely different. The Aztecs believed that the original Salvadorans spoke like children, and dubbed them the "Pipil," Nahuatl for "children."

Around the 10th century AD, the Mayan civilization mysteriously collapsed. Historians disagree on the cause, but many now believe that the urban population became too large to support and city resources were stretched to a breaking point.

Mayan culture enjoyed a brief revival during the **Post-Classic Period** (900 to 1400 AD). Commerce replaced religion as the dominant social force and an incredible nautical trade network coordinated as many as 4,000 boats on the sea at one time. Mayan cities throughout Central America shipped goods to one another this way.

By the 14th century, provincial revolt in many cities toppled the central social authority and the Mayan civilization declined again. Mayan city-states battled each other for the next two centuries, and by the time the Spanish arrived, many of the cities of this once-great civilization had been deserted.

By the 16th century, five main tribes had made their way into El Salvador. The three earliest arrivals, the Pok'omáme, the Chorti and the Lenca, were concentrated in the country's eastern regions. The Lenca were the largest group, settling in what would become Usulután, San Miguel and La Unión departments, and spreading as far north as Chalatenango. They spoke the Potón language, and left behind many of their words in the names of Salvadoran towns. A group known as the Ulúa arrived later and established a few smaller settlements in the same region.

■ **The Pipil.** El Salvador's largest indigenous group arrived from Mexico around 900 AD, just as the Maya reign was coming to an end, and quickly became the largest group in the region. Pipil populations were concentrated in the central and western areas of El Salvador, in the region bordered by the Río Lempa and the Río Paz.

More warlike but less scientifically advanced than their Mayan forebears, the Pipil lived within a society organized into city-states that resembled Mayan city-

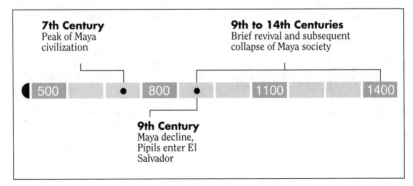

7th Century
Peak of Maya
civilization

9th to 14th Centuries
Brief revival and subsequent
collapse of Maya society

500   •   800   •   1100   1400

9th Century
Maya decline,
Pipils enter El
Salvador

In The Beginning

They say the earth was spinning in space, humming in the silence. Darkness penetrated the borders of everything. All was black; black earth and black sky. The cold stretched throughout the frigid caverns of the Nothing.

Emptiness.

Death blanketed the world. Nothing flew, nothing floated, nothing moved. No rivers, no valleys, no mountains. There was only the sea.

One day Teotl rubbed two *achiote* branches together and produced fire. With his hands he sprinkled fistfuls of sparks that scattered themselves throughout the emptiness, forming stars. The mystery was populated with points of light.

Suddenly in the highest reaches of the heavens appeared Teopantli, the Reformer who rules the universe. He emerged smiling, enveloped in a cascade of light.

Teotl threw a final handful of fire, which condensed down below into a ball of light: that was Tónal, the good father Sun.

But among the noise of the cocoons of life bursting open, of the worlds being engulfed in their orbits, of the explosions of light, Teopantli cried.

And his tear fell, remaining suspended. It turned white and began to spin. That was Metzti, the good mother Moon. And so she is sad. She projected her light onto the earth and it was no longer empty. The seas were pounding against the coasts. There were mountains and canyons. Wild beasts bellowed from the barren mountaintops. The moon's pale light shone upon two lions in combat. Lizards scurried among the ponds and vines. The rivers writhed like giant white serpents.

Life was singing.

—Pipil Creation Myth

states. Cuscatlán, which means "Land of Happiness," was the largest of these, and served as the Pipil capital, located where the city of Antiguo Cuscatlán is today. Sonsonate and Ahuachapán are two other modern Salvadoran towns that began as large Pipil city-states. The ruins of Tazumal, San Andrés and Joya de Cerén are all remnants of the Pipil civilization.

The Pipil operated within a corn-based agricultural economy and grew beans, tobacco, cocoa, pumpkins and gourds in communally-owned fields known as *calpullis*. All of these crops were cultivated without the use of the wheel, the plow or domesticated cattle. The Pipil were among the first Meso-American groups to abolish human sacrifice, and they limited use of the death penalty to punishment for murder, adultery and sacrilege.

Contact and Conquest

Ever since 1513, when Vasco de Balboa gazed west from Panama and became the first European to see the Pacific Ocean, the influence of the Spanish and the *conquistadors* has been ingrained in the history of the Americas. The Spanish approached Central America both from the south across the Panamanian isthmus, and from the north in Mexico, where Hernán Cortés conquered the Aztecs in 1521. In 1522, four ships piloted by Andrés Niño sailed into the Gulf of Fonseca. The sailors who disembarked on the island of Meanguera became the first Europeans to set foot in what would one day become El Salvador.

■ **De Alvarado's Campaign.** In 1523, Cortés sent Pedro de Alvarado, one of his principal commanders, to investigate rumors about civilizations in Central America that were said to be as rich as

> ## "A Good Four Fingers"
>
> In the first battle between the Spanish and indigenous warriors, a Pipil archer named Atonatl fired an arrow through Pedro de Alvarado's left knee. The wound left the Spanish commander limping on a leg that was shorter than his other by "a good four fingers," according to a letter he wrote to Cortés. Atonatl became a national hero.

the Aztec. De Alvarado left Mexico with 100 cavalry, 150 foot soldiers, several thousand indigenous allies and strict instructions to conquer the area peacefully, if at all possible.

After overrunning the Maya-Quiché of Guatemala and establishing a capital there, de Alvarado began his invasion of El Salvador. He crossed the Río Paz near La Hachadura in Ahuachapán department in 1524. By the time his army arrived, many towns had already been deserted, either because their inhabitants had died from European diseases or because they had scattered into the countryside in fear of de Alvarado's already well-established reputation for ruthlessness. When de Alvarado's troops finally faced off against Pipil warriors near Acajutla, the Pipil emerged victorious. Soon thereafter, a demoralized Pedro handed over leadership of his forces to his brother and left for Mexico, where he died fifteen years later and 40,000 *pesos* in debt.

In 1525, the Spanish moved into the Pipil capital of Cuscatlán, which had been left empty by its 10,000 inhabitants. Native tribes continued to resist the Spanish, though, and soon forced the evacuation of the newly-established villa of San Salvador.

Before long, the momentum shifted again. The Spanish exploited the lack of unity that plagued native forces in El Salvador, just as they had when they battled the Aztec in Mexico. Each small tribe confronted the Spanish independently, rather than joining together into a unified front. By 1540, the Spanish gained complete domination over what is today El Salvador and incorporated it into the Spanish Captaincy-General of Guatemala.

The Colonial State

Realizing that El Salvador's wealth lay in its incredibly fertile volcanic soil, the Spanish quickly set up an agricultural society in El Salvador that was typical of its colonies in the New World. Throughout the land, they constructed plantations to grow cotton, balsam, cacao and indigo.

Good fortune for the Spanish brought misery for the indigenous populations. The Spanish settlers enslaved natives to work on plantations and instituted brutal labor systems. One system, a Caribbean import known as the *encomienda,* gave a Spaniard the right to demand labor and tribute from indigenous people in exchange for "educating" them and converting them to Christianity.

Indigenous laborers succumbed by the thousands to overwork, undernourishment and European diseases.Only 77,000 of El Salvador's original 500,000 inhabitants survived a plague in 1578, and by the end of the 16th century fewer than 10,000 indigenous people were left alive in El Salvador. Since there wasn't enough of a labor force left to work the *encomiendas,* the Spanish experimented with other labor systems. They eventually settled on *haciendas,* large plantations in which workers quickly became indebted to rich landowners.

■ **Colonial Society.** The early plantation culture was split into distinct social classes based on race. At the top of the cultural ladder sat the pure Europeans, either *peninsulares* (born in Spain) or *criollos* (born in the New World). Next came the Spanish-indigenous *mestizos,* who were allowed some administrative duties but could not own land, horses or guns in order to prevent them from rebelling. Next to the bottom were the *zambos,* with black and indigenous parents. The bottom class was reserved for purely native blood and the handful of blacks imported from Africa and the Caribbean.

> ### Blacks in El Salvador
>
> You don't see many blacks in El Salvador today because no more than 10,000 black slaves were imported to El Salvador during the colonial period. The long sea journey made African slaves expensive to import just to harvest indigo during its two-month season. Also, a planned slave rebellion in San Salvador in 1625 that was narrowly averted made authorities wary of importing any more slaves than was absolutely necessary.

The Catholic Church preached humility and subservience to the natives, telling them to bear the burdens of this life while holding out for a future paradise. Native religions were destroyed, old celebrations forbidden, temples toppled and gods replaced. Ironically, the indigenous peoples' most vocal defenders in this era were also representatives of the religious orders. Father Bartolomé de las Casas spent most of his 92 years in the 16th and 17th centuries defending the native tribes of El Salvador. "I prefer someone not baptized," he once said, "than dead and Christian."

At first, trade in cacao boomed when the Spanish replaced the chili peppers and corn in the original recipe for chocolate with sugar. It soon faltered, though, when so many indigenous workers died that there weren't enough left to work the cacao plantations. An economic depression that lasted for most of the 17th century was replaced by an agricultural boom in the 18th century, spurred by European demand for indigo. At one point, more than 90 percent of all indigo exported from Central America came from El Salvador.

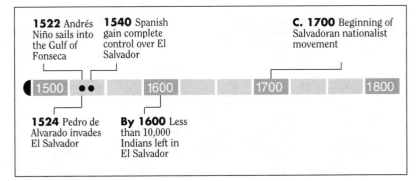

1522 Andrés Niño sails into the Gulf of Fonseca

1540 Spanish gain complete control over El Salvador

C. 1700 Beginning of Salvadoran nationalist movement

1500 ●● 1600 1700 1800

1524 Pedro de Alvarado invades El Salvador

By 1600 Less than 10,000 Indians left in El Salvador

The 18th century also saw the beginnings of Salvadoran nationalism, as tension began to mount between the Old and New Worlds for a variety of reasons. Many inhabitants of Central America felt that the colonies were run exclusively for the benefit of Spain. The Spanish Crown imposed high taxes, restricted sea trade to royal ships and demanded tribute. In addition, the abuse of indigenous peoples ran contrary to the orders of the Crown, adding fuel to the political fire.

By the end of the 18th century, many patterns were already in place that would haunt El Salvador for centuries to come. A wealthy, Europeanized elite ruled society and looked down on a mixed-blood majority that it viewed as almost sub-human. The economy was expanding rapidly but depended on exports for its wealth. As a result, land became El Salvador's most valuable commodity, rather than something used to benefit everyone. The Church supported the status quo as native populations were decimated through disease and abuse. Finally, the military was well on its way to becoming an autonomous, privileged class; a law called the *fuero militar* was enacted to exempt members of the armed forces from the jurisdiction of Spanish courts.

Independence

Colonial resentment against Spain and Guatemala City, the Crown's appendage in the New World, continued to grow into the 19th century. A plunge in indigo profits, due in part to high taxes imposed by Spain, only made matters worse. When Napoleon invaded Spain in 1808, the Crown demanded huge sums from its colonies to fund its battles and to help return the deposed Ferdinand VII to the throne.

Spain's decision to rely upon its colonies to support a war on the other side of the sea infuriated the people of Central America, and eventually led to the collapse of the Spanish Empire. In 1811, Father José Mathías Delgado led El Salvador's first uprising against Spanish rule. The insurrection shook cities throughout the country, but ultimately failed. Delgado succeeded in setting the revolutionary machinery in motion, however. In 1814, Pedro Pablo Castillo, vice-mayor of San Salvador, led a second unsuccessful revolt against the Crown.

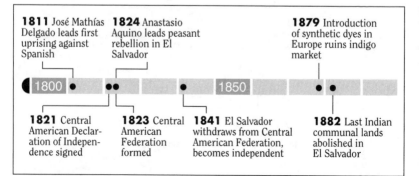

1811 José Mathías Delgado leads first uprising against Spanish

1824 Anastasio Aquino leads peasant rebellion in El Salvador

1879 Introduction of synthetic dyes in Europe ruins indigo market

1800 • •• • 1850 • •

1821 Central American Declaration of Independence signed

1823 Central American Federation formed

1841 El Salvador withdraws from Central American Federation, becomes independent

1882 Last Indian communal lands abolished in El Salvador

Soon after Napoleon's abdication in 1814, King Ferdinand VII returned to the throne and proceeded to persecute anyone in Central America who was suspected of advocating independence. But the revolutionary spirit lived on and Mexico, inspired by the success of the French and American revolutions, declared its independence from Spain in February 1821. On September 15 of that year, representatives of every Central American nation met in Guatemala City to sign the Declaration of Independence from Spain. September 15 is still celebrated as a national holiday throughout Central America.

The countries of Central America initially aligned together under Mexico, in what was known as the Mexican Empire. The Empire was short-lived, however, as the people of Central America discovered that life was just as unbearable whether Spain or Mexico was giving the orders. When many of the allied countries decided to break free from the empire, Mexico sent troops to El Salvador and laid siege to San Salvador. Soon, however, the empire collapsed entirely.

■ **The Central American Federation.** The Central American Federation, signed on July 1, 1823, was the next attempt at regional solidarity. Manuel José Arce, a creole who had helped settle Delgado's uprising peacefully, was appointed president of an alliance that included El Salvador, Guatemala, Honduras, Nicaragua and Costa Rica. José Mathías Delgado wrote the federation's constitution which made the Central American Federation the first nation in the New World to abolish slavery.

Despite the revolutions, the plight of ordinary peasants changed little through the first part of the 19th century, and El Salvador suffered frequent uprisings. In 1824, a *campesino* named Anastasio Aquino led a peasant rebellion near Zacatecoluca. Rallying under the cry "Land for those who work it!" Aquino's hastily-assembled army of 4,000 managed to capture Zacatecoluca and San Vicente. The ragtag troops, mostly peasants from local *haciendas,* were quickly subdued, and Aquino's head was displayed in a tree near San Vicente as a warning to other potential revolutionaries.

Civil unrest, among other things, led El Salvador to withdraw from the Central American Federation in 1841. By 1842, the Central American Federation collapsed under the combined weight of cultural disunity and political differences. From then on, each small Central American nation was on its own.

Señor Walker: Wrong Country, Wrong Agenda

In 1855, American adventurer William Walker declared himself president of Nicaragua, re-establishing slavery in the process and declaring English the country's new official language. The United States quickly recognized Walker's government. The rest of the countries of Central America, meanwhile, feared a North American colony in their midst and banded together in an unusual display of solidarity. Soon they sent Walker packing. Apparently the would-be filibuster didn't learn his lesson, though, because five years later he returned and tried to seize power in Honduras. There, he was captured and executed. His gravestone in Trujillo, Honduras reads, "William Walker: *Fusilado*" (Shot).

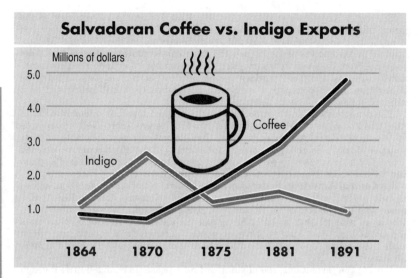

Salvadoran Coffee vs. Indigo Exports

Millions of dollars

5.0
4.0
3.0
2.0
1.0

Coffee

Indigo

1864   1870   1875   1881   1891

Early Nationhood

El Salvador was constituted as a "free, independent and sovereign nation" in 1841. Its early years were marked by struggles for political power and numerous short wars with its neighbors, including battles with Honduras in 1845 and Guatemala in 1844, 1851 and 1863. Many Salvadoran presidents, including Francisco Malespín and General Gerardo Barrios, came to power through coups or invasions from neighboring countries. Meanwhile, the Salvadoran population and economy grew slowly through the end of the 19th century, until coffee arrived on the country's plantations.

■ **Coffee.** The introduction of synthetic dyes in Europe in 1879 caused indigo prices to plummet. Coffee arrived just in time, though, and demand had just begun to skyrocket. The impact of this unremarkable bean on Salvadoran culture can't be overestimated; the coffee industry was and still is almost singlehandedly responsible for many of the country's economic and social imbalances.

Coffee caused land ownership to be concentrated in the hands of the country's elite even faster than had occurred with indigo. Coffee couldn't be cultivated where indigo was grown; it flourished on the high, cool hillsides where the country's few indigenous people still happened to live and own land.

The government supported the coffee growers' ravenous appetite for more and more land, and in 1882 it passed a law abolishing the last vestiges of indigenous communal landholdings. Displaced peasants were forced to choose between working on coffee plantations for extremely low wages or migrating to neighboring countries such as Honduras.

The Salvadoran economy soon became dangerously dependent on the growth and export of coffee, to the exclusion of all other crops. Domestic manufacturing and food production fell sharply as coffee production rose, from 50 percent of El Salvador's exports in 1882 to 76 percent by the turn of the century.

The History of Coffee

Coffee's crucial role in Salvadoran history is made more interesting by the plant's own unusual history. The word coffee is said to come from Kaffa, the province in southern Ethiopia where the intoxicating plant was discovered. According to legend, in 850 AD a goatherd named Kaldi was tending his flock by the shores of the Red Sea. He noticed that after his goats ate the red beans off a certain bush, they romped especially playfully. He tried the beans himself, and soon became the world's first caffeine addict.

Regardless of its source, coffee became popular throughout Ethiopia, although it was used mostly as a food—people would chew the leaves and fruit for a buzz of energy and to dull hunger pangs. Arabs began importing the beans more than 1,000 years ago and are credited with inventing the brewing process. Coffeehouses all over Mecca were decried by priests who said that coffee, as an intoxicating beverage, was prohibited by the Koran. Soon coffee made its way to Europe when a Dutch trader stole a single plant and brought it to Holland in 1616. London's first coffeehouses were open by 1652.

Less than a century later the valuable plant was smuggled yet again, this time to the New World. In the 1720s, a French naval officer stole a single coffee seedling from a bush in the Jardín de Plantes, the royal gardens of Paris, and took it with him on a boat to the Caribbean. When drinking water on the voyage ran low the officer was forced to share his ration with the seedling, which survived and went on to spawn the island's coffee industry.

Coffee's final journey was to the South American mainland. When a Brazilian soldier visited French Guiana, he was given a bouquet as a farewell present from the governor's wife. One wonders just how fond a farewell it was, because inside the bouquet the wife had hidden a single, priceless coffee plant. Thus the Brazilian coffee industry—today the world's largest—was born. Coffee eventually made its way north to El Salvador, and was being cultivated in earnest by the middle of the 19th century.

BACKGROUND

For their part, the coffee growers saw themselves as the economic saviors of El Salvador. After all, they did bring enormous wealth into the country. Most of this money, however, was reinvested in the coffee industry or taken abroad. Little was paid in taxes or redistributed to benefit the other sectors of the Salvadoran economy. There was no incentive to pay coffee workers any more than bare survival rations, since the peasants couldn't afford the crop they grew anyway. Peasant resentment toward the unequal distribution of wealth grew steadily, and the government responded by increasing the size and strength of its police force.

By the end of the 19th century, an enormously unequal distribution of wealth had developed in El Salvador. While landowning *cafetaleros* earned upwards of $200,000 each year, their workers toiled for barely $2.50 per week. In 1890, one-half of one percent of the Salvadoran population controlled 90 percent of the country's wealth.

Into the 20th Century

■ **Development and Unrest.** Urban development in El Salvador took off in the early 20th century, thanks in part to the emerging urban middle and working classes—in the 1920s El Salvador was the largest importer of structural steel in Central America. Around the same time, the first *sindicatos,* or workers' unions, began to appear in the cities. Displaced peasants strongly supported these urban leagues.

Rural areas, on the other hand, remained underdeveloped. The government built just enough infrastructure in the countryside to grow and extract coffee, and didn't spend much money on educating the populace. Schools weren't considered necessary, for example, since literacy wasn't a prerequisite for coffee-harvesting. In response, urban college students often traveled into the countryside to set up schools where they tutored *campesinos* in everything from mathematics to politics.

The government felt threatened by actions to organize peasants and it soon declared labor organizations illegal. Peasants who attempted to organize unions were imprisoned, tortured and killed. The National Guard, founded in 1912 for the purpose of keeping order in the countryside, was seen as an avenue to power and prestige by the emerging urban middle and lower classes.

The world economic depression in the 1920s reduced demand for luxury items like coffee, and exports fell sharply. In El Salvador, where coffee exports accounted for 95 percent of the country's revenue, almost half of the rural work force was suddenly unemployed. Support for leftist causes increased, sparked by earlier land grabs and recent layoffs. Militant unions in the western coffee-producing areas claimed 80,000 members, and in 1930 the Salvadoran Communist Party was founded. The government responded to the "communist threat" with more arrests, beatings, tortures and killings.

■ **Araujo's Short Tenure.** The presidential election of 1931 was won by Arturo Araujo, a little-known *haciendado* who paid his workers twice the going rate and who had established a worker's clinic on his *hacienda*. The surprise victor discovered that it was easier to make campaign promises to improve the lot of the common man than it was to fulfill them, and he was ousted in a coup the same year by his vice president, General Maximiliano Martínez.

La Matanza

Civil unrest grew after Araujo's deposition. The Martínez regime violently repressed strikes and demonstrations and perpetrated enormous electoral fraud in the 1932 election to ensure its own victory.

All the while, the Salvadoran Communist Party quietly gathered support and planned an armed uprising for January 22, 1932. The government learned about the uprising ahead of time, though, and newspaper headlines warned the country of the planned rebellion days before it was to take place. Following an informant's

Late 1920s World economic depression, coffee prices plunge

1931 Arturo Araujo elected president, deposed by General Martínez

1940s Economy begins to improve

1900   1925

1912 National Guard Founded

1930 Salvadoran Communist Party founded

1932 Indigenous uprising in western El Salvador, sparks *La Matanza*

1950 Constitution written

Uncle Sam Takes an Interest

The United States replaced Great Britain as the premiere world power in the early 20th century, and began investing heavily in El Salvador. The United States saw all of Central America as an important region in which to gain a foothold, since the area was the best location for building a canal between the Atlantic and Pacific Oceans, as well as a source of cheap labor. US investment in El Salvador rose from $1.8 million in 1908 to $34 million by 1930.

tip-off, the government arrested three leaders of the uprising, including Faribundo Martí. Many communist sympathizers continued their preparations for the uprising anyway.

On January 20, the Izalco Volcano lit up the skies as machete-wielding peasants occupied towns in the western coffee-growing highlands near Ahuachapán, Sonsonate and Santa Ana. The uprising was centered around indigenous villages and set loose decades of rage and resentment. About 100 local government officials and wealthy landowners were dragged out of their homes and offices and killed by peasant rebels, who looted shops and began to celebrate their "victory" almost immediately.

Soon, however, the government struck back. Soldiers and paramilitary organizations like the *cafetalero*-organized "White Guards" retook towns within days, inflicting heavy losses on the poorly-organized rebel troops. Although the government controlled the region within a week of the initial uprising, it continued to attack peasants with astonishing and calculated brutality, with the full support of the oligarchy and the Church.

■ **Backlash.** Soldiers executed anyone suspected of having links to the uprising, starting with the leaders. José Feliciano Ama, a rebel leader from Izalco, was hanged in front of an assembly of local schoolchildren. Soon, government troops targeted anyone who had indigenous features, dressed like a *campesino* or carried a machete. All were shot on the spot.

In Juayúa, the headquarters of the uprising, government troops killed all the men, women, children and dogs. Peasants, guilty or not, were forced to dig their own graves in the town plaza, lined up with their thumbs tied behind their backs and shot with machine guns mounted on the backs of trucks. In all, tens of thousands of peasants were slaughtered over the next week in an event that came to be known as *La Matanza* (The Massacre).

> "*The Red Horse of the Apocalypse appears to signify the sinister glitterings of World Communism, which with the roars of indomitable fiends, with the din of violent torment, with the rage of merciless flames and the vapor of human blood brandishes its many arms, crazily seeking to topple the ancient structure of Civilization.*"
>
> — Church edict, 1932

BACKGROUND

The Original Revolutionary

The man whose name was adopted by the FMLN was an early Salvadoran revolutionary who struggled to bring socialism to his country. Augustín Faribundo Martí was raised in an upper middle class family in the early 20th century and became a lawyer. He became involved in politics early on, and for the duration of his short life Martí was jailed and exiled repeatedly in his struggles against the conservative forces of the Salvadoran government.

In the late 1920s, Martí went to Nicaragua to fight alongside César Augusto Sandino, who was struggling to expel the US Marines who had occupied the country. Though the two were fighting for different causes—Martí for socialism and Sandino for nationalism—Martí came to admire the Nicaraguan leader, calling him the "world's greatest patriot."

When it became clear to Martí that Sandino would not embrace socialism, he returned to El Salvador in the early 1930s during a period of great civil unrest. Martí was thrown in jail just before *La Matanza* for his role in plotting the uprising. As the army combed the countryside and killed thousands of suspected communist sympathizers, Martí was executed by a firing squad for sedition and rebellion. When asked by a priest just before his execution whether he had any sins to confess, Martí answered no.

In fact, nobody knows exactly how many people died in *La Matanza*; estimates vary from 10,000 to 50,000. Some sources claim that the army simply didn't have enough ammunition to kill more than 10,000 people. Most historians estimate the total was close to 30,000—nearly two percent of the Salvadoran population at the time.

Through the decades, the events of 1932 have fallen prey to selective memory. Regardless, its effects are still felt in modern-day El Salvador. Nearly an entire rural generation was wiped out, and El Salvador's indigenous population has never really recovered. Since then, indigenous Salvadorans have found it difficult to escape the mindset that being of native descent is somehow inherently dangerous. Aside from certain special occasions, they rarely wear their traditional dress or speak their native languages. Finally, *La Matanza* set in place a model for dealing with popular unrest that would be followed for decades to come.

Aftermath

Reeling from the twin blows of the Depression and *La Matanza*, El Salvador entered a decade-long Dark Age in the 1940s under General Martínez. The government declared a national state of siege and halted the few political freedoms that it had granted in the previous two decades. Union and political opposition activity was suspended; anyone who opposed the status quo was persecuted as a communist. The government instituted a national ID card system, shut down the independent press and gave the National Guard the right to search without a warrant. Coffee prices plunged in 1932, causing many unemployed peasants to flee into the northern departments and over the border into Honduras.

■ **Life Under the General.** Martínez, who discovered early on that a facade of democracy was sufficient to keep the United States content, kept power through the 1930s by rigging elections. Ironically, his success in eliminating the threat of a peasant uprising ultimately led to his own downfall. Without a common enemy to unite the government and the country's aristocracy, Martínez and his former supporters bickered over the pace of industrialization and economic diversification.

Before long, university students and laborers called renewed strikes. In a show of strength by El Salvador's emerging middle class, the strikes soon brought the country to a halt. When Martínez finally resigned in 1944, he left behind a legacy of centralized political power and a powerful military apparatus that was better at policing internal "threats" than it was at defending against external forces.

When the Depression ended with the 1930s, the Salvadoran economy began to pull out of its tailspin. Modernization efforts forged ahead and roads, including the Panamerican Highway, were built across the country. The Salvadoran government managed the economy more closely, but mostly for the benefit of the rich. US economic influence grew as well, in spite of Roosevelt's non-interventionist "Good Neighbor" policy. As El Salvador passed into the 1940s, many sectors of its economy were finally beginning to thrive.

Modernization

The Salvadoran economy continued to grow through the middle of the 20th century in a surge of "progress" that masked festering social ills. Wealthy Salvadoran investors developed roads, factories and an electrical network. Much of the development was meant to reduce the country's dependence on the growth and export of

---

MAXIMILIANO HERNÁNDEZ MARTÍNEZ (1882-1966)

El Brujo

Maximiliano Hernández Martínez was the iron-fisted general known as the author of *La Matanza* in 1932. He is also remembered as "El Brujos" (The Sorcerer) for his often outlandish "scientific" beliefs that he occasionally forced upon the Salvadoran populace.

Martínez received some training as a lawyer in El Salvador near the turn of the century, but soon left for a military education in Guatemala. After assuming the presidency, Martínez presided over the killing of thousands of peasants in 1932. Martínez justified his actions by explaining that "In El Salvador, I am God."

Martínez was also interested in the occult, believed in sorcery and held seances in his home. He had strange remedies for everything. Once, when the country was in the throes of a smallpox epidemic, Martínez ordered that red cellophane be placed on all the street lights in the city, since he believed that colored light would cleanse the air and stop the disease from spreading.

"It's good for children to go barefoot," he remarked. "That way they can better receive the beneficial emanations of the planet. Plants and animals don't use shoes." Another time he was overheard saying "it's a much greater crime to kill an ant than a man. While the man has an eternal soul, the ant is dead forever."

Twelve years after *La Matanza*, Martínez resigned the presidency and went into exile in Honduras, where he lived on a farm. At the age of 88, El Brujo was stabbed to death by his chauffeur.

coffee. The elite, perfectly content with coffee revenues, were divided on how best to proceed, although few were pleased at the prospect of being taxed to finance the change.

Many new jobs, mostly in San Salvador, provided work for a growing middle class. Despite this, the country's distribution of income became even more skewed, since most Salvadorans were still too poor to participate in the rising consumer economy.

■ **Cotton and Sugar.** New crops were planted on what little land remained uncultivated. Cotton was grown in coastal areas cleared in the 1950s. From 1935 to 1965, 110,000 hectares had been converted to the production of cotton. Sugarcane was planted in valleys that were too low for coffee and too high for cotton. Cultivation of sugarcane increased from 8,500 hectares in 1960 to 33,200 hectares in 1975.

The surge in production of these crops were the final two nails in the coffins of small landowners, who were forced off what little land they had left. Staple food crops were pushed aside in favor of cotton and sugar, and the country became more dependent on imported food. With better machinery and larger farms the new crops required fewer workers during harvest season, and unemployment increased.

The new constitution of 1950 promised "liberty, health, economic well-being and social justice" to every Salvadoran. It provided for some reforms, including a 48-hour workweek, an 8-hour day and the right to vote for the country's women. However, the constitution promised more than the government was able to deliver. At the same time the Cuban Revolution of 1959 struck fear into the hearts of oligarchies everywhere and boosted hopes of leftist revolutionaries.

Some political opposition was allowed during this period, and urban labor organizations enjoyed some measure of freedom. But politics in the countryside was repressed by the National Guard, which had become a private army of the *cafetaleros*.

■ **The Christian Democrats.** The middle class gained a new voice with the founding of the Christian Democratic Party (PDC) in 1960, filling in the political void between the communists and the right-wing Party of National Conciliation (PCN). The PDCs sought social change through agrarian reform, and were frequently the target of government repression during their early years. Two years after the boycotted 1962 elections (in which university students nominated a donkey for president), the PDCs won the first-ever opposition seats in the National Assembly. PDC candidate José Napoleon Duarte was elected mayor of San Salvador and was twice reelected.

Through the 1960s and early 1970s, fear of another uprising grew among the elite and more money was funneled to the military. With money and political influence, the military was evolving into an independent political force, increasingly immune to the normal rules and values that guided the rest of society.

In the late 1960s, the National Democratic Organization (ORDEN), a paramilitary civilian vigilante group, was founded and supported by elements of the military and aristocracy. Trained by the National Guard, ORDEN set out to combat the "growing specter of communism," in the process showing just how frightened El Salvador's elite had become.

JOSÉ NAPOLEÓN DUARTE (1926-1990)

JFK, the Pope and Duarte

José Napoleón Duarte is one of El Salvador's most recognizable political figure and was, for a time, its most popular. His political career made him a legend among Salvadorans through his efforts to slow military growth and to moderate political extremism. But by the end of his term as president, Duarte's administration had lost popular support and his efforts were generally perceived as a failure.

Duarte hailed from simple roots. His mother, who didn't have enough money to send José to a good school, convinced priests at Catholic schools to provide scholarships for Duarte and his brother. His father later won a fortune in the national lottery and used the proceeds to send Duarte to the US to study at the University of Notre Dame in Indiana.

When he returned to El Salvador, Duarte became active in domestic politics at a time when scant political opposition was allowed by the government. After helping found the Christian Democrat Party (PDC) in the early 1960s, Duarte was elected mayor of San Salvador. His popularity soared when his administration managed to install street lights in the capital. The most popular photos in Salvadoran homes at the time were portraits of JFK, the Pope and Duarte.

In 1972 Duarte ran for president of El Salvador against a military leader. When it became clear that Duarte had won a majority of the votes, the military imposed a three-day blackout and clamped down on all opposition. Duarte was beaten and sent into exile, where he remained until the end of the decade.

After his return to El Salvador in the early 1980s, Duarte served with members of the military on two juntas. Since the death squads remained active during this time, many felt that Duarte undermined his claims to moderation by participating in a government that allowed such activities.

Duarte ran for president in 1984 against ARENA party candidate Roberto d'Aubuisson, and won in a close vote. He promised to end the civil war and to quash paramilitary groups that operated throughout the country. Though Duarte brought the rebels briefly to the negotiating table for peace talks in La Palma, his administration soon became corrupt and ineffective and in the end accomplished almost nothing.

Towards the end of his term as president, Duarte was diagnosed with terminal cancer. He promised to survive the duration of his term, which he did, and to write a sequel to his autobiography when the war was over. After Duarte's death in 1990, though, the war continued and the sequel was left unwritten.

The Soccer War

In 1969, an old rivalry between El Salvador and Honduras erupted into a brief war, momentarily shifting attention from El Salvador's deteriorating political situation. The battle was caused by a number of issues, including a long-standing dispute over the exact location of a border between the two countries and the huge numbers of Salvadorans who had migrated into Honduras.

By the late 1960s, more than 300,000 Salvadorans had settled in Honduras, and many Hondurans resented losing their jobs to the hard-working immigrants. In addition, the two countries differed on how to apply rules relating to the emerging Central American Common Market. Salvadoran companies competed strongly against their Honduran counterparts, which slowed Honduran efforts to industrialize. Finally, rich Honduran landowners sought a scapegoat for land imbalances in their own country, and focused attention on the easiest target: Salvadoran immigrants.

Honduras began to expel Salvadorans in the late 1960s, causing the Salvadoran press to trumpet allegations of mistreatment at the hands of Honduran authorities. Tensions peaked around the June 1969 World Cup playoffs between the two countries, and erupted into war on July 14. Throughout the four-day war, the only organized call for peace was a rally staged by the Salvadoran Communist Party in San Salvador. Begun under the pretense of "protecting the human rights of Salvadoran settlers," the war ended when the Organization of American States arranged a cease-fire. By August, Salvadoran troops returned home to a "victory celebration" staged in the capital in an official attempt to salvage some national pride.

■ **Who Won?** The "Soccer War," as it came to be known, left 3,000 dead, 6,000 wounded and caused $50 million in damage. Relations between the countries worsened and Honduras closed its borders to Salvadorans, blocked shipments of Salvadoran goods and stopped buying Salvadoran products. As Salvadoran emigrants returned home, land pressures and unemployment increased.

In the end, the Salvadoran military was the only group that benefitted from the war. The "effectiveness" of the armed forces had been demonstrated, and Colonel Sanchez Hernández rode a wave of nationalistic fervor into the presidency in the 1970 elections. The military-allied PCN received 60 percent of the vote versus 28 percent for the PDCs. Nonetheless, repression, torture and disappearances of dissidents continued.

1960 Christian Democratic Party founded

1964 Christian Democrats win seats in National Assembly, Duarte elected mayor of San Salvador

1969 El Salvador attacks Honduras in Soccer War

1975 El Salvador hosts Miss Universe pageant

1950   1960   1970   1980

1959 Cuban Revolution

1962 Elections boycotted by all opposition parties

Late 1960s ORDEN founded, Honduras begins to expel Salvadoran immigrants

1972 Col. Molina elected president over Duarte

1977 Oscar Romero appointed archbishop

The Turbulent 1970s

The United National Opposition, a coalition of the Christian Democrats and other leftist groups, nominated Duarte for president in the 1972 elections. The coalition fought governmental harassment in an uphill campaign battle and was stunned when the official vote count signaled that Duarte had been elected president. The government's Federal Election Board, however, announced that PCN candidate Colonel Arturo Molina had won.

This blatant fraud sparked a coup attempt on March 25 by young military officers who had lost patience with the corrupt government. Duarte called upon his supporters to confront the troops of the entrenched military who were advancing on the younger officers, but few responded. The coup failed and Molina assumed the presidency. Duarte, meanwhile, was hunted down by the military, beaten and exiled to Venezuela for his role. As a result of the loss, support for the Christian Democrats faded in the 1970s, and the best opportunity for political moderates to take power in years was lost.

■ **Social Chaos.** A rising tide of government-sponsored violence and intimidation in the 1970s was countered with attempts by the left to organize and retaliate. The opposition increasingly saw revolution as the only way to affect change in the country, as they formed numerous clandestine paramilitary groups which would eventually unite into a guerrilla army in the early 1980s. Arms from Nicaragua and Cuba began to filter into the hands of various resistance groups, including some which financed their operations by kidnapping and ransoming rich Salvadorans. By 1979, the left was responsible for ten percent of all political killings and their followers demanded millions of dollars in ransom. Underground left-wing political groups also sprang up, replacing older leftist parties silenced since the 1972 election fraud.

Since legitimate political opposition was all but impossible, the left began a grass-roots effort to organize peasants. Trade unions, *campesino* organizations and student groups staged strikes, marches, rallies and sit-ins. Radical student groups at the National University prompted Molina to close down the campus in 1972 with tanks and planes. When the university re-opened a year later, it was run by a Molina-appointed rector. By the end of the decade, the country's economy had become paralyzed by unrest and foreign investment had dried up.

By 1975, members of the oligarchy had become terrified for their safety and looked for ways to protect their livelihood. Soldiers, ex-soldiers and rural landowners joined together into pro-government paramilitary groups similar to ORDEN, such as the White Warrior's Union (UGB) and FALANGE. They responded to the Church's increasingly leftist stance with pamphlets bearing messages like "Be a patriot! Kill a priest!" The Jesuit University of Central America in San Salvador was bombed repeatedly.

Reform efforts by the government were continually undermined by the right. Molina met fierce resistance from landowners when he attempted to limit landholdings in San Miguel and La Unión departments to 86 acres, which would have required the government to break up many large farms. Eventually, the government relented and made the land reform voluntary. A 1973 cartoon in El Salvador showed one grade-school student leaning over to another and whispering, "El Salvador must be the largest country in the world because they've been carrying out agrarian reform for ten years and it's still not finished!"

OSCAR ARNULFO ROMERO Y GALDAMES (1917-1980)

The Voice of the Voiceless

El Salvador's archbishop in the late 1970s, Oscar Arnulfo Romero was a revolutionary advocate for the dispossessed and repressed. He spoke out frequently against the army's blatant disregard for human rights and was criticized for aligning himself too closely with the political left. When the country's right felt that Romero's weekly homilies threatened their own interests, he was assassinated.

Romero was considered a political conservative when chosen in 1977 by Rome to serve as archbishop of El Salvador, the country's highest position in the Catholic Church. He had been groomed by the oligarchy, it was understood, and was expected to keep quiet. Romero replaced Archbishop Chávez, a politically liberal leader who had moved the Church toward the political left.

But soon after Romero's ordination, Father Rutilio Grande, Romero's friend and a well-known advocate of peasant rights, was gunned down on a country road. Despite a request from Romero, the government refused to investigate. This incident, along with Romero's frequent interaction with peasants whose families had been affected by army campaigns, caused him to reconsider his political views.

Romero soon gained the support of the country's underclass. His sermons were broadcast throughout the country and as many as 75 percent of all Salvadorans would tune in every week to hear him speak. Rightist forces felt threatened by Romero's growing influence and repeatedly bombed the radio station that broadcast Romero's words.

Many of Romero's homilies were directed against the army's violence and human rights abuses. Romero believed that the Church had an obligation to speak up for those who were otherwise silenced.

"When a dictatorship seriously violates human rights and attacks the common good of the nation," he explained, "when it becomes unbearable and closes all channels of dialogue, of understanding, of rationality—when this happens, the Church speaks of the legitimate right of insurrectional violence."

When the right accused Romero of directing the Church to undermine the government, Romero disagreed and responded, "the Church is not against the government. The truth is that the government is against the people and we are with the people."

Romero also denied that he was a leftist himself, as the government contended, although he did agree with much of what the left advocated. "I don't call them the forces of the left, but the forces of the people," he said. "Their voice is the voice of anger resulting from social injustice. What is called the left is the people. It is the people organized, and its cry is the cry of the people."

A day before he was killed, Romero addressed his sermon to the country's soldiers and called on them to reconsider their role in society: "I issue a special entreaty to the army, the National Guard, police and military. Do not kill your fellow peasants, your brothers and sisters. No soldier is obliged to obey an order which is against the law of God."

This address, seen by the armed forces as a direct call to mutiny, sealed Romero's fate. As he was giving mass in the Divine Providence Cancer Hospital on March 24, 1980, Romero was shot in the heart in front of the entire congregation. Soon afterward, Roberto d'Aubuisson, founder of the ARENA political party and one-time presidential candidate, was implicated in the murder.

Father and sons, near La Unión

Steep street, Chalatenango

> More than 100,000 people attended Romero's funeral. As mourners moved across the Plaza Gerardo Barrios in front of the San Salvador Cathedral, army snipers atop the Presidential Palace opened fire, killing dozens. Many consider Romero's assassination and the tragedy at his funeral to be the real beginning of the civil war.

■ **The Church Changes its Stance.** In the midst of the growing political turmoil, members of the Catholic Church were agitating for change as well. Under the guidance of Archbishop Oscar Romero and the Liberation Theology he espoused, the Church became involved in the political struggle, usually on behalf of the left. Priests went into the countryside to educate *campesinos* and to organize them into cooperatives and unions. For their efforts, members of the Catholic clergy were targeted by right-wing groups, and dozens of priests were killed. Many later joined rebel groups in frustration.

General Carlos Humberto Romero, a conservative functionary of the right (no relation to the archbishop), was elected president in 1977. Thousands of dead people were counted as having voted for Romero, and some villages registered more voters than their entire populations. Many in the country interpreted the elections as a sign that the oligarchy was digging in and tightening its hold on power.

Soon after the election results were announced, protestors occupied the Plaza Libertad in San Salvador to call for new elections. Thousands camped out. Day by day the crowds grew, until 60,000 sat facing the Metropolitan Cathedral. The scene was a carnival of protest with political speeches, live music and food for sale.

On February 28, the army surrounded the plaza and ordered the crowd to disperse within ten minutes. In response, protestors sang the national anthem. Soldiers opened fire and sent volleys of tear gas into the plaza. Dozens of protesters were killed, including many who fell trying to seek shelter in the Metropolitan Cathedral. Foreign news crews captured the event, and Oliver Stone used the stunning footage in the opening credits of his movie *Salvador*. In all, between 80 and 300 people died around the plaza. In the days following the attack, enraged crowds burned cars and government offices in the capital.

■ **Revolution in Nicaragua.** The Sandinista revolution against the US-backed Somoza dictatorship in Nicaragua in 1979 is often credited as one of the major sparks that ignited the Salvadoran civil war. Crowds in San Salvador supported the left, cheering "Romero y Somoza, son la misma cosa!" ("Romero and Somoza are the same thing!") The Salvadoran army, meanwhile, shifted its allegiance between the center and the right and was uncomfortable siding too strongly with

---

IN THE NEWS

Missed Universe

In 1975, the Salvadoran government spent more than one million dollars preparing to host the Miss Universe pageant. Peaceful student demonstrations in the streets of San Salvador attended by as many as 50,000 people were staged in protest of the decision to host the event. Police opened fire on the marchers, killing dozens and wounding many more.

either side. With a communist insurgency around the corner and Reagan at the helm, the US government soon took a particular interest in El Salvador's internal affairs.

General Romero eventually lost support from all sides. The oligarchy and the US considered him incompetent in the face of opposition, and the army didn't see him as useful any longer. On October 15 1979, Romero was deposed in a coup by army officers.

Civil War

A civilian-military junta was appointed to replace General Romero. This group of army officers and prominent civilians was perceived as the country's best hope of avoiding an imminent civil war. The junta attempted some reforms, promised democratic elections and invited the nascent guerrilla movement to join in talks with the government. But few reforms were initiated and the paramilitary violence continued. Soon, the civilian members of the junta resigned in frustration. Although other juntas followed (including one with Duarte, who had returned from exile in 1980), none were able to affect change.

On January 22, 1980, the streets of the capital were filled with the largest peaceful protest march in El Salvador's history. Over 220,000 people demonstrated against the death squads, disappearances and killings. Suddenly, in the middle of the march, shots rang out from above the Presidential Palace. Dozens of protestors were gunned down as the crowd scattered. Most witnesses blamed government soldiers for opening fire without provocation.

■ **The Final Straw.** Two months later, on a Sunday afternoon in the middle of mass, Archbishop Romero was shot and killed by a lone gunman. Leftist supporters felt that if even the archbishop wasn't safe in El Salvador, all hope for a negotiated peace was lost.

By October, five guerrilla groups had united under the banner of the Faribundo Martí National Liberation Front (FMLN) and the civil war began in earnest. A handful of leftist political parties withdrew from the political process and formed the Democratic Revolutionary Front (FDR), which became the political wing of the FMLN. At roughly the same time, Duarte was sworn in as president with the support of the US government.

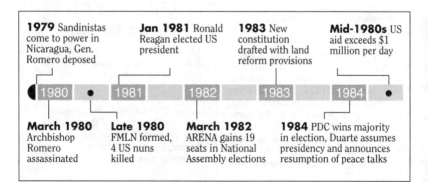

1979 Sandinistas come to power in Nicaragua, Gen. Romero deposed

Jan 1981 Ronald Reagan elected US president

1983 New constitution drafted with land reform provisions

Mid-1980s US aid exceeds $1 million per day

1980 ● 1981 1982 1983 1984 ●

March 1980 Archbishop Romero assassinated

Late 1980 FMLN formed, 4 US nuns killed

March 1982 ARENA gains 19 seats in National Assembly elections

1984 PDC wins majority in election, Duarte assumes presidency and announces resumption of peace talks

On December 2, four US churchwomen who had come to El Salvador to work with victims of the war disappeared on the road from the Cuscatlán airport. Their car was found the next morning near Zacatecoluca, burned and without license plates. The bodies of the women, who had been raped and shot to death, were discovered in a shallow grave nearby.

Suddenly the civil war was more than just a Salvadoran problem. Despite a suggestion by then-US Secretary of State Alexander Haig that the nuns were killed when they tried to run a roadblock, the US suspended $25 million in military and economic aid pending an official investigation. The aid was resumed barely two months later, though, when the FMLN launched a series of major attacks.

The FMLN's "final offensive" in January 1981 helped the rebel movement gain credibility as a fighting force. The rebels made initial advances in northern and eastern El Salvador, forcing the government to abandon talk of reform and to focus its efforts on fighting.

When Ronald Reagan became president of the United States, a zealous fear of Soviet-style communism gaining a foothold in Central America spurred the US to pump millions of dollars of aid to El Salvador. US loans to the Salvadoran government jumped from $5.9 million in 1980 to $533 million in 1985. By 1985, when Congress threatened to block aid to El Salvador in response to its failure to control the activities of the death squads, Reagan declared that the government had made "good progress" in stopping human rights abuses. That same year the Salvadoran Catholic Church announced that government troops were responsible for 3,059 political assassinations during the first six months.

■ **Rise of the Right.** The elections for the National Constituent Assembly in March 1982 were proclaimed a success for Salvadoran democracy and used by the US to justify its decision to provide more aid. But others maintained that the elections were merely a media event, and blamed the results on voting inflation and transparent ballot boxes. As then-US Ambassador Robert White said, "No power on earth can convince a poor unlettered *campesino* with a numbered ballot in his hand that the military commander of his district will not know for whom the vote was cast."

BACKGROUND

ROBERTO D'AUBUISSON (1943-1992)

Man of the Right

Roberto d'Aubuisson, who died from cancer in 1992 at age 45, was a man of great contradictions. He was both a populist and an extremist, a presidential candidate and a disgraced co-conspirator in the assassination of Archbishop Romero. Above all, though, the founder of the ARENA party was the country's premier anti-communist throughout the war, as well as one of the chief organizers and supporters of El Salvador's death squads.

D'Aubuisson was raised in a lower-middle-class family, entered military school at 15 and was sent abroad to Taiwan and the US to learn how to combat communist insurgencies. At one point d'Aubuisson worked under General José Medrán, founder of ORDEN, El Salvador's first organized death squad.

Throughout his career, d'Aubuisson was almost as fiercely xenophobic as he was anti-communist. In his campaign against Duarte's moderate politics and the administration's close association with the US, d'Aubuisson alleged that Duarte and US President Carter had conspired to turn

(continued on next page)

the country over to communism just like in Nicaragua. When evidence emerged that Nicaragua was supporting the Salvadoran guerrillas, d'Aubuisson advocated a retaliatory attack against El Salvador's larger southern neighbor.

Despite his extreme views, d'Aubuisson was also an effective campaigner and public speaker. He was an imposing figure, too, with a bullet-proof vest, high-heeled boots, jeans and a pistol always tucked into his waistband. His short, muscular frame was surrounded by a constant entourage of bodyguards. The vest and bodyguards accompanied him everywhere after a sniper's bullet grazed him in 1982.

But d'Aubuisson is most remembered for his fiery rhetoric. In a deep voice, with jaws clenched and r's rolling hard, he would refer to then-President Duarte as "El Loco Duarte," and repeatedly curse US politicians and the foreign press.

In one of his better-known campaign tactics, d'Aubuisson would take a watermelon (whose color represented the PDC's official green) and chop it in half with a single blow of a machete to show how—like the watermelon—the PDCs were "green on the outside, but red [communist] on the inside." When d'Aubuisson began his campaign for the presidency, he continued to express his extremist political views by threatening to napalm villages and vowing to free the army of any human rights restrictions.

D'Aubuisson's legacy is tied to his involvement in the assassination of Archbishop Romero in 1980, his constant efforts to undermine any moderate political force in the country and his ARENA party. When the army broke in on d'Aubuisson and others plotting to assassinate Romero, d'Aubuisson tried to eat certain incriminating papers. After being sent briefly into exile, he was allowed to return in part because the US government at the time was more concerned with the threat of a communist takeover than they were with state-sponsored terrorism. D'Aubuisson was so closely tied to the death squads that then-US Ambassador Robert White described him to Congress as a "pathological killer."

Despite ARENA's shady beginnings, d'Aubuisson's political party has prospered. D'Aubuisson began the party after failing to spur a coup to overthrow the 1980 military junta which included Duarte. Initially, he became known for television appearances in which he would hold up photos of suspected terrorists. Not coincidentally, the appearances would be followed by death squad attacks.

When ARENA came to power in the Constituent Assembly in 1982, his shadowy paramilitary friends resurfaced in the assembly building. In his 1984 campaign for the presidency, d'Aubuisson promised to exterminate guerrillas within three months of convening a new National Constituent Assembly, and promised to seize Duarte and try him for treason.

D'Aubuisson's political views mellowed shortly before his death, just months after the government and rebels agreed to the peace accords. He seemed to realize that, in the long run, his extreme views could actually harm his party's popularity, and moved himself more behind the scenes. President Cristiani later credited d'Aubuisson with making the agreements possible, and said that without his support radical elements in ARENA would never have allowed the talks to take place.

The recently-founded Republican National Alliance (ARENA) gained a surprising 19 seats in the assembly. ARENA, representative of the radical right just as the FMLN represented the radical left, had paid a US advertising firm $200,000 to run its campaign. The investment paid off. Roberto d'Aubuisson, the party's founder, was elected president of the assembly, reflecting El Salvador's recent shift to the right in the

IN THE NEWS

Old Fears

The 50th anniversary of *La Matanza* in early 1982 prompted 1,000 police to conduct a house-to-house search in San Salvador in fear of a memorial uprising.

face of the leftist insurgency. In 1982, the assembly appointed Dr. Alvaro Magaña, a banker, temporary president of El Salvador, although he was more of a figurehead than a legitimate leader. A year later the assembly drafted a new constitution.

■ **Failed Land Reform.** A key issue in the new constitution was land reform, a three-phase program initiated in 1983, supported by the US and written by the same US law professor who had drafted South Vietnam's land-reform program during the Vietnam war. The first phase, in which farms over 1,250 acres (15 percent of El Salvador's farmland) were to be turned into cooperatives, ultimately created large farms that were less productive than the private farms they replaced. The second phase, which would have redistributed holdings between 500 and 1,250 acres, was never implemented. The third phase was designed to give peasants ownership of small parcels of land that they had previously rented or share-cropped. By that point, 150,000 people were supposed to have benefitted from the land reform program. In fact, less than 1,000 land titles were ever handed out.

When land reform was begun, right-wing landowners were enraged. Many peasants who applied for land titles were murdered or disappeared. Rodolf Viera, head of the Salvadoran Land Reform Institute, was gunned down after speaking out against the right-wing backlash. Before the land reform program totally collapsed, the assembly voted to allow landowners to own up to 262 hectares each. ARENA claimed victory for having stifled the program.

■ **Guerrilla Tactics and the Army's Response.** Through the early 1980s the FMLN continued to strengthen its control over northern and eastern El Salvador. Berlín and San Miguel were both occupied by guerrilla forces in 1983. The rebels, numbering 10,000 in 1984 compared with 50,000 government troops, staged successful attacks on military garrisons and important economic targets. The guerrillas destroyed the enormous Cuscatlán bridge over the Lempa River in January 1984, despite 400 government soldiers on duty to protect it. Soon FMLN attacks in western El Salvador threatened the country's all-important coffee industry.

Guerrilla attacks on the country's infrastructure were an attempt to undermine the government by demolishing the country's basic economic lifelines. In the end, though, these attacks damaged the FMLN's reputation almost as much as they damaged El Salvador's roads, bridges, buses, dams and power lines.

The army was fortunate that public confidence in the FMLN declined as the war progressed, because even with the help of US-trained quick-reaction battalions and surveillance photos showing the location of guerrilla troops, efforts to contain the revolution were often half-hearted and never very successful. When the army launched indiscriminate attacks against civilians whom it believed supported the guerrillas, they undermined confidence in both the government and the US policy of providing arms.

As early as 1981, more than 300,000 Salvadorans had fled to neighboring countries or to the US. Large parts of Chalatenango, Morazán, and Cabañas departments were left nearly deserted.

■ **Duarte's Return.** Salvadorans attached considerably less hope for peace to the 1984 elections than they had to the elections two years earlier. The FMLN refused to participate and hampered voting in areas under its control, and owners of radio stations were repeatedly threatened by paramilitary groups which warned them against broadcasting advertisements for the Christian Democrats. The US, which feared ARENA's virulently conservative platform, supported Duarte. Duarte won in a run-off with just over half the vote and became El Salvador's first freely-elected president in over 50 years. At the same time, the Christian Democrats won a majority in the assembly and announced plans to initiate social reforms.

With the momentum of a resounding victory, Duarte soon announced the resumption of peace talks with the guerrillas, to be held in the small town of La Palma in Chalatenango department. But after two rounds of talks no agreement could be reached, and each side accused the other of being unwilling to compromise. In the remaining years of his presidency, Duarte repeatedly clashed with the radical right and the military, and was unable to bring about the end of the war or any meaningful reforms.

■ **The War Continues.** By the mid-1980s, the enormous US military funding began to show results as the army gradually regained control of areas once dominated by guerrillas. US-supplied jets gave El Salvador the most powerful air force in Central America and allowed the army to strafe and bomb large parts of guerrilla territory. When US aid to El Salvador peaked in the late 1980s, more than $1 million a day was being funneled to the Salvadoran government, and most of it was re-channeled to fight the war. Such enormous sums made El Salvador the fifth-largest recipient of US aid in the world. As fighting between the army and the FMLN dragged on, many Salvadorans came to believe that victory for either side was unlikely to come anytime soon.

The FMLN expressed a desire to participate in elections scheduled for late 1989, the same year George Bush became president of the US. The rebels asked that voting be postponed for six months, in order for them to have sufficient time to prepare for an election, and that both sides agree to an immediate 60-day cease-fire. The government refused to postpone the elections. In response, the FMLN killed more than 40 people in an election-day attack on the National Guard headquarters in San Salvador.

Despite a law that made voting mandatory, a combination of voter apathy and fear kept more than half of all Salvadorans away from the polls. For the first time in a decade, the FMLN didn't attack polling stations, although they did bomb power stations and black out 90 percent of the country. Rubén Zamora, a leftist leader recently returned from self-imposed exile, ran for president as the candidate of the Democratic Convergence Party (PDC).

ARENA candidate Alfredo Cristiani, a wealthy businessman raised on one of the country's largest coffee plantations and educated at Georgetown University in the US, was elected president. The US perceived Cristiani, who had a cleaner record than did his mentor d'Aubuisson, as a political moderate. ARENA hoped he would be able to help the party shed its rabidly conservative image acquired when d'Aubuisson was at the helm.

■ **A Chance at Peace.** In September 1989, the government and the FMLN began another round of peace talks at the collective request of other Central American nations. In October, negotiations were cut short when a bomb ripped through the headquarters of the Salvadoran Workers' National Union Federation (FENESTRAS), killing ten and wounding 29. The FMLN blamed the army and refused to return to the bargaining table. Within a month the guerrillas had launched a new offensive that reached the streets of the capital.

The government declared a national state of siege as it launched a counter-offensive in the capital. When the situation seemed as bad as it could get, six Jesuit priests were killed on the campus of the University of Central America on the morning of November 16, 1989. Their bodies, along with those of their housekeeper and her young daughter, were found riddled with bullets in their dormitory. The audacious murders, immediately pinned on the army, were reminiscent of Archbishop Romero's assassination almost a decade earlier. Many people wondered whether the cycle of violence would start all over again.

Despite the turmoil, peace negotiations began again in early 1990. This time the UN mediated the talks, but was unable to help the two sides agree on the accountability and future role of the country's military. By the end of the year fighting had resumed. The FMLN shot down a government plane with a Soviet surface-to-air missile in late 1990 and, in January 1991, rebels downed a US military helicopter on its way to Honduras. Two US servicemen who survived the crash were subsequently executed by the FMLN, prompting the US to resume military aid.

IN THE NEWS

The Jesuit Case

Five soldiers, three lieutenants and Colonel Guillermo Benavides, then head of the military academy, were charged with the Jesuit murders. There were rumors that higher-ranking officers had participated in the plot, but no hard evidence was available to prosecute them.

The prosecution fought a long battle to bring the case to trial. Even President Cristiani was frustrated at the embarrassing lack of progress, and asked Britain's Scotland Yard and the Spanish police to help in the investigation. In May 1990, important evidence disappeared, including Benavides' diary. By January 1991, two state prosecutors had resigned to protest interference by the army and the Attorney-General.

When the case reached the Supreme Court in April of that year, two lieutenants and all five soldiers were acquitted for having followed orders. Benavides and the other lieutenant were found guilty of the killings and sentenced to 30 years in jail, the maximum penalty allowable. Fourteen months later, in March 1993, both were set free under the government's General Amnesty law.

Peace

By the beginning of the 1990s, leaders and supporters of both sides were exhausted by the endless fighting. The turning point in negotiations came when the government accepted demands that it purge the armed forces. On September 25, 1991, representatives of the Salvadoran Government and the FMLN signed the New York City Accords at the United Nations headquarters, under the auspices of the UN and the Catholic Church. In this preliminary agreement, the FMLN secured the rights for peasants to permanently occupy land controlled by the guerrillas, and a bi-partisan National Commission for the Consolidation of Peace (COPAZ) was organized to oversee the peace process and the FMLN's formal introduction to the political process.

The final peace agreements, known as the Accords of Chapultepec, were signed on January 16, 1992 in Mexico. A two-year timetable was established to implement a long list of reforms and changes in both the government and the FMLN. The government agreed to reduce the size of its 30,000-strong active forces by one-half, and to disband its 17,000-member rapid-deployment battalions. The notorious National Guard and Treasury Police, both implicated in death squad activities, were also to be disbanded. Intelligence services were transferred to civilian control, forced army recruitment was ended and entrance requirements for military service were made stricter.

Most importantly, the accords required the government to purge officers and judicial officials accused of human rights abuses and corruption, and to enact constitutional amendments that redirected the mission of the military toward defending the country from external threats instead of internal ones. A National Council of the Judiciary (CNJ) was created to evaluate the competency of all judges.

Land reform provisions required a transfer of all holdings over 245 hectares, with preference for land to be given to ex-combatants. A new civilian police force, the National Civil Police (PNC), was created to replace the old, discredited National Police. An Office of the Counsel for the Defense of Human Rights was to take over monitoring of the human-rights situation after the United Nations Mission to El Salvador (ONUSAL) left the country. A National Truth Commission was to be established to investigate past human rights abuses by both sides and to propose a list of recommended actions which the government agreed to adopt. The FMLN, for its part, agreed to lay down its arms in a five-stage demilitarization process and to be reborn as a political party.

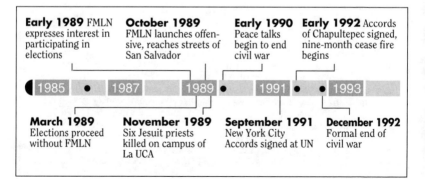

Early 1989 FMLN expresses interest in participating in elections

October 1989 FMLN launches offensive, reaches streets of San Salvador

Early 1990 Peace talks begin to end civil war

Early 1992 Accords of Chapultepec signed, nine-month cease fire begins

1985 ● 1987 1989 ● 1991 ● ● 1993

March 1989 Elections proceed without FMLN

November 1989 Six Jesuit priests killed on campus of La UCA

September 1991 New York City Accords signed at UN

December 1992 Formal end of civil war

■ **Cease-fire.** A nine-month cease-fire between government and rebel forces, mandated by the peace accords, began on February 1, 1992, under the supervision of 1,000 UN troops. A crowd of 30,000 leftist supporters gathered in the Plaza Gerardo Barrios to celebrate the first day without fighting while Radio Venceremos, the clandestine wartime voice of the FMLN, broadcast freely from the roof of the Metro-

> After 13 years of strict rules forbidding rebels from drinking any alcohol, former FMLN troops celebrated for four days straight in San Antonio, near the Guazapa Volcano, and drank the town dry.

politan Cathedral. A 40-foot FMLN banner hung across the entrance to the cathedral. Two blocks away, meanwhile, government supporters welcomed Cristiani back from the peace talks, watched a fireworks display and danced until dawn.

On December 15, a formal ceremony marking the end of the war was attended by Cristiani, FMLN leaders, the UN Secretary-General and Central American heads of state. That same day, the FMLN was registered as an official political party. After more than a decade of bloodshed which killed one percent of the Salvadoran population, left countless more wounded or indigent and drove nearly 15 percent of the population abroad, the civil war was over.

■ **The Elections of the Century.** March 1994 saw the first presidential, legislative and municipal elections in El Salvador since the end of the conflict. Two thousand election observers watched as campaign rhetoric flew. ARENA warned landowners that the FMLN wanted to nationalize all their holdings and claimed that an El Salvador run by the left would end up with food-rationing books like Cuba. The FMLN countered by pointing out how they had been putting their lives on the line for the sake of their country for the duration of the war, while ARENA seemed to discover voters only at election time.

The presidential election pitted Rubén Zamora of the Center-Left Coalition, representing the FMLN and other left-wing groups, against Armando Calderon Sol, a conservative lawyer, co-founder of ARENA and two-time mayor of San Salvador who had been linked to death squad activities while working with d'Aubuisson.

A light turnout tarnished the elections and the Supreme Electoral Tribunal was accused of making voting difficult for rural voters. *Campesinos* were required to vote in departmental capitals rather than in municipalities closer to home.

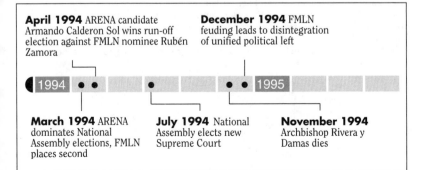

April 1994 ARENA candidate Armando Calderon Sol wins run-off election against FMLN nominee Rubén Zamora

December 1994 FMLN feuding leads to disintegration of unified political left

March 1994 ARENA dominates National Assembly elections, FMLN places second

July 1994 National Assembly elects new Supreme Court

November 1994 Archbishop Rivera y Damas dies

Registration was particularly difficult since many rural records had been destroyed during the war. More than 70,000 people were unable to vote because their birth certificates could not be located.

Looking Ahead

Close results in the first round of voting required a run-off between ARENA and FMLN presidential candidates. In the end, pervasive distrust of the new FMLN political party and the lingering specter of communism convinced the electorate to side with ARENA, despite its links to the death squads. When the second round of voting was complete, Calderon Sol emerged with 68 percent of the vote and became El Salvador's new president. ARENA won 39 seats in the Legislative Assembly, groups sympathetic to the FMLN won 21 seats, the PDC won 18 and other groups took the remaining six seats. UN observers declared the election free of fraud, but some watchdog groups claimed otherwise.

In July 1994, a new Supreme Court was elected by the assembly, and no members of the previous court were returned to office, fulfilling the recommendations of the UN-sponsored Truth Commission. In late September, former soldiers stormed the Legislative Assembly demanding severance pay for 30,000 of their comrades out of work as a result of the peace process.

As 1994 progressed, internal squabbling soon threatened to split up the groups comprising the FMLN political party. By late 1994, the political left was in complete disarray as extremist elements broke from former rebel leader Joaquín Villalobos, who tried to toe a moderate political line. Supporters from all sides encouraged Villalobos to dissolve the FMLN once and for all. Villalobos, meanwhile, had other concerns as he was sent to jail on charges of libeling a prominent businessman. The Supreme Court later dismissed the charges and ordered his release.

In November, Archbishop Arturo Rivera y Damas, one of the late Archbishop Romero's strongest supporters, died of natural causes. Rivera y Damas followed in the footsteps of Romero by giving regular homilies that denounced human rights abuses and played a major role in bringing the government and rebels together to sign the 1992 peace accords. President Caldeòn Sol attended the wake for the archbishop, but said that he did not agree with all that Rivera y Damas stood for.

Disappearances in El Salvador had completely come to an end by the close of 1994. Political murders were also on the decline, although several public figures (including leftist leaders) have been killed under suspicious circumstances in the last year. The UN announced that the country's security forces continued to commit human rights abuses, but that their efforts to control such abuses had improved. All of this diverted attention from President Calderón Sol, who had an otherwise unremarkable beginning in his struggle to end corruption and crime.

Geography

El Salvador is the smallest country in Central America—roughly the size of Massachusetts. It is 260 kilometers long east to west, 100 kilometers wide north to south and has 320 kilometers of Pacific coastline. It's conceivable to drive the length of the country in a day, although the roads may dictate otherwise. El Salvador's size and shape has earned it the affectionate nickname *El Pulgarcito* (The Little Thumb) of Central America.

El Salvador is divided roughly into three geographical regions running east to west. The Sierra Madre mountain chain fills the **interior highlands** bordering Honduras and Guatemala. The mountains are low and old, and are sparsely populated. The **central region** consists of high valleys separated by mountains and volcanoes. Most of El Salvador's major cities and its best farmland, including many coffee plantations on the lower volcanic slopes, are located here. The **coastal plain** is narrow but fertile, dotted with a few port cities and farms and lined with beaches. The coastal mountain range borders it to the north.

■ **Earthquakes & Volcanoes.** El Salvador's hyperactive geography is a direct result of its location along the Cinturón del Fuego (Belt of Fire), a ring of volcanoes and fault zones that encircles the Pacific Ocean. According to historical records, there have been at least 50 destructive earthquakes in Central America since 1520, caused by shifting of the earth's plates and volcanic eruptions. Earthquakes are most frequent in the central highlands, which unfortunately is where most of the country's largest cities are located. There are 14 large volcanoes in the country, although many are extinct. The largest are the Santa Ana (2,365m), San Vicente (2,181m) and San Miguel (2,129m) volcanoes. Periodic eruptions over the centuries have covered the country in ash, and usually coincide with earthquakes.

About 90 percent of El Salvador is blessed with incredibly fertile volcanic soil. The Río Lempa, the country's only large river, was formed by volcanic eruptions and has created a 24-kilometer wide alluvial plain in southeast El Salvador. The landscape is dotted by a few large lakes including the Lago de Ilopango, just east of San Salvador. The dazzlingly blue Lago de Coatepeque lies next to Cerro Verde and the Izalco and Santa Ana Volcanoes west of San Salvador. Geysers are scattered throughout the country and provide some of the country's electricity.

El Salvador's Tallest Volcanoes

Meters

2,300
2,200
2,100
2,000
1,900
1,800
1,700

Izalco San Salvador Cerro Verde San Miguel San Vicente Santa Ana

■ **Political Divisions.** El Salvador is divided into 14 **departments**, each with its own capital. Departmental capitals are usually the largest city in the department, and often share the department's name. **San Salvador**, the nation's capital, sits in the middle of the country in the department of the same name.

The rest of the country (as well as this book) is divided into three main regions. The **western region** contains Ahuachapán, Santa Ana, Sonsonate and La Libertad departments. The **northern region** contains Chalatenango, Cabañas and Cuscatlán departments. The **eastern region** is made up of San Vicente, La Paz, Usulután, San Miguel, Morazán and La Unión departments.

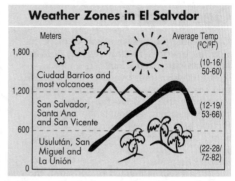

Weather Zones in El Salvdor

Meters		Average Temp (°C/°F)
1,800		(10-16/ 50-60)
	Ciudad Barrios and most volcanoes	
1,200	San Salvador, Santa Ana and San Vicente	(12-19/ 53-66)
600	Usulután, San Miguel and La Unión	(22-28/ 72-82)
0		

Climate

El Salvador is situated in the tropics, where the climate remains more or less constant throughout the year but rainfall changes greatly with the seasons. In fact, the temperature changes more from day to night than it does from season to season. El Salvador spans three different weather zones (see table above).

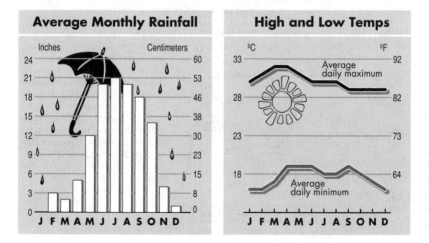

Average Monthly Rainfall

Inches — Centimeters

	Inches	Centimeters
24		60
21		53
18		46
15		38
12		30
9		23
6		15
3		8
0		0

J F M A M J J A S O N D

High and Low Temps

°C — °F

	°C	°F
33	Average daily maximum	92
28		82
23		73
18	Average daily minimum	64

J F M A M J J A S O N D

The **rainy season**, known as *invierno* (winter), runs from mid-May to mid-October. Rain comes in predictable spurts, usually in late afternoon, and drenches some parts of the country more than others. The rains brings out the best of the country's foliage—the greens are especially green—but many backcountry roads become impassable. The **dry season**, or *verano* (summer), begins in mid-November and continues through mid-April. Flowers bloom across the country, but the weather is still hot. The short periods in between summer and winter are transitional seasons, similar to spring and autumn in zones farther from the equator.

Environment

El Salvador's incredible natural beauty is threatened by pollution, deforestation, and the effects of a devastating civil war. In light of the problems, there's hope that political peace will allow the country to focus some attention on the environment and save its few remaining resources.

> Plans are underway to reforest the Guazapa Volcano, a guerrilla stronghold devastated by the fighting, in memory of the 75,000 Salvadorans killed during the war. One tree will be planted in this "reconciliation forest" for each victim.

■ **What Little is Left.** El Salvador's environment has been under attack from the moment Europeans set foot in the country. The UN estimates that El Salvador has already lost an astronomical 95 percent of its natural forests at the second-highest rate of deforestation in the world. The country's virgin forest has been so thoroughly depleted that the remaining five percent is no longer sufficient to meet domestic demand, so wood for construction is now imported from Honduras. Many animals that once thrived in the forests, especially wild cats and monkeys, are now extinct. Erosion depletes 20 percent of the country's topsoil base every year, and has left up to three-quarters of the land useless.

Limited access to fresh water is also a problem. During the 1980s, the water table in San Salvador dropped more than one meter per year. To meet demand, water was redirected from a river 130 kilometers away. Eventually, though, that source turned out to be polluted.

Environmental Statistics

■ Salvadoran farmland is only half as productive as it was 30 years ago.

■ Five types of fresh water fish, three kinds of amphibians, 21 reptiles, 68 birds and 18 mammals have become extinct in El Salvador.

■ Ninety percent of the rivers in the country are polluted.

■ **Public Health.** It's occasionally taken public health disasters to focus attention on El Salvador's environment. Each year, pesticides banned in the US but still used in El Salvador kill thousands of people. Shoals of dead fish wash up on shore at the end of the cotton-growing season when the rains flush pesticides out to sea. During the war, bombs dropped into jungles ignited uncontrollable forest fires that left the soil bare, contributing to erosion.

In November 1990, sulfuric acid explosions in Soyapango, near San Salvador, burned through tin-roofed homes in the area. The government said nothing, but reporters discovered that toxic waste was "stored" in steel drums scattered around a nearby facility. The government responded by handing out antihistamines.

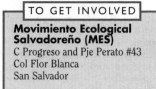

TO GET INVOLVED

Movimiento Ecological Salvadoreño (MES)
C Progreso and Pje Perato #43
Col Flor Blanca
San Salvador

Foreign companies have contributed to the debacle by looking to El Salvador and other Central American countries as storage facilities for waste that would need special treatment back home. A Texas-based company tried to ship toxic ash to La Unión, claiming that the material was harmless and would make good housing foundations. This attempt to "help" the people of La Unión would have brought enough heavy metal to make anyone living on it deathly sick.

Finally, the absence of environmental regulations and the inability to enforce laws contribute to the losses. Some rivers are polluted with pesticides that are used excessively or illegally. Forests are destroyed for fuel, since high tariffs have made oil difficult to import for many years, and skyrocketing populations further strain resources that are already stretched to the breaking point.

■ **Hope.** As bleak as it may seem, there is still hope for El Salvador's battered environment. The Laguna El Jocotal in San Miguel department is being monitored as part of a wildlife restoration project. The area around Trifinio, at the juncture of El Salvador, Honduras and Guatemala, will be developed with money from the Inter-American Development Bank, although there's some fear that Bosque Montecristo may be damaged in the process. And, perhaps most significantly in a country torn by political strife, politicians from the left and right are beginning to agree that the environment can't wait much longer.

People

El Salvador is a small but crowded country. Almost everyone speaks Spanish, and little of the original indigenous cultures survive. El Salvador's small upper class is mostly of European descent, while the majority of peasants are *mestizos* (mixed blood) or the descendants of indigenous peoples.

Of approximately five million Salvadorans, about half live in or around the cities, which are crowded and growing quickly. The incredible population density—250 people per square kilometer—is made worse by a 2.2 percent annual growth rate. As a result nearly half the population is under 15 years old. At the present rate, El Salvador's population will double by the year 2025. Life expectancy is about 65 years and infant mortality is 49 per 1,000 (1990).

■ **Cultural Groups.** El Salvador can be roughly divided into three ethnic groups, which also tend to correspond to social classes. Salvadorans of pure European descent comprise about one percent of the population but most of the country's upper class. *Mestizos,* who make up 89 percent of the population, are of mixed European and indigenous descent, and form part of all the social classes. Native Salvadorans comprise just ten percent of the population, are usually poor and are limited to parts of the southwest and southeast.

■ Indigenous Inhabitants. El Salvador's indigenous population is mostly descended from the Pipil tribe. Since the Spanish arrived, they have frequently been repressed for raising their political voice and for resisting the appropriation of their lands (which has often meant siding with the left). They became increasingly isolated as the country adopted the language and customs of the Spanish. Today El Salvador's remaining indigenous populations struggle to protect their communities from cultural extinction.

Native Salvadorans (meaning those of indigenous descent) aren't easy to spot on the streets, partly because *La Matanza* in 1932 killed much of El Salvador's indigenous population. After the massacre, native people learned to dress in European clothes, cut their hair and speak Spanish in public. Many fear that by reasserting their traditional culture they will be inviting another crackdown. In recent years, there's been a limited revival of indigenous culture—due in part to the sale of native handicrafts—but the government doesn't do much to help.

> **TO GET INVOLVED**
>
> **Salvadoran National Association of Native People (ANIS)**
> C Obispo Morroquín
> Oficina Antigua Adjuana #5
> Sonsonate
> Tel 451-1721

■ Women. Most women in El Salvador lead a difficult life that hasn't changed for centuries despite war, famine and political upheaval. Salvadoran women have more difficulty finding employment, struggle against abusive and legally-sanctioned traditions and frequently bear children at such a young age that they are too busy raising families to strive for change. Only recently has their situation slowly begun to improve.

Women struggle to find work throughout the country. With 20 percent more women out of work than men, many *Salvadoreñas* resort to selling fruit and making *pupusas* on the street. Marital violence and the treatment of women as second-rate citizens, although evident in every country, is a particular problem in Latin America. A provision remains in El Salvador's civil code that requires a man to protect his wife and a wife to be obedient to her husband. There is also a history of sexual abuse in the countryside, where young, uneducated women work for wealthy landowners who control their pay and their lives. A 1971 survey indicated that one-third of all 14-year-old girls in the Salvadoran countryside had become pregnant at least once.

The war has also scarred the lives of many women. The death of husbands and fathers left many women and girls to tend households—often filled with children—by themselves. Without a second income, these women struggle to find work to support their remaining family members.

Despite the war, the past decade has brought hope for Salvadoran women. Women fighting alongside men in the guerrilla armies gave many men a newfound respect for their female companions. The country's upper class, including many Salvadorans educated abroad, now includes more women professionals than ever before. Nearly 30 percent of the country's doctors and attorneys, and an even larger percentage of dentists and high school teachers, are women.

BACKGROUND

TO GET INVOLVED

Still On The Move

More than one in four Salvadorans—about 1,300,000 altogether—abandoned their homes and villages at some point during the civil war, and some half million who are still in the country have never returned. Of the rest, about 150,000 are in the United States and more than 250,000 emigrated to Mexico. Church-run resettlement villages were established during the civil war, but they were only a temporary cure. If you're interested in getting involved, contact:

Creative Associates (USAID)
Blvd El Hipodromo
Pje 1 #124
Col San Benito
San Salvador
Tel 298-1540, 224-6347

Christian Committee of the Displaced
23a C Pte #1520
San Salvador
Tel 226-3717, 225-5853

Foundation for the Displaced
University of Central America
Autopista Sur
San Salvador
Tel 224-0011, ext 133

Fundación Habitat
C Pacaraina #20
Col Miramonte
San Salvador
Tel 226-0816

International Rescue Committee
41a Av Sur and 12a C Pte #2137
San Salvador
Tel 271-0924

UN High Commissioner for Refugees
73a Ave Sur #232
Col Escalón
San Savlador
Tel 298-1809, 298-1810

The pill is gradually becoming the country's most frequently-used contraceptive, although the nation's gynecological wards are filled with an alarming number of women injured during poorly-performed abortions. Public hospitals in El Salvador, influenced by the Church, still refuse to give abortions.

Finally, the legal system shows signs that the rights of women will be guarded more closely. The country's labor code protects pregnant women from performing dangerous jobs, although this is occasionally used as grounds for discrimination. The 1983 constitution includes a provision guaranteeing equality for men and women in the eyes of the law. As a practical matter, though, many of these laws are rarely enforced.

Religion

The Catholic Church has always been extremely powerful in Latin America, and El Salvador, with a population
more than 80 percent Christian, is no exception. In
recent decades, Liberation Theology has influenced the
Church and has been at the basis of its struggle with the
government and the army.

Liberation Theology, espoused by Rome in the mid-1960s, is essentially an
attempt by the Church to make Catholicism more accessible to the poorer, working
classes, and to make them more politically aware by instructing them to improve
their lot during this life instead of waiting for a future paradise. Beginning in the
late 1960s, the Church organized base communities throughout the country that
brought people together to worship and to take political action. As these base communities became more and more revolutionary and threatened landowners and the
oligarchy, community members were frequently repressed, jailed and killed.

■ **The Church Against the Army.** The army first began its campaign against the
Church in the 1970s, just as Liberation Theology began to take hold. Jesuit priests
were targeted from the beginning, but the frequency of terrorist acts rose sharply
when Oscar Romero became archbishop and began preaching the new gospel in
earnest. By the late 1970s, when the army raided towns to search for communists,
soldiers frequently attacked peasants who belonged to the Church.

The campaign continued throughout the civil war. When the FMLN attacked
the capital in November 1989, the army rounded up hundreds of Church leaders
and charged them with having sheltered guerrillas. Relations between the Church
and the military deteriorated quickly, until six Jesuit priests were murdered at the
University of Central America later in the month. The investigation which followed led to the historic decision to prosecute military officers. In all, some 600
priests or Church sympathizers were murdered during the war.

Today the Church operates various social programs, but most are less politically oriented than they once were. An arm of the Church distributes international
aid, and another operates an orphanage. The Church's legal aid office investigates
human rights abuses in the country, in spite of frequent threats by the army. The
late Archbishop Arturo Rivera y Damas, a less charismatic leader than his fiery
predecessor, moved the Church to the political center and eased away from its
sponsorship of Liberation Theology.

Festivals

El Salvador's many festivals are religious and cultural events that bring
communities together, providing a common occasion to preserve and participate in religious traditions, eat and
dance in the streets. The most important festivals are the *fiestas patronales*
(patron festivals) dedicated to each
town's patron saint.

Of all the festival dances in El Salvador,
you're most likely to see the Baile de
Los Historiantes (Dance of the
Historiantes). The story told through the
dance mixes themes from pre-Columbian
religious life with scenes from Spain
under Muslim domination. At one point
God intervenes to help the Christians
defeat the Moors.

> **"The Church's position concerning the conflict is clear: the Church is on the side of those who suffer and is against prejudice."**
>
> — Archbishop Rivera y Damas, in reply to an accusation that his homilies divide the people of El Salvador

VOICES FROM THE WAR

The festivals originated when the Spanish arrived and imposed Catholicism on native tribes. Now many towns carry both a Catholic and an indigenous name, such as Concepción Quetzaltepeque. Most, but not all, festivals are celebrated during the dry season (November through April). Outside the major cities, few people go to work for the duration of the festival.

Festivals are exciting affairs. Preparations begin a full 15 days ahead of time to give people time to prepare food and drinks, including *chicha,* which has to ferment. Vendors sell local food specialties, including *tamales, pan de torta* (a sweet bread similar to pound cake), chicken soup and plenty of sweets. Groups play traditional music and religious icons are carried soberly through the streets. During most festivals a young "queen" is crowned to preside over the celebrations.

■ **Important Holidays.** Huge **Christmas** celebrations throughout the country typically include three additional activities. First, children dress up and sing at the church and various houses. Next an image of the Virgin Mary is carried house to house to solicit donations for the church. Finally a mass known as the Misa de Gallo (Rooster's Mass) is held at midnight on Christmas Eve. San Salvador celebrates one of the country's biggest festivals, called the **Fiestas Agostinas**, from the last week of July through the first week of August.

Thursday and Friday during the week before Easter Sunday, or **Semana Santa**, are also popular times to celebrate. In some cities with especially large festivals, Salvadorans participate in the Procession of the Crosses by walking across the town to visit mock-ups of the "14 Stations of the Cross," tracing Jesus' route to the Crucifixion. Izalco and Texistepeque both have famous Semana Santa celebrations.

Education

El Salvador's educational system, and especially its public schools, has never been very effective. Rural schools have always been scarce, and consequently much of the rural population is illiterate. The civil war only made matters worse, since many schools were closed for the decade while government spending was redirected to the army.

Universities in the country have experienced other, non-financial problems. Underground movements, especially the FMLN, have always used the country's university system as an ideological springboard. The army, meanwhile, has been hypersensitive to criticism levied by professors and students, and has occasionally attacked campuses.

Students have always been at the forefront of political change in El Salvador. In 1944, students helped bring down the Martínez dictatorship by organizing a general strike. In 1989, the FMLN used the National University as a base to launch raids on the capital. The army responded by bombing and invading the campus.

■ **Problems with the Military.** The army, for its part, has always reacted badly to criticism from intellectual circles, and has, traditionally associated universities with the liberal ideology it so fiercely opposes. The paranoia is at least partially justified at the National University, where relaxed entrance requirements allow many lower-caliber students to enroll, including many from poorer families. The university, perceived as more of a political center than a research institution, graduates few students but is filled with left-wing student groups.

The army has infiltrated or attacked university campuses twice since the beginning of the civil war. In 1980, army troops overran the National University and killed 22 students. Soldiers were repeatedly stationed at the entrance of the National University throughout the 1980s.

The Jesuit-run University of Central America ("La UCA"), more prominent than the National University, wasn't immune to attack either, as the murder of the six Jesuit priests there in 1989 demonstrated. That same year, La UCA's printing press was dynamited by the military after scholastic journals included articles that were interpreted as sympathetic to the FMLN.

Public education is supposed to be free but really isn't, since many parents are unable to afford the school materials their children need to attend. Only 15 percent of Salvadoran students make it to secondary school, including 6 percent of rural students versus 62 percent of urban students. Only 30 percent of the country's rural schools offer classes through the fifth grade. The deficient system has produced an undereducated populace; about half the work force has not studied beyond the third grade, and three in five people in rural areas are illiterate.

During the civil war, the education system suffered losses it could little afford. About 2,000 schools closed in the first two years of the war, leaving more than 100,000 chil-

---

TO GET INVOLVED

World Organization for Education
Avenida Los Sismiles
Metrocentro Norte
San Salvador
Tel 225-1277

Foundation for the Development of Education
Final Av Masferrer Sur
#701
Col Maquilishuat
San Salvador
Tel 223-5707

Educational Statistics

■ According to UNESCO estimates, literacy among Salvadorans over the age of 15 was 73 percent.

■ About 70 percent of El Salvador's children in the primary school age-group were enrolled.

■ Only 15 percent of children old enough for secondary schooling were enrolled.

(1990)

dren on the streets. Per-capita spending on education dropped 66 percent from 1978 to 1987 as the government shifted its resources towards fighting the FMLN. Leaders of teachers' unions have been targeted and killed for decades by interest groups sympathetic to the army and other conservative causes.

The peace accords can only benefit the country's education system. Student groups, following the lead of the FMLN, have accepted the peace accords. The army now has fewer enemies at the country's universities. Unfortunately, the money once used to support the school system isn't likely to be used for that purpose again anytime soon, since so much of the rest of the country now needs rebuilding as well.

Politics and Government

■ **Structure.** The Salvadoran government has a unicameral legislature elected every three years, with members eligible for re-election. A president serves one five-year term and cannot be re-elected. The Supreme Court is the third branch of government. Municipalities are governed by popularly-elected mayors.

■ **Background.** Political power in El Salvador derives from various sources. The wealthy minority has traditionally supported right-wing politics and the military in undermining efforts at political reform. The military and the US government, through its embassy in El Salvador, have their own agendas and are able to wield control through force and money, respectively. Although the country has always had an enormous underclass, it has never been able to organize effectively and has been repressed for decades.

The Salvadoran government has been traditionally right-wing and fiercely anti-socialist. Since coffee became the country's dominant crop and a few wealthy families gained control of most of the country's plantations, coffee money was funneled to right-wing political causes to curry favor with the military and to discourage the rise of leftist parties that advocated land reform.

El Salvador's left, backed by the peasants, has had few opportunities to gain political power. When the chances have appeared, as with Duarte's victories in 1972 and 1984, either the military has stepped in or the right has made compromise impossible through its support of death squads.

In addition to the military and right-wing politicians, the US government, via its embassy, has been the other main player in Salvadoran politics. For the entire civil war, the US supplied arms to the once-backwards military and kept the government afloat with regular loans that were eventually forgiven. The army needed weapons and airplanes to fight the guerrillas, especially since soldiers were initially reluctant to fight outside of a nine-to-five, Monday through Friday schedule. The government, meanwhile, had steered most of its budget to the military and needed cash just to stay afloat.

■ **Recent Changes.** The last twenty years have seen a tremendous upheaval in Salvadoran politics. The rise of the Christian Democrats in the mid-60s was a partial victory for the left, since Duarte and his clique were moderate and represented the country's lower and upper-middle classes. The rise and subsequent legalization of the FMLN represents a further step in the democratization of Salvadoran politics.

The peace accords have started to open the political process to moderate forces and have reduced the influence of the military, the US embassy and the most strident right-wing politicians. Leftist leaders are now able to confront the government more easily and safely, although death squads are occasionally blamed for continuing political murders. The US embassy, with much less aid to distribute, carries a smaller stick. And the military, stripped by the peace process of many of its most notorious generals and without a significant internal threat to confront, has given hints of support for the political process.

Political Q & A

■ **Q:** How could ARENA stay in power after being connected with the death squads and the army during the civil war?

■ **A:** The guerrillas overestimated the sympathies of most Salvadorans. When the FMLN declared, "If everyone doesn't eat, no one eats" and proceeded to sabotage the country's infrastructure, peasants were the first to feel the squeeze. When coffee plantations were bombed and *campesinos* left without work, their already difficult life became unbearable.

Second, although ARENA sympathizers were involved in death squad attacks, the targets were chosen randomly and affected only certain families. Other families, stung by guerrilla sabotage near their villages, were glad to see the army clear the area at almost any price.

Third, ARENA had money and a charismatic leader. Owners of the country's coffee plantations stood to lose everything if the guerrillas won the elections, so they poured money into right-wing causes. D'Aubuisson was a popular figure, in spite of his reputation, and many Salvadorans didn't associate his shady past with the party he represented.

ARENA's recent victory can be ascribed to a combination of the ruling party's political experience, financial advantage and a lingering distrust of the newly-legalized FMLN. This distrust was mostly thanks to ARENA's savvy campaign rhetoric, which presented the vote as a choice between a strong, albeit tarnished, political giant and a ragtag bunch of communist ex-terrorists.

■ **Q:** Why didn't the FMLN succeed in overthrowing the government?

■ **A:** The main reason the guerrillas were unable to achieve their goal of bringing the government to a standstill was the air power supplied by the US. For the guerrillas to instigate a general popular uprising, they had to present themselves as a reasonable alternative government to the one currently in power, which they were ultimately unable to do. As a result, their support among the masses fell below the level necessary to unseat the government.

In the early stages of the war, the FMLN was able to present itself as a viable political alternative by taking control of towns for days or even weeks at a time, as the government army struggled to figure out how to retaliate on a nine-to-five schedule. But when the US kicked in by providing the army with jets which enabled the air force to bomb large targets like rebels control centers, everything changed.

From that point on the guerrillas were unable to operate in large groups, since these groups were easily spotted from the air and bombed by the government's jets. Where once they were able to seize entire towns, the best the FMLN could do now was to plant a bomb and run. Large-scale assaults and face-to-face confrontation with the army were out of the question.

The guerrillas, essentially, were reduced to roving bands of terrorists. To many, the FMLN's actions began to seem almost as unacceptable as the atrocities committed by the army and the death squads. As the majority of poor Salvadorans started to feel the effects of the FMLN's continued attempts to disrupt the things on which day-to-day life depended—such as buses, bridges and roads—popular support for the guerrilla movement waned.

Political parties

■ **National Conciliation Party (PNC).** A right-wing party created by the military. Colonel Arturo Molina, the PNC candidate for president in 1972, was opposed by Duarte of the Christian Democrats. Duarte was defrauded of the win and exiled.

TO GET INVOLVED

Human Rights Organizations

Many human rights organizations set up shop in El Salvador during the war, and their work is far from over. If you're interesting in helping out, contact:

Tutela Legal del Arzobispado
(Church office that deals with human rights)
1a C Pte
Seminario San José de la Montaña
San Salvador
Tel 226-2085, 224-4427, 224-0492

University of Central America Human Rights Office
Universidad Centroamericana
Autopista Sur
San Salvador
Tel 224-0011

United Nations Observer Force in El Salvador (ONUSAL)
Hotel El Salvador
87a Av and 15a C Pte
Tel 298-0014

Committee of Families for the Liberation of Political Prisoners and the Disappeared
C Gabriela Mistral
Casa 614
Col Centroamerica
San Salvador

Committee of Mothers and Relatives of Prisoners, Disappeared and Assassinated
C Gabriela Mistral
Casa 617
Col Centroamerica
San Salvador

Committee of Mothers of the Disappeared
Santa Eugenia 122
Pje San Miguelito
Tel 222-9023

Government Human Rights Commission
Paseo General Escalón
87a Av Sur
Bloque 2 #226
San Salvador
Tel 223-7443

Amnesty International USA
322 8th Av
New York City, NY 10001
Tel 212/807-8400
Fax 212/627-1451

In the end, opposition to the military strengthened as opponents became convinced that an armed insurrection was the only way to achieve political change. The PNC was gradually replaced by ARENA.

■ **Republican National Alliance (ARENA).** Founded in 1981 by army major Roberto d'Aubuisson and Armando Calderon Sol, ARENA brought together right-wing politicians and the army. ARENA gained popularity when President Duarte was unable to bring an end to the war or reverse the country's economic decline. In 1988, ARENA gained control of the National Assembly and a year later Cristiani, a protege of d'Aubuisson's, became president. The party has traditionally stood for nationalism and anti-communism, and is composed of many factions, including some conservatives who oppose any settlement with the FMLN.

■ **Christian Democratic Party (PDC).** Moderate and reformist, opposed to class conflict, party of the middle class, pro-civilian control. The liberal PDC, founded in the mid-60s and led for many years by José Napoleon Duarte, lost support for not being able to bring peace to the country while it retained power. During the mid-1980s, the PDC under Duarte aligned itself closely to the military to avoid being accused of sympathizing with the left.

Duarte failed in part because his administration was perceived as corrupt, because the continuing human rights abuses angered the US Congress and because the war dragged on. PDC vote counts have dropped in every election since the early 1980s.

■ **Democratic Convergence Party (CD).** A handful of socialist and liberal democratic parties formed the Democratic Convergence in 1988 to participate in the 1989 election campaign. Leftist leaders Rubén Zamora and Guillermo Ungo were placed in charge. The party had some support in the larger cities. When the FMLN was legalized for the 1994 election, the Democratic Convergence joined with other leftist parties, including the FMLN, to support Zamora's bid for the presidency.

■ **Faribundo Martí Front for National Liberation (FMLN).** Both a political party and former military force, the FMLN was an umbrella organization for many leftist organizations that weren't large enough to stand on their own. For most of the civil war, Joaquín Villalobos lead the major rebel organizations. Early on, the FMLN joined with the Democratic Revolutionary Front (FDR), a collection of dissident leftist groups.

Four guerrilla groups forged an alliance with the FMLN and agreed to support Rubén Zamora in his campaign for president in 1994. Zamora shaved his beard for the election to appear more clean-cut. Prior to the campaign, Zamora made fundraising trips to the United States, and discussed the economy and the social system, rather than the war, in advertisements. As the election approached, elements of the FMLN actually renounced Marxism.

The transition from warfare to politics was difficult for the FMLN and its supporters. Each of the leftist parties that comprised the FMLN backed a separate candidate in the 1994 San Salvador mayoral elections. After the election, in which the left placed second with 32 percent of the votes, the FMLN struggled to prevent its constituency from splintering off into separate political parties. Eventually, though, Marxist and moderate factions found it impossible to coexist under the same title, and the party was dissolved in December 1994

> "Soldier, why risk your life for a miserable salary? We're all poor here. Defect now."
>
> — Guerrilla graffiti

> "My country is a small country
> Tiny
> So infinitesimal
> That I don't know where they fit
> All the dead."
>
> — Unknown Salvadoran

> "Tremble, tremble communists!
> Because the people have awakened.
> They've understood, they've understood
> Who is the enemy."
>
> — ARENA campaign song

VOICES FROM THE WAR

Economy

In El Salvador, opportunities are few, pay is low and bloated government bureaucracies empty the treasury and raise barriers and rules that make it difficult to get things done. Since so much of the land is cultivated for coffee, the country doesn't produce enough food to feed people at home. So while the rich profit from selling coffee abroad, the poor pay a high price to buy the foods they need to survive.

■ **Production in Reverse.** Salvadorans have a reputation as hard workers, but their skills are not so easily applied at home. Work is difficult to find, especially outside the capital, jobs on farms don't pay very much and the minimum wage is universally ignored. Though the average Salvadoran earns around $1,400 a year, most peasants don't make even half that much.

The country's agricultural system has two main markets: foreign countries which buy coffee and a large Salvadoran population which needs food. Coffee plantations take up huge amounts of land, but earn money that returns only to the coffers of the owners who pay their workers low wages and ignore tax requirements. Corn and other staple food crops are rarely farmed, since they are worth much less than coffee. As a result, El Salvador has imported beans, corns and wheat since the 19th century.

■ **Effects of the War.** The war devastated the economy. The FMLN, fighting under the slogan "Either we all eat or no one eats," sabotaged the coffee industry and much of the country's infrastructure. In all, the rebels destroyed more than 70 bridges and 35 percent of the country's buses. Underproduction cost the economy $2 billion each year. The government responded by devoting up to half of its budget to battling the guerrillas.

With the fighting finally over, the Salvadoran economy can only improve. Government reforms are opening the market to international investment and are making Salvadoran companies more competitive. The government is also borrowing money, with international help, to rebuild its infrastructure.

El Salvador's economy has traditionally been strong—as recently as 1970, El Salvador was the most industrialized nation in Central America. The government, spurred on by the fiercely capitalistic ARENA party, is pursuing important structural reforms. The Cristiani government eliminated price controls on many consumer products, made importation easier and removed controls on foreign currency exchanges. In 1992, three banks were privatized, the Hotel Presidente was sold off and the government launched an $81 billion national reconstruction program.

The international community has responded positively to the reform program. The United States Agency for International Development (USAID) administered programs worth $200 million in 1992, the US government wiped out nearly $500 million of the Salvadoran national debt and the International Monetary Fund and the World Bank have provided some large loans. In addition, El Salvador and Guatemala recently established a free-trade zone.

If the country remains politically stable, the economy will continue to grow throughout the end of the 1990s. The government still has a few significant headaches to deal with that make business more difficult, such as a crumbling road system and an antiquated telephone network. But there's work to be done, and construction is booming.

Economic Statistics

Agriculture	Agriculture employs 35 percent of El Salvador's workforce, including seven percent of its male workers.
Cash Crops	The country's main cash crops are coffee, sugar cane and cotton. Corn, rice and beans are its principal food crops.
Land	Half of all landowners in El Salvador own less than 2.5 acres each. Put together, these holdings comprise less than five percent of the country's total area.
Minimum Wage	Industry and commerce: $3.50 per day. Agriculture: $2 per day.
Unemployment	An estimated fifty percent of El Salvador's workforce was unemployed in 1991.
Economic Growth	From 1980 to 1991, El Salvador's economy grew by 1.1 percent. In 1993 alone, it grew by five percent.

El Salvador in the Arts

■ **Movies About El Salvador.** *Salvador* (1986) depicts recent Salvadoran history through the eyes of an American journalist. Oliver Stone's movie is engrossing but fanciful, and at times crosses the line into utter fiction. Whatever its shortcomings, it does give a vivid picture of the chaos of life in El Salvador during the early 1980s. *Romero* (1989) stars Raul Julia as Archbishop Romero. The movie moves slowly but manages to show Romero's struggle and death in a straightforward, almost hypnotic way. In the end, it's more effective than *Salvador* at getting its point across, although less entertaining. Plus, bonus points if you can spot the same actor who plays a "bad guy" in *Salvador* but a "good guy" in *Romero*.

■ **Documentaries.** Many documentaries have also been made about the Salvadoran civil war. ***Making the News Fit*** (Cinema Guild, 1984, 27min) uses El Salvador as an example of how media bias can alter public views of news events. ***El Salvador: The Seeds of Liberty*** (Maryknoll World Video Library, 1981, 24min) focuses on the murder of the American nuns, and includes interviews with famous Salvadoran figures. ***Guazapa*** (Northstar, 1984, 37min) shows how guerrillas lived and fought on the slopes of the Guazapa Volcano, through the eyes of a reporter who lived with them for six weeks. ***Witness to War: An American Doctor in El Salvador*** (First Run Features, 1985, 30min) began as American doctor Charlie Clements' book about his work with Salvadoran peasants during the war. The documentary is well-known but ends up being as much about Clements, a Quaker who finds his neutrality sorely tested, as it is about the guerrillas he treats.

■ **Books About El Salvador.** Most history books on El Salvador focus on the civil war and its historical framework. ***Latin America: A Concise Interpretive History*** (1972), by E. Bradford Burns, is a good introduction to Latin American history. Tina Rosenberg's ***Children of Cain: Violence and the Violent in Latin America*** (1991) is a well-written, chilling account of the author's first-hand experience with Latin American violence from Chile to Guatemala, with a great chapter on El Salvador. Jeremy Paxman's ***Through the Volcanoes*** (1985) and Patrick Marnham's ***So Far From God*** (1985) each have a chapter on the authors' travels through El Salvador. Liisa North's ***Bitter Grounds: Roots of Revolt in El Salvador*** (1985), Philip Russel's ***El Salvador in Crisis*** (1984) and Jenny Pearce's ***Promised Land: Peasant Rebellion in Chalatenango, El Salvador*** (1986) all deal with the civil war and its causes in detail. ***Mirrors of War*** (1985), published by Zed Books, is an excellent collection of poetry and prose excerpts by Salvadoran authors writing about the civil war.

ROQUE DALTON (1933-1975)

The Pen and the Sword

Leftist writer Roque Dalton was a revolutionary and a prolific writer who joined the FMLN near its inception. Although Dalton escaped death and long-term imprisonment many times, he eventually died at the hands of his own comrades.

The son of a Salvadoran mother and an American father, Dalton received international acclaim for his writing. He wrote 15 books in all, most while in exile in Mexico, Cuba and Czechoslovakia. For much of Dalton's life, many of his books were banned in El Salvador for their leftist slant.

While still in El Salvador, Dalton was jailed repeatedly and earned a reputation for escaping under unusual circumstances. In 1960, the right-wing government of Colonel José Maria Lemus fell in a coup days before Dalton was to be executed. Later, an earthquake that rocked the capital opened a hole in Dalton's cell large enough for him to escape through.

Despite the acclaim his writing received, Dalton focused his attention on the revolution. In the early 1970s, he decided to return to his country and join the rebels in their struggle to overthrow the government. He joined a group called the People's Revolutionary Army (ERP) that included Joaquín Villalobos, future leader of the FMLN.

Dalton had difficulty adapting to the regimented rebel lifestyle and fell out of favor with the ERP. Soon, in a move the rebels would later regret, Villalobos and others accused Dalton of spying for the CIA and sentenced him to death. Dalton was executed along with another comrade by a firing squad on May 10, 1975. Their bodies were left at El Playón, the notorious death squad dumping ground. News of Dalton's death rocked the country's intellectuals, many of whom sympathized with the rebel cause but condemned the murder.

Years later, at the conclusion of the civil war, Villalobos discussed the situation more openly. He said that the rebel command made a mistake by killing Dalton, and thereafter preferred to incarcerate rather than execute its suspects. In a postwar interview about Dalton's death, Villalobos commented, "If there [was] one part of the history of our organization that I would like to erase, it would be this."

BACKGROUND

■ **Salvadoran Authors.** Both **Curbstone Press** (321 Jackson St, Willimantic, CT, 06226; tel 203/423-5110) and the **Latin American Literary Review Press** (2300 Palmer St, Pittsburgh, PA 15218; tel 412/351-1477) offer books by Latin American authors in translation, including some by Salvadoran authors.

Salvador Salazar Arrué, writing under the pen name Salarué, was one of the founders of the modern Central American short-story genre. *Cuentos de barro* (Tales of Mud, 1934) is his most famous book. **Claudia Lars** was born in 1899 under the name Carmen Brannon de Samayoa. She went on to become one of Central America's outstanding poets. Her works include *Poesía última 1970-1973* (Latest Poetry 1970-1973, 1976) and *Canciones* (Songs, 1960).

Claribel Alegría was born in Nicaragua in 1924 but considers herself a Salvadoran. She has published many books of poetry dealing with daily life in Central America, including the celebrated collection *Sobrevivo* (I Survive, 1978). She has also written novels, including *Cenizas de Izalco* (Ashes of Izalco, 1966) and *Flores del volcán* (Flowers from the Volcano, 1982). **Manlio Argueta** is one of El Salvador's most famous literary figures. The novelist and poet lived for a time in exile in Costa Rica because his works were so revolutionary and controversial. He is the author of *Un día en la vida* (One Day of Life, 1981) and *Cuscatlán, donde bate la mar del sur* (Cuscatlán, Where the South Sea Beats, 1983).

Roque Dalton was one of El Salvador's most famous and politically-aware poets. He was one of the founders of the left-wing People's Revolutionary Army (ERP) and was killed by his fellow revolutionaries after being fingered as a CIA spy. His books of poetry include *Poémas clandestinas* (Clandestine Poems, 1975) and *Las historias prohibidas del pulgarcito* (Prohibited Stories of Tom Thumb, 1975). *Poetry and Militancy in Latin America*, published by Curbstone Press, describes Dalton's views on the relationship between poetry and political participation.

Basics

Before Going

When to Go

A few factors to consider in planning a trip to El Salvador are airplane ticket prices, the timing of festivals and national holidays and the climate. Ticket prices are much higher from December to mid-January and from July to mid-September, and empty seats are scarce. The big festivals are Semana Santa (the week before Easter), Christmas and the San Salvador city festival during the first week of August, which basically closes down the capital. Commerce grinds to a halt during these periods and everyone either celebrates or relaxes, so it's not a good time to cross a border or to have to deal with officialdom. Tourist spots and beaches are packed during holidays, and most hotel rooms are booked. Finally, since the timing of downpours are fairly predictable during the rainy season (mid-May through mid-October), they shouldn't make much of a difference if plan your daily schedule accordingly.

Packing

Two words: *pack light*. Heed the old correspondent's axiom: "Lay out everything you think you will need on the bed, then take half of that and twice as much money." Or, "Never take more than you could carry at a dead run for a kilometer." Besides, where will you put all your souvenirs if your bag is already stuffed?

■ **Carrying It All**. Internal-frame **backpacks**, the "soft" kind, are the choice of most long-term travelers. They're tough, flexible and usually more comfortable than external-frame packs. They don't protect your possessions as well, but smaller ones have the added benefit of being easy to cram under bus seats or in overhead racks. External-frame **backpacks** are more suited to the trail than the bus. More outside pockets mean easier access and organization, but the exposed frames are easily bent and more awkward.

Convertible packs, the curious offspring of backpacks and suitcases, are a cheaper alternative to a full backpack. They're good if you don't plan to go far off the beaten track. Otherwise, you'll find that they resemble suitcases more than backpacks, since the shoulder straps and hip belt aren't meant for long hikes. Convertible packs usually travel better than backpacks, simply because they're designed with baggage handlers and luggage racks in mind. Take a **suitcase** only if you plan to stay in nicer hotels and have someone else carry your bags most of the time. **Day packs** are good for short trips when you don't want to carry all your stuff with you. Stuff a tough nylon knapsack into your bigger bag.

■ **Clothing**. You don't need many clothes to travel. One set in addition to what you're wearing should be enough, plus a few extras:
- One **sweater, fleece or light jacket** for higher altitudes.
- One or two pairs of **long cotton pants**. Jeans are hot, heavy and take forever to dry.
- One or two pairs of **shorts**. For men, a swimsuit that doubles as a pair of shorts is ideal.
- One or two **light long-sleeved shirts**, including one collared shirt that can pass as "dressed up" if the need arises.
- Two to four **T-shirts**.
- Plenty of **underwear and socks**.
- **Rain gear**. A poncho or waterproof jacket is essential during the rainy season.
- **Swim suit**.

> Salvadoran fashion runs the spectrum from fancy Western styles to purely functional work clothing. Most men wear long pants and an unbuttoned long shirt, even if it's hot outside. Women often wear heels, skirts and blouses. Everyone occasionally wears jeans, but few people wear short pants.

■ **Footwear**. If you plan to do a lot of walking, invest in a good pair of hiking boots. Make sure they fit well and break them in early. A pair of light sneakers or sandals are good for relaxing or exploring the beach.

■ **Bedding**. A sleeping sack (a dark-colored sheet folded lengthwise and sewn across the bottom and partway up the side) is the most versatile sleeping arrangement. A sleeping bag is necessary only if you plan to go camping at higher altitudes. You can also buy a hammock in San Salvador to string up on the beach. Bring your own pillowcase to store dirty clothes in during the day or to replace dirty ones in hotels.

■ **Toiletries**
- **Toothbrush**.
- **Toothpaste**.
- **Dental floss**.
- **Soap**. A bar in a plastic container, or liquid soap.
- **Shampoo/conditioner**. Seal inside a ziplock bag— these things seemed to be designed to come open inside backpacks.
- **Nail clippers/file**.
- **Personal medicines/prescriptions**. Try to keep medications in their original, labeled containers to avoid border hassles ("But officer, I swear they're for headaches!"). Carry copies of the prescriptions for each medicine you are carrying, along with the dosage and the generic name in case you need a refill. Diabetics should take their own sterile needles plus certification of their condition.
- **Contraceptives**.
- **Tampons**.
- **Towel**.

■ **First Aid Kit**. Some kind of medical kit is essential for every traveler who plans to leave major cities. They can be purchased as a unit or assembled on your own. Preassembled kits are available at many outdoor recreation stores, are compact but expensive and usually contain instructions on using the contents. Their contents are geared more towards wilderness-related injuries, so if you buy one you'll probably still want to add some items of your own.
- A brief **personal medical history** that describes your blood type, any specific medical conditions, recent illnesses and prescriptions you are taking.
- **Diarrhea medications**. Take two: Pepto-Bismol and Immodium tablets.
- **Thermometer** in a hard case (some airlines prohibit mercury thermometers).
- **Tweezers**.
- **Calamine lotion** for insect bites and rashes.
- **Anti-fungal powder** for athlete's foot.
- **Antibiotic cream** or salve.
- **Band-Aids** in different sizes.
- **Moleskin** for blisters.
- **Sterile gauze pads**.
- **Adhesive cloth tape**.
- **Elastic (Ace) bandage** for sprains, small or medium size.
- **Pills** for malaria (Chloroquine, etc.), pain (aspirin, Tylenol, Advil), motion sickness (Dramamine), colds (Sudafed, Actifed), antacid tablets (Maalox).

What Makes a Good Gift?

Nothing breaks the ice as well as a gift. Small, unpretentious gifts are best, especially ones from back home such as souvenir T-shirts from your city, state or university. Any other objects with a characteristic logo or picture are fine too, like postcards, buttons and photographs. Children appreciate pens and notebooks, especially if they can't easily afford them for school.

BASICS

▪ Essentials

- **Glasses/contact lenses**, if needed, plus replacement pairs.
- **Insect repellent**.
- **Flashlight**.
- **Film**. Both slide and print film is available in San Salvador at a few photo shops. There are also plenty of places to process film, though slides may be a hassle. Even small towns have places that sell and develop film, but the stock may be stale and all photo finishing is shipped to the capital anyway. The best things to do, then, is to bring your own film and wait until you get home to develop it.
- **Locks**. One combination lock for cheap hotel-room doors, plus a few smaller padlocks to secure your bags. Available cheap from many street vendors in the capital. A cable lock is also useful to lock your bag to something sturdy for short periods or at night.
- **Name tag** securely attached to your bag.
- **Photocopies** of your passport and plane ticket. Leave one set at home.
- **Repair kit** including duct tape (the ultimate repair tool—to avoid taking a whole roll, wrap some around a pencil or something else that's skinny); extra batteries for flashlight and camera; scissors (maybe on Swiss army knife); sewing kit or strong thread and a few needles; spare flashlight bulb.
- **Spanish-English dictionary/phrasebook**.
- Any **special equipment** you may need: camping equipment (tent, sleeping bag, compass, sleeping pad, cooking equipment); snorkeling equipment; a surfboard in a travel case.
- **Sunglasses**.
- Waterproof **sunscreen**.
- **Swiss army knife**. No traveler should be without one. They often include tweezers and scissors.
- **Toilet paper**.
- **Travel alarm clock** or a digital watch with a loud alarm.
- **Wallet-size** photos of yourself, and pictures of your family.
- **Water bottle** for hiking and long bus trips. Camping water bottles (Nalgene) and bicycle water bottles both work well—just be sure they close securely.
- **Ziplock bags**. Great for storing just about anything.

▪ Maybes.

- **Books**. Thick paperbacks are lightest and last longest.
- **Flip-flops** for dirty shower stalls.
- **Hand towel**.
- **Journal** plus pens, paper and envelopes to write letters.
- **Pack cover**. To protect your pack from rain and to discourage thieves.
- **Shortwave radio**.
- **Vitamin supplements**.
- **Walkman** with tapes and extra batteries.
- **Washing supplies**, including detergent, clothesline.
- **Water purification tablets** or a water filter.

Top: View from Hotel de la Montaña, Cerro Verde
Bottom: Playa El Espino

Top: Young vendors, La Libertad
Bottom: *Turicentro* pool, Quetzaltepeque

ID Cards

Student identification cards aren't likely to be helpful in finding deals in El Salvador, but some offer basic insurance and access to special plane fares that make them worthwhile. Entrance fees to museums and such are already inexpensive, so you'll find that your university ID is just as useful (or useless) in many situations.

The International Student Identity Card (ISIC), though, offers benefits that justify its $15 cost. These include an emergency toll-free hotline, limited medical coverage and access to low airplane fares through Council Travel, STA and others travel and educational organizations. The International Youth Card, available to anyone under 26, offers some of the same benefits as the ISIC card. An International Teacher Card is available to educators. For info on these cards, inquire at a local university, contact Council Travel or STA, or call 800/438-2643 in the US.

Health & Travel Insurance

Be sure to straighten out potential complications with health insurance before you leave. Your best bet is to go with your own insurance company, provided it covers you while you're out of the country. The International Student Identity Card carries limited protection which is worth the price of the card. Also, some credit cards

Insurance Checklist

■ **Before Going**
- ✓ Make sure your insurance company covers travel abroad.
- ✓ Understand if and how you will be reimbursed for treatment abroad—most foreign doctors won't accept your insurance card and will require you to pay cash on the spot.
- ✓ See which activities, if any, are not covered under your policy. These tend to be more dangerous pursuits like rock climbing and motorcycling.
- ✓ Always carry your policy number, proof of insurance (an insurance card) and the telephone number of your carrier.

■ **If Something Happens...**
- ✓ Keep all receipts.
- ✓ Report thefts and muggings to the police as soon as they occur and get a copy of the police report.
- ✓ Contact your embassy or consulate for more serious matters like surgery. They can give you the names of reputable doctors and help arrange payment of large bills from your insurance company or your relatives.

BASICS

Travel Insurance Companies

Access America International
PO Box 90315
Richmond, VA 23230-9315
Tel 800/284-8300

Carefree Travel Insurance
PO Box 9366
100 Garden City Plaza
Garden City, NY 11530
Tel 800/323-3149

Europe Assistance Ltd.
252 High Street
Croyden, Surrey
Great Britain CRO 1NF
Tel 01-680-1234

HealthCare Abroad
Wallach & Co Inc
107 West Federal Street
PO Box 480
Middleburg, VA 22117-0480
Tel 800/237-6615

International SOS Assistance
PO Box 11568
Philadelphia, PA 19116
Tel 800/523-8930

**International Travelers'
Assistance Association**
PO Box 10623
Baltimore, MD 21285-0623
Tel 800/732-5309

Teletrip
3201 Farnam Street
PO Box 31685,
Omaha, NE 68131-0618
Tel 800/228-9792

Travel Assistance International
1133 15th Street NW, Suite 400
Washington DC 20005
Tel 800/821-2828

Travel Guard International
1145 Clark St.
Stevens Point, WI 54481-2980
Tel 800-782-5151

Travel Insured International
PO Box 280568
East Hartford, CT 06128-0586
Tel 800/243-3174

offer insurance packages. Finally, there are specialized travel insurance companies which cover just about everything that could possibly happen while traveling, from flight delay reimbursement and lost baggage protection to emergency medical evacuation and repatriation of remains. Their premiums tend to be more expensive, so shop around for the best deal.

Pre-Travel Immunizations

Some of the medications on this list below are just recommended, but others are more certain to save you pain and suffering. Some contraindications (limitations) exist for pregnant women, young children and people with certain medical conditions, so ask your doctor if you're not sure. Record every vaccination you receive in an International Certificate of Vaccination (the "yellow health card"), which is available from most public health departments. Travelers' clinics, usually associated with universities or government health clinics, are excellent sources of information and most give vaccinations.

■ Required Vaccinations/Tests:

AIDS A negative HIV test is required for anyone over 18 who is planning to move to El Salvador permanently. Contact a Salvadoran embassy for details.

Yellow fever A certificate of vaccination for yellow fever is required for anyone older than six months who is entering from an area considered infected, such as Panama and much of South America. *(Single dose, good for ten years)*

■ Recommended Vaccinations:

Malaria Chloroquine phosphate pills taste terrible, but since no chloroquine-resistant mosquito strains have yet invaded El Salvador, they are your best source of protection. Chloroquine is available in its generic form or under the brand name Aralen. *(One 500mg pill per week, beginning two weeks before entering the country and continuing four weeks after returning home)*

Cholera Even though El Salvador is considered a cholera-free country, some doctors recommend a cholera vaccine. The vaccine is only about 50 percent effective, and is considered by many to be more dangerous than the disease itself. Since it isn't required to enter the country, the vaccine is recommended only for people with weak stomachs or for those who plan to spend extended periods in rural areas. *(Single dose, good for six months)*

Hepatitis A (Infectious Hepatitis) A shot of gamma globulin (GG) is recommended for all travelers, especially those planning to spend time in rural areas with poor sanitary conditions. During an extended visit, a booster dose every four to six months is necessary. Get this shot as close as possible to the time you leave, but ask your doctor about how other immunizations that are received at the same time might interfere with it. *(Single dose, good for about six months)*

Typhoid Vaccination with the oral vaccine Ty21a is recommended for people visiting rural areas, for those staying longer than three weeks and for adventurous eaters. An injected vaccination is also available. *(Four pills taken over one week, good for five years; two shots at least four weeks apart, good for three years)*

Rabies A preexposure vaccination with the human diploid cell rabies vaccine (HDCV) or the Rabies Vaccine Adsorbed (RVA) is only recommended for anyone anticipating frequent contact with wildlife. Speak with your doctor about this, since it is expensive. *(Two shots administered over one month)*

Routine Immunizations The standard sequence of childhood immunizations should all be updated before traveling anywhere in the developing world. Check with your doctor for any of these you might need, including tetanus/diphtheria, measles, mumps, rubella, influenza, pneumococcal, poliomyelitis (a booster dose of the oral polio vaccine OPV or inactivated polio vaccine IPV) and a measles booster for anyone born after 1956. Schedule doctors' visits early, since some of these immunizations can't be administered together or require follow-up shots.

Volunteer Opportunities

El Salvador's turbulent political history has given rise to many grass-roots volunteer groups. Most have a leftist slant and welcome volunteers from abroad.

Christians for Peace in El Salvador (CRISPAZ) have been sending volunteers to El Salvador to promote literacy and health care for ten years. CRISPAZ is ecumenical but is open to anyone. They also publish a quarterly news and analysis magazine called SALVANET. Volunteer positions last at least one year. *(1135 Mission Rd, San Antonio, TX 78210; tel 210/534-6996)*

The Committee for Solidarity with the People of El Salvador (CISPES) began in 1980 in opposition to US involvement in El Salvador and has evolved into a sizable activist organization. They are very left-leaning and make no bones about their affiliations with the FMLN. Write them for information about their programs dealing with social justice and human rights. *(19 W 21st St #502, New York, NY 10010; tel 212/229-1290)*

The Fellowship on Reconciliation Task Force on Latin America and the Caribbean offers a volunteer program on which you can work with poor majorities on nonviolence education and human rights efforts. Costs such as travel, food and lodging are not included, and applicants must be at least 21. FRTFLAC also runs the Resource Center for Nonviolence in Santa Cruz. *(515 Broadway, Santa Cruz, CA 95060; tel 408/423-1626)*

The International Solidarity Center (CIS) in San Salvador houses the Mélida Montes Language School (see Studying in El Salvador) and acts as a "reference point for international solidarity." The center was started in part by CISPES and places volunteers throughout El Salvador working with grassroots organizations, marginal communities and special-interest groups. *(Urb Padilla Cuéllar, Pje Los Pinos #17, San Salvador; tel 225-0076)*

The National Central American Health Rights Network sends delegations to El Salvador and other Central American countries to perform health assessments and investigate health conditions. Tours run about 10 days and cost $700-$800, including everything but airfare. *(11 Maiden Lane, Suite 10D, New York, NY 10038; tel 212/732-4790)*

Partners of the Americas pairs US states with specific areas of Latin America to plan and carry out programs in rural development, health and education. Louisiana is paired with El Salvador, but the programs should be open to anyone who is interested. *(1424 K St NW, Washington DC 20005; tel 202/628-3300)*

Peace Brigades International have offered programs promoting nonviolence and democracy in El Salvador since 1987. They accept Spanish-speaking volunteers for a minimum of 7 months, and prefer people over 25. *(2642 College Ave, Berkeley, CA 94704; tel 510/540-0749)*

Salvadoran Universities

Universidad Centroamericana José Simeon Cañas (UCA)
(Public)
Autopista Sur and Jardines de Guadalupe
San Salvador
Tel 273-4400

Universidad Americana
(Private)
Centro Professional Feria Rosa
San Salvador
Tel 279-0680, 223-9691

Universidad Francisco Gavidia
(Private)
Alam Roosevelt #3031
San Salvador
Tel 224-5962, 223-9704)

Universidad El Salvador
(Public)
Ciudad Universitaria
San Salvador
Tel 225-8826

Studying in El Salvador

To study in a Salvadoran school or university you are required to produce a certified high school diploma, a passport, a copy of your birth certificate and a medical certificate. If you write well in advance of the time you plan to go and ensure that your university will accept transfer credits, you can save yourself some money. The University of Central America is the best university in El Salvador.

▪ Language Schools

AmeriSpan Unlimited offers Spanish classes starting at $345 for two weeks, which includes travel insurance, homestay and two meals a day. Classes have a maximum of four people and meet for four hours a day. Optional airport service and excursions cost more. *(PO Box 40513, Philadelphia, PA 19106; tel 800/879-6640)*

The Mélida Anaya Montes Language School is run by CISPES. The language program is $177.50 per week or $710 per month, including homestay and two meals a day. Political and cultural discussions and field trips are included. *(CISPES, 19 W 21st St #502, New York, NY 10010; tel 212/229-1290)*

▪ Other Educational Opportunities

Central American Mission Partners (CAMP) is a non-profit humanitarian organization that runs an educational study tour of Central America. The tour covers many angles of the history and culture of Central America, focusing on the role of the Church. The $1,350 fee covers airfare, hotel accommodations and other arrangements. *(PO Box 10206, Oakland, CA 94610; tel 510/644-8077)*

Other Useful Organizations and Publications

■ **General Resources**

DataCenter is a storehouse of information on worldwide social issues, focusing on Latin America and the Third World, human rights and Right to Know issues. The data is available through a public-access library, research and clipping services and computerized information services. *(464 19th St, Oakland, CA 94612-2297; tel 835-4692)*

The Overseas Development Network has a great list of publications about volunteering throughout the Third World, including *The Peace Corps and More: 120 Ways to Work, Study and Travel in the Third World* for $10. *(Publications Department, 333 Valencia St, Suite 330, San Francisco, CA 94103; tel 415/431-4204)*

The South American Explorers Club has a wealth of information on all of Latin America. Their humorous quarterly newsletter/catalog *South American Explorer* is filled with travel guide listings, trip reports and other goodies. Membership benefits include discounts on catalog items and travel assistance. They'll be glad to send you information on a particular destination. *(126 Indian Creek Rd, Ithaca, NY 14850; tel 607/277-0488; yearly membership $30)*

Third World Resources has the best resource list going, with dozens of organizations, books, periodicals, pamphlets and films. Their *Resource Center Bulletin* is published quarterly. *(464 19th St, Oakland, CA 94612-2297; tel 800/735-3741)*

Volunteers for Peace offers workcamps in Ecuador, Cuba, Guatemala, Mexico and Costa Rica, and publish a resource list of volunteer opportunities in Latin America. *(43 Tiffany Rd, Belmont, VT 05730; tel 802/259-2759)*

■ **Travelers with Disabilities**

The Information Center for Individuals with Disabilities assists disabled travelers with fact sheets, newsletters and disabled-friendly travel agent lists. *(Fort Point Pl, 27-43 Wormwood St, Boston, MA 02210-1606; tel 617/727-5540)*

Mobility International USA provides information on handicapped travel around the world and has a list of publications and videos. It also offers exchange programs specifically for travelers with disabilities. *(PO Box 10767, Eugene, OR 97440; tel 503/343-1284; yearly membership $20)*

The Society for the Advancement of Travel for the Handicapped has a list of tour operators and other information geared to disabled travelers. For handicapped-travel information on a specific destination such as El Salvador, send them $2 and a self-addressed stamped envelope. *(347 5th Ave, Suite 610, New York, NY 10016; tel 212/447-7284; yearly membership $45, students and senior citizens $25)*

Travel Industry and Disabled Exchange promotes disabled travel through booklets and newsletters. *(5435 Donna Av, Tarzana CA 91356; tel 818/343-3786; yearly membership $15)*

■ **Other Publications**
The Diabetic Traveler is a quarterly newsletter. *(Box 8223 RW, Stamford, CT, 06905; tel 203/327-5832; yearly subscription $18)*
The International Gay Travel Association can provide you with a list of member travel agencies. *(PO Box 4974, Key West, FL 33041; tel 800/448-8550)*

Internet Resources
The rapidly-expanding world of the Internet provides contact with over 20 million people around the world, so odds are you can find people interested in Latin America, Central America and El Salvador. Large bulletin boards like Compuserve and America Online are good places to communicate.

Internet Lists

- Some of the information posted on these lists is in Spanish.
- sub: address to join the list
- list: address to post a message on the list
- On Your Own: jjb9e@uva.pcmail.virginia.edu

Center for Information, Documentation and Research Aid in El Salvador at the University of Central America
 cidai@huracan.cr
Central America General
sub: listserv@ubvm.bitnet
list: centam-l@ubvm.bitnet
Latin American Database Interest Group
 ladbad@unmb
Latin America General
sub:lasnet-request@emx.utexas.edu
list: lasnet@emx.utexas.edu
 lasnet@utxvm.bitnet
 nicbbs@bitnic.bitnet
Latin American History
 hlatam@syncorva.cortland.edu
 h123ahg@mailhost.tcs.tulane.edu

Latin American Poetry
 postmast@unalcol
Latin American Music
 crjh@asuacad
Latin American and Caribbean Folklore
 sub/list: follac@ccwf.cc.utexas.edu
Rocky Mountain Council for Latin American Studies
 cneas@unmb
The New York Transfer News Collective is a non-partisan, non-profit newsgroup that distributes "all the news that doesn't fit" concerning Latin America. You can connect by modem (212/675-9690 or 212/675-9663) to access news services, an online library, discussion groups and articles on many Latin American countries and related topics. The minimum three-month subscription costs $40; a year costs $125. (sub: nyt@blythe.org; information: info@ blythe.org)

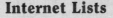

(Lists courtesy of Michael Blackmore)

BASICS

"Usenet News," the world's largest computer bulletin board with over 5,000 topics, is also a great resource. There you can talk to people in newsgroups like Travel, Society and Culture of Latin America and Society and Culture of specific countries (none yet for El Salvador, though).

Coming and Going

Visas & Embassies

To enter El Salvador, you need one of two documents. A **tourist visa**, available from Salvadoran embassies abroad, is good for the life of your passport minus one year. They're free to Americans but cost more to some other nationalities, and require two photos, some background information and a few days' processing time. In El Salvador, refer visa problems to the Office of Immigration, second floor, Federal Building, Centro de Gobierno *(Mon-Fri 8am-12pm, 1:30-4pm)*.

The new **tourist card** is a handy alternative. It's available for $10 at borders and the airport and is good for six months. Citizens of Great Britain and Germany don't need a visa or tourist card to enter. Citizens of the US, Canada and Australia do.

Salvadoran Embassies Abroad

Canada
209 Kent St
Ottawa, Ontario K2P 1Z8
Tel 613/238-2939

Costa Rica
Av 10, C 33
San José
Tel 224-9034

Germany
Burbacherstr. 2
DW-5300
Bonn 1
Tel 228/22-1351

Guatemala
12a C 5-43, Zona 9
Guatemala City
Tel 32-5848

Honduras
2a Ave Nte #205
Col San Carlos
Tegucigalpa
Tel 32-5045

Mexico
Ave Las Palmas #1903
Lomas de Chapultepec
Mexico DF
Tel 596-7366

Nicaragua
Ave del Campo #142 and
  Pje Los Cerros
Reparto Las Colinas
Managua
Tel 74892

Panama
Via España # 124
Edifico Citibank, 4th floor
Panama City
Tel 233020

United Kingdom
5 Great James St
London WC1N 3DA
Tel 071-430-2141

United States
2308 California St NW
Washington DC 20008
Tel 202/265-3480, 265-
  9671

46 Park Ave, 3rd floor
New York, NY 10016
Tel 212/289-3608

104 S Michigan Ave #423 Chicago, IL 60603 Tel 312/332-1393	425 Ingraham Bldg 25 Southeast 2nd Ave Miami, FL 33131 Tel 305/371-8850	1136 International Trade Mart New Orleans, LA 70130 Tel 504/522-4266
6655 Hillcroft #212 Houston, TX 77081 Tel 713/270-6239	2412 W 7th St, 2nd floor Los Angeles, CA 90013 Tel 310/608-4343	870 Market St San Francisco, CA 94102 Tel 415/781-7924

Visas to Leave El Salvador

Visa requirements change, so check with your embassy in El Salvador to see if you need a visa to enter any of the three neighboring countries. Most embassies require your passport, a few passport-sized photos, a small fee and a few days to process a visa.

▪ To Guatemala

Don't need visa: US, Canada, Central American countries, some European countries. A $5 tourist card available at the border is valid for three months.

Do need visa: Australia, New Zealand, other Latin American countries, other European countries. The visa costs $10.

▪ To Honduras

Don't need visa: US, UK, Canada, Australia, New Zealand, Japan, most Western European countries. If you're from one of these countries you can stay for 30 days without a visa. Then you can apply for an extension at an immigration office, and can stay up to 90 days before you have to leave and re-enter the country.

▪ To Nicaragua

Don't need visa: US, Spain, England, some European countries, some South American countries, Guatemala, El Salvador, Honduras. Residents of these countries will receive a 30-day tourist card.

Do need visa: Canada, Australia, New Zealand, some European countries. The visa costs $25 and is valid to enter Nicaragua for 30 days. After you enter the country, it's good for a 30-day stay. Visas can be extended twice, for 30 days more each time, at the immigration office in Managua. After that you have to leave and re-enter the country.

Foreign Embassies in El Salvador

All are in San Salvador
except the US embassy,
which is in nearby Antiguo
Cuscatlán.

Argentina
79 Av Nte #704, Apt #384
Col Escalón
Tel 224-4238

Brazil
Edif la Centroamericana,
  5th floor
Alam Roosevelt #3107
Tel 223-1214

BASICS

Belize
Cond Médico B
Local 5, 2nd floor
Tutunichapa, Urb La
    Esperanza
Tel 226-3588

Chile
Pje Belle Vista #121
Between 9a C Pte and 9a C
    Pte Bis
Col Escalón
Tel. 223-7132

Colombia
C El Mirador #5120
Col Escalón
Tel 279-3290, 279-3204

Costa Rica
Edif la Centroamericana,
    3rd floor
Alam Roosevelt #3107
Tel 279-0303

Ecuador
Blvd. Hippódromo #803
Col San Benito
Tel 224-5921

France
Pje A 41-46, Apt 474
Col La Mascota
Tel 223-0728

Germany
3a C Pte #3831,Apt 693
Col Escalón
Tel 223-6140

Guatemala
15a Av Nte #135 and C
    Arce
Tel 271-2225

Honduras
67a Av Sur #530
Col Flor Blanca
Tel 271-2139, 221-2234

Italy
1a C Pte and 71a Av Nte
    #204
Tel 223-7325

Japan
Av La Capilla #615
Col San Benito
Tel 224-4597

Mexico
Pje 12 and Av
    Circunvalación
Col San Benito
Tel 298-1079, 278-1084

Nicaragua
72a Av Nte
and 1a C Pte #164
Tel 223-7729, 223-9860

Panama
55a Av Nte #2838
and Alam Roosevelt
Tel 223-7893

Peru
Edif. La Centroamericana,
    2nd floor
Alam Roosevelt #3107
PO Box 1620
Tel 223-0008

Spain
51a Av Nte #138
Between 1a C Pte and Alam
    Roosevelt
Tel 223-7961

United Kingdom
Edif. Inter Inversion
Pas Gen Escalón #4828,
    Apt 1591
Tel 298-1763

United States
Final Blvd Santa Elena
Urb Santa Elena
Antiguo Cuscatlán
Tel 278-4444

Uruguay
Edif Intercapital, 1st floor
C La Ceiba and Pas Gen
    Escalón
Tel 224-6661

Public Holidays

January 1	New Year's Day
March, April	Semana Santa (Holy Thursday, Good Friday, Easter)
May 1	Labor Day
First week in June	Corpus Christi
June 29-30	Bank holiday
August 1-6	Festival of El Salvador del Mundo (San Salvador)
September 15	Independence Day
October 12	Columbus Day
November 2	All Souls' Day
November 5	First Call of Independence (1811)
December 24-31	Christmas

By Air

■ **To and From the US**. The least expensive flights to El Salvador from the US are from the gateway cities of Miami, Houston, Los Angeles, New Orleans, New York, San Francisco and Washington DC. Prices for a round-trip ticket start around $500, but vary depending on when you go and where you leave from. Prices during the high season (December to mid-January and July to mid-September) are up to 50 percent more expensive.

To get the cheapest ticket possible, check the travel and classified sections of major newspapers for deals on flights, or give a call to a reputable budget travel agency. **Council Travel** (800/800-8222, 212/661-1450) and **STA Travel** (800/777-0112, 213/937-5714) are the two of the largest budget travel organizations, with many regional offices throughout the US. A local favorite in the eastern US for tickets to Central America is **Peace Frogs** (804/977-1415).

Airhitch's Target Flight Program (212/864-2000) also might be able to save you money on a flight to El Salvador, although you have to be flexible with your departure date since they work on a space available system. Living near the air-

Questions to ask when purchasing an airplane ticket:

✓ Can I change my return date? What's the charge?
✓ If the ticket has an open-ended return date, how long is the ticket good for?
✓ Is there a special student fare? How can I qualify?
✓ Is there a charge for stopping over in another city along the way? How long can I stay in the stopover city?
✓ Can I return from a different city than the one I traveled to originally?
✓ What do I do if my ticket is lost?

Air Deals to Central America

TACA (El Salvador), Aviateca (Guatemala), Copa (Panama), Lacsa (Costa Rica) and Nica (Nicaragua) offer a coupon system for traveling around Central America that allows you to buy a group of connected tickets for less than you would pay for individual tickets. The **Mayan Airpass** program (TACA, Aviateca and Lacsa only) is useful for flights between destinations in Mexico, Guatemala, Honduras and El Salvador and costs $75 per coupon (most flights require one coupon), with a minimum purchase of four coupons. The **Visit Central America** program can be a good deal for round-trip travel from the US if you're planning to travel to more than one country in Central America. Call TACA for details.

port helps, too. Finally, **consolidators** buy blocks of unused tickets and resell them to individuals, often at substantial savings (see Airplane Ticket Consolidators box).

■ **To and From Canada**. Flights from Canada to Central America are routed through the United States. Travel CUTS (416/977-3703) is Canada's budget travel giant, and you don't have to be a student to use their services.

■ **To and From the UK**. The cheapest flights from the United Kingdom originate in London. Many discount "bucket shops" advertise in papers like the Sunday Times, the Evening Standard, Time Out or TNT. Make sure the shop is bonded before you buy a ticket. Council (071/465-0484) and STA (071/937-9962) both have offices in London.

■ **To and From Continental Europe**.Your best bets for inexpensive fares from the rest of Europe to Central America are from Amsterdam, Brussels, Frankfurt and Athens. It might be cheaper if you travel through London. Council Travel and STA both have offices in France (CT:142/662087; STA:142/61-0001) and Germany (CT:211/329088; STA:496/9430191). Iberia in Spain has flights to San Salvador five times a week.

■ **To and From Australia and Asia**. Coming from Australia and Asia, flights through Miami and Los Angeles are least expensive. STA has offices in Australia (03/347-4711), New Zealand (09/309-9723) and Hong Kong (725-3898).

■ **To and From South America and Mexico**. Flying to El Salvador from South America is a little more interesting. The two fastest routes are to fly directly to either Managua, Nicaragua or San José, Costa Rica and then on to El Salvador. There are direct flights to Mexico from El Salvador twice a week.

Toll-Free Airline Numbers in the US

American	800/433-7300
Continental	800/231-0856
TACA	800/535-8780
United	800/538-2929.

Airplane Ticket Consolidators

Euram	800/848-6789
UniTravel	800/325-2222
Travac	800/872-8800
TFI	800/745-8000
Fly Cheap	800/359-2432

Airline Offices in San Salvador

Aerolineas Argentinas
Alam Roosevelt #3006 and 57a Av Nte
Tel 224-3936

American Airlines
Edif Montecristo, 4th floor
Tel 298-0666

Continental Airlines
55 Av Sur
Centro Roosevelt
Edif D, 5th floor
Tel 223-8968, 239-9501

COPA (Panama)
Alameda Roosevelt and 55a Av Nte #2838
Tel 223-2042, 271-2333

LACSA (Costa Rica)
43 Av Nte #216
Between Alam Roosevelt and 1a C Pte
Tel 298-1322

Mexicana
Av La Revolución
Hotel Presidente
Tel 271-5936, 271-5950

TACA International Airlines
Plaza Las Americas
Edif Caribe
Tel 222-244/224-0044

VARIG (Brazil)
Urb La Esperanza, 2nd Diagonal and Pje #5
Edificio Diagonal, 4th floor
Tel 226-0840, 225-8526

■ **Around Central America**. Flying between the countries of Central America is easy and getting easier, since the airlines of these countries are working together to offer special packaged travel (see Air Deals to Central America box).

■ **Airport Transportation**. Cuscatlán International Airport is located 44 kilometers from San Salvador, and getting to and from the city is a pain in the neck. The drive to the airport takes a little under an hour by taxi without traffic. Taxis and microbuses run between the city and the airport and will be waiting for you just outside the terminal. Prices are inflated (taxi $11.50, 35min; microbus $2.50-$10, 45min), so the best option may be to split the cost of a taxi with others. **Acacya** microbuses run daily from San Salvador to the airport. *(3a C Pte and 19a Av Nte #1107; tel 271-4937/8; 6, 7, 10am, 2pm; $2.50 one way)*

■ **Departure Tax**. It will cost you a whopping $20 to leave El Salvador by plane.

By Bus

■ **To and From Guatemala**. Puerto Bus and Tica Bus both operate out of San Salvador (see San Salvador). Buses to the border also leave San Salvador's Terminal de Occidente. At the border, you can cross and pick up a Guatemalan bus on the other side. International buses to Guatemala City also leave from Santa Ana (see Santa Ana).

A number of international buses run from Guatemala City to San Salvador. Melva International (3a Av 1-38, Z9, Guatemala City, tel 02/310874) has service through the border at San Cristóbal and through Santa Ana in El Salvador. The trip takes about five hours.

■ **To and From Honduras**. Tica Bus runs from El Salvador all the way to Panama through Honduras, Nicaragua and Costa Rica (see San Salvador). Regular non-international buses run from San Salvador to the northern border at El Poy. You can also ride to the border at El Amatillo from San Salvador, San Miguel, La Unión or Santa Rosa de Lima. The border at Sabanetas northeast of Perquín in Morazán department is supposed to open in 1995, though roads there are so bad that only local buses will make the trip. If you cross by foot, cross early enough to catch a Honduran bus on the other side.

From Tegucigalpa, Honduras, Tica Bus has regular international service to El Salvador (17a C between 7a Av and 8a Av; tel 387040, 386587). In Comayagüela, Honduras, buses leave from near the Mercado Zonal Belén.

By Car

Driving to El Salvador from the US means passing through Mexico, which requires drivers to buy insurance and obtain a permit to return (both are available at the border). Be warned: unleaded fuel can be difficult to find in Mexico, and the trip to El Salvador will take at least three days from the US border.

Foreigners are required to show a license and proof of ownership at the Salvadoran border, but you shouldn't have to pay anything at all. With these documents you're allowed 15 days in the country. To stay longer than that you need to go to the Ministry of Transit and pick up a *permiso de circunvalación al dentro del país*, (permit for driving within the country), good for 30 days. Bring your documents, plus a photocopy of your license and $2.85. *(Departamento General de de Tránsito, Autopista Norte; tel 226-4840; Mon-Fri 8am-12pm, 2-4:30pm, Sat 8-11:30am)*

El Salvador's Best Drives

Some of El Salvador's roads may be bad, but the scenery is almost guaranteed to be beautiful. Here are some of our favorites, in no particular order:

■ **Road from Panamerican Highway through San Jorge to Coastal Highway.** This paved road connects the Panamerican Highway just west of San Miguel to the Coastal Highway east of Usulután. Along the way it winds up and over the gently-sloping base of the San Miguel Volcano. The volcanic soil turns the road maroon in parts, and fences made from piled lava rocks line rich coffee estates. If you come from the north, there's a stunning view of the southern coastal plains as you pass over the base of the volcano.

■ **Road from San Salvador west to Sonsonate.** Soon after you turn off the Panamerican Highway at El Poliedro, this road crosses a small river where people bathe and wash clothes. As it passes into wide, flat plains, the distinctive triple peaks of Cerro Verde and the Izalco and Santa Ana Volcanoes come into view on the right.

■ **Panamerican Highway from San Salvador to Santa Ana.** The wide divided highway is lined with overhanging trees, and passes through El Salvador's rich western farmlands. Notice on the right how even the hillsides are cultivated.

■ **Road from Panamerican Highway northeast to Quetzaltepeque.** This road passes through an enormous dried lava flow that continues up the slopes of the San Salvador Volcano to the south. The blackened, jagged wasteland is striking in the middle of the surrounding green farmland.

■ **Road to Cerro Verde.** For sheer oohs and ahhs, this steep road might just take the prize. In a few short kilometers up to the top of Cerro Verde you're treated to views of Lago de Coatepeque glittering to the east, the Izalco cone and Cerro Verde itself. The road is narrow and winding, but at least it's paved. There are a few places to pull over to admire the vistas.

■ The approaches to many Salvadoran cities and towns, especially those up in the mountains, are often as scenic as the towns themselves. Apaneca, La Palma, Metapán and Ciudad Barrios have some of the most beautiful approaches.

Borders

There are seven land borders where you can enter and leave El Salvador. Immigration offices are officially open 8am-5pm, but many border guards live at their posts, so you may be able to cross outside these hours. Try to arrive at the border as early in the day as possible to improve your chances of crossing and to give yourself time to arrive at the next town by nightfall. At the border, people will likely mob you with offers to change money or to help you with your paperwork. There aren't any banks, so you may need to change money on the noisy black market(see Money) , but since there isn't any paperwork to worry about with a tourist card, you can just ignore the other half of the crowd.

It may be tempting (and not particularly difficult) to slip across the border without going through all the proper channels. But you're just asking for trouble if you do that, since when you leave they'll look for the entrance stamp. Take the extra time to get all the right stamps and signatures or a tourist card.

International Borders	
Guatemala	La Hachadura (Ahuachapán). A.k.a. Puente Arce. Las Chinamas (Ahuachapán). A.k.a. Puente El Jobo. Currently closed, to be reopened in 1995. San Cristóbal (Santa Ana). Anguiatú (Santa Ana). A.k.a. Paso de la Ceiba.
Honduras	El Poy (Chalatenango). Sabanetas (Morazán). To be opened in 1995. El Amatillo (La Unión). A.k.a. Puente Goascorán.

While There

Business Hours

In Latin America, business hours are flexible. During lunchtime (12-2pm) you'll find many shops and offices closed. Here are some rough guidelines for when you can expect certain businesses to be open:

■ **Antel**. In San Salvador, you can make international calls Mon-Sat 7am to 9pm. In smaller cities, 8am to 4pm.

■ **Banks**. Mon-Fri 9am to 12pm, 1:45 to 4pm.

■ **Government offices**. Mon-Fri 8am to 4pm

■ **Post offices**. The main post office in the Centro de Gobierno is open Mon-Fri 7am to 5pm, and Sat 7am to 12pm. The express-mail service in the same building is also open during these periods.

■ **Restaurants**. Since Salvadorans are early risers, breakfast usually starts around 6am. Lunch is served from 11am to 2pm and dinner from 5 to 9pm. When there's music and drinking, some restaurants will stay open much later.

■ **Shops**. Mon-Sat 8am to 12pm, 2 to 6pm. Department stores generally don't close for lunch.

Time/Electricity/Measurements

El Salvador is one hour behind Eastern Standard Time and six hours behind Greenwich Mean Time. Since the country is along the equator, it doesn't have daylight savings time.

The country runs on 110 volts, the same as Mexico and the US. You'll have trouble finding a third (grounding) hole, so bring a three-to-two prong converter if you have something important that needs to be plugged in.

El Salvador operates on the metric system, with a few exceptions. Fuel is sold by the gallon, and weights are occasionally measured in *libras* ("pounds," equal to 0.48kg) as well as in kilograms.

Safety & Security

Although crime is certainly a problem in El Salvador, especially since the end of the war, you're unlikely to encounter any trouble if you take some simple precautions and stay alert. Youth gangs and bandits armed with guns from the civil war cause problems. However, a new and effective police force now patrols the streets of the country and is visible even in the smallest towns. Prepare yourself by learning about the dangers in advance and by taking extra precautions with how you carry your baggage and money.

The war is over and political violence has almost completely subsided; most crime today has little to do with politics. Theft is now the most common problem,

IN THE NEWS

Power Line Blues

Rebel troops destroyed thousands of power lines during the war in an attempt to undermine El Salvador's infrastructure. Since the rebel army was a fraction of the size of the government army, attacks on the country's electrical system affected everyone and made the rebels seem bigger than life.

All of this made work as a Salvadoran power repairman no fun at all. Teams of electricians worked throughout the civil war to repair damaged power lines in huge, labor-intensive operations. Since rebels often booby-trapped the area around the downed lines, electricians frequently waited for hours while a team of explosive experts combed the area.

Electricians were flown throughout the country to work on downed lines, and labored under army helicopters which hovered overhead to defend against ambushes. If you keep an eye out for them, you'll spot telephone and electrical poles throughout the country that were knocked down by the FMLN and hastily clamped back together by power repairmen.

especially in large cities where crowds fill the sidewalks, buses are packed and markets are teeming with people. Crowded public places are pickpocket hunting grounds. Beaches are another place where theft is common, since bags are often left unattended.

■ **Preparation**. The best source of information about the specific dangers in the country is your embassy in El Salvador. Contact them as soon as you arrive, or in advance if you're planning a long stay. The US State Department has an automated fax service (tel 202/647-3000) and an electronic bulletin board (tel 202/647-5225) which provide security bulletins for every country. Shortwave radios are also a convenient way to keep up to date with the big news once you're there.

■ **Staying Safe**. There are a few basic rules of action to keep in mind while traveling. When you arrive in San Salvador with your bags, take a cab to your hotel to avoid pickpockets on buses, who know that recently-arrived foreigners are often the easiest targets. If you're staying at a questionable hotel, try locking your bags to the frame of your bed when you leave your room. Needless to say, always lock your hotel door, even if you have to buy your own lock.

Avoid unsafe parts of towns, parks, and bus and train stations, especially after dark, but also during the day. Ask the hotel manager where it is safe to walk in the city. Walk with authority and only peek at your guidebook when you're out of sight. If you need to put your bags down, watch them closely or lock them up to something solid. If you ever feel threatened, forget your inhibitions and howl. Attention is your best defense.

■ **Carrying Valuables**. How you carry your valuables is as important as watching where you go. If you must wear jewelry, wear cheap stuff that nobody would want. Carry your most important things—travelers' checks, some cash, passports, and airplane tickets—in a money

IN THE NEWS

The New Good Guys

El Salvador's new National Police Force (PNC) is one unquestionably positive consequence of the peace accords. The country's police were once so poorly-trained, corrupt and violent that most Salvadorans routinely avoided them, even when they had nowhere else to turn.

The new National Police are an enormous change for the country. Unlike their predecessors, they are not under army command, and their composition—20 percent former guerrillas, 20 percent former police members and 60 percent civilians—helps ensure that they aren't partial to any particular political wing. Members are also required to undergo a psychological exam intended to weed out the most notorious offenders from both sides of the conflict.

The National Police are clean-cut, usually with a beige top and navy pants, and they carry pistols in contrast to the rifles used by the old police force. The government constructed a new police academy to train them, foreign governments are chipping in with funding for the pick-up trucks they drive and a reassuring one in ten are women.

---

belt or a pouch that fits under the waistline of your pants. Split up the rest of your money—put some cash deep in your luggage and the remainder in another part of your clothing, such as under the insoles of your boots. That way, even if you're robbed of everything you're carrying, you'll still have some cash left.

Smart travelers often stick some cash in their socks, underwear, bra or into extra pockets sewn inside their clothing. Pockets closed with short strips of Velcro are more difficult (and noisy) to pick, and bags made of heavy nylon are harder to slash open.

■ **Dangers for Women**. El Salvador is as *macho* as much of the rest of Latin America, so women travelers face special problems and should take extra precautions. You're especially likely to be pestered if your hair is light and your complexion is fair, but wearing skimpy clothing will make any woman's life more difficult.

Latin men often hiss or proposition women as they pass on the street. Ignore them and avoid eye contact—any sort of response will be seen as a come-on. If you ever feel threatened, move away quickly and yell to attract attention.

■ **In the Water**. Though El Salvador's shores have a reputation for shark attacks, they don't happen often enough to worry about. Rip tides, though, are a real danger. These strong outward currents can quickly pull even strong swimmers away from the beach. You can't swim against them, but they don't pull you under the water and tend to fizzle out where the waves break, so don't worry about being pulled completely out to sea. If you get caught up in one, try not to panic—just remember to float and try to swim parallel to the beach. When the rip tide dies out, you can return to the beach by swimming at a 45-degree angle to the shore.

Health

The best advice on staying healthy abroad is simply to pay attention to how you feel. You know your body better than anyone else; if anything feels out of whack, it probably is. Always seek qualified medical help whenever possible. If this means going out of your way to get to a large city, do it. Most health hazards involve unsanitary food and water, so be careful about what you eat and drink. Beyond that, get your immunizations, cover yourself with bug spray and don't get too much sun, and you should be all right.

A medical kit is essential (see Packing). Cover any cut or scratch you receive immediately with a band-aid and antibiotic ointment, since a routine infection could become worse if it is ignored. For more serious problems, your embassy should have a list of recommended doctors, many of whom speak English and were trained in the West.

Some symptoms of disease don't show up for a while, so it may be difficult to associate something you picked up along the way with an illness that shows up after you return. Doctors routinely misdiagnose travel-related illnesses, since they rarely see many of them. So keep a close eye on your general state of health for about six months after you return and get a blood test on your next trip to the doctor.

■ General Health Concerns

Food and Drink Remember the four keys to safe eating and drinking under unsanitary conditions: "Peel it, boil it, cook it or forget it."

Peel fruits and vegetables whenever possible. Drinking unpurified water is probably the easiest way to slip up and catch something nasty, so watch everything you drink. Don't drink anything that doesn't come in a sealed bottle opened in front of you, and steer clear of all ice except in the best restaurants. Don't hesitate to ask if the water in your drinks has been boiled. Carbonated and alcoholic drinks are safe if they are not mixed with any contaminated water or ice, as are yogurt and coffee or tea made with water that has been thoroughly boiled. Dairy products can be a problem if they were made with unpasteurized milk. Any fruit juice or ice cream product that uses unpurified water is also a potential problem.

If you're cooking your own food, you should boil questionable beverages for at least ten minutes, filter them through a specialized water filter (no T-shirts) or use purification tablets. Chlorine tablets like Puritabs or Steritabs and iodine tablets such as Potable Aqua all work well. Five drops of tincture of iodine (2%) per quart or liter of water will also kill just about everything in there within 30 minutes. Careful, though, since too much iodine can make you sick. Powdered drink mixes help the chemicals go down more smoothly.

The food at many roadside stands may look tempting, but remember you're taking your health into your own hands. Sometimes, it comes down to a choice between eating questionable food or going hungry: the risk is yours.

BASICS

Travelers' Diarrhea is a fact of life in the developing world. Since diarrhea robs your body of fluids and electrolytes, drinking lots of clean fluids at the first sign of gastric distress is the first step towards feeling better. Try weak tea with a little sugar or flat, watered-down soda. Bland soups go down reasonably well, too. Unspiced foods such as bananas, rice, beans and potatoes provide protein and vitamins. Avoid other solid foods and milk until you feel better.

SYMPTOMS: an intestinal tract that feels like it's full of club soda.

TREATMENT: Pepto-Bismol, Kaopectate, Lomotil, Immodium AD. If more severe, persistent symptoms develop like nausea, vomiting, stomach cramps, fever or bloody stool, you may have dysentery (see below). With any of these symptoms, the ingredients in Lomotil and Immodium are potentially dangerous (Pepto-Bismol is OK, though). Seek medical attention if you think you have something worse than diarrhea.

Studies have shown that a single 500mg dose of the prescription antibiotic ciprofloxacin decreases the length of bouts of travelers' diarrhea significantly. Some doctors advise travelers to carry ciprofloxacin or other quinoline-class antibiotics.

Mosquitoes The best strategy is to avoid being active at times during the day and in places where mosquitoes are most prevalent: dawn, dusk and night, and in the hot, damp regions along the coast and in the jungle. The greatest risk is below 600 meters during the rainy season. Mosquitoes almost never climb above 900 meters and are less prevalent during the dry season. Wear long-sleeved shirts and long pants to cover as much skin surface as possible whenever you can.

Only buy repellents containing DEET, the most effective chemical repellent. A solution with a 12-30 percent concentration of DEET is recommended, since too little isn't effective and too much isn't particularly good for you. Lotions last longer and are more compact than sprays. Also, consider a personal mosquito net that can be slung over a hammock or a bed.

Dehydration is an excessive loss of body fluids that can be caused by strenuous activity, diarrhea or high altitude. If you are sweating and thirsty, chances are you're dehydrated already. The easiest way to stay hydrated is to drink almost continuously, usually more than you think you need.

SYMPTOMS: very little urination, dark yellow urine, dry mouth, headache.

TREATMENT: drink water or rehydration mixtures (see Travelers' Diarrhea).

Heat Cramps occur when you lose too much salt by perspiring, usually from strenuous activity in hot weather.

SYMPTOMS: muscle cramps, sweating.

TREATMENT: drink slightly salted water (one teaspoon of salt in one quart of water), rest.

Heat Exhaustion, also known as heat prostration, is an extreme case of dehydration. Body temperature is usually not much higher than normal at this stage, but without attention this may lead to heatstroke.

SYMPTOMS: pale, clammy skin, excessive sweating, rapid breathing and pulse rate, nausea, dizziness.

TREATMENT: administer fluids and salts (see Traveler's Diarrhea), lay person down in cool place, loosen tight clothing, raise feet slightly above head. Seek medical attention if condition does not improve.

Kitchen Cure for Montezuma's Revenge

Mix one cup of fruit juice (for potassium) with one teaspoon of honey or corn syrup (for glucose) and a pinch of table salt (for sodium). This mixture should be no more salty than tears. In a second glass dissolve one teaspoon of baking soda in eight ounces of water. Drink alternately from each glass until you aren't thirsty anymore or until both are empty, whichever comes last. Keep this up throughout the illness.

Heatstroke is a potentially life-threatening condition which occurs when the body becomes unable to regulate its own temperature under extreme heat stress. Internal organs are threatened as body temperature rises and water and salt are depleted.

SYMPTOMS: body temperature in excess of 104 degrees Fahrenheit (40 degrees Celsius), hot, dry and flushed skin, lack of sweat, rapid and strong pulse, confusion, unconsciousness.

TREATMENT: move person to coolest place possible, remove clothing, apply cool water to skin, wipe with cool damp cloths, seek medical attention immediately.

Sunburn occurs amazingly fast when you're close to the equator. An hour or two near the middle of the day, even with sunscreen, can turn you into a living chili pepper. Gradually increase your exposure time to the sun over the course of a few weeks, starting with no more than half an hour. Always wear sunscreen (at least SPF 15) and don't forget to reapply it after sweating or swimming. Wear long sleeves, loose, light-colored clothing and a hat whenever possible.

SYMPTOMS: according to severity, redness, swelling, blisters.

TREATMENT: calamine lotion or other sunburn-relief gels, cold compresses and pain medication such as aspirin. More severe cases with blistering may require medical attention.

■ Insect-borne Diseases

Chagas' Disease (American Trypanosomiasis) is transmitted by the nocturnal reduviid ("kissing") bug. Take care when sleeping in mud, adobe brick or palm thatch buildings, especially with cracks or crevices in the roof and walls. Lather on the DEET and string up the mosquito net.

SYMPTOMS: swelling of the eyelid, "pink eye," rash and fever.

TREATMENT: seek medical attention for testing as soon as possible. Past a certain point, Chagas' Disease becomes untreatable and may cause long-term damage to the heart and internal organs.

Dengue Fever (Breakbone or Dandy Fever) is transmitted by *aedes* mosquitoes. No vaccines are available, but luckily the disease tends to be relatively benign and to eventually run its course. It is more prevalent around the Cerron Grande Dam, north of San Salvador, than in other parts of the country.

SYMPTOMS: flu-like, including severe, sudden fever, headache and pain in muscles and joints. Often accompanied by vomiting, nausea, swollen lymph nodes and a pale rash or flushing of the face. The fever usually comes in two to three day cycles, separated by a day-long period of remission.

TREATMENT: stay hydrated, rest, seek medical attention.

Encephalitis (Japanese Encephalitis) is a viral infection transmitted by mosquitoes. It occurs primarily in rural areas of the tropics during the rainy season. Most people who are infected show no symptoms, and symptoms that do appear resemble those of other insect-borne infections. If any of these occur suddenly or together, see a doctor.

SYMPTOMS: weakness, stiffness, muscle soreness, delirium, vomiting. Fever, chills and headache often begin suddenly. Convulsions, paralysis and coma may follow without treatment.

TREATMENT: stay hydrated, seek medical attention immediately.

Leishmaniasis (Dum-Dum fever or Kala Azar) is one of a number of tropical parasitic diseases transmitted through the bite of sandflies. More serious internal conditions may take months or even years to appear. Sandflies are most active at night.

SYMPTOMS: small (1-2 cm) sores on the face that won't heal, followed by fever and swelling of some internal organs.

TREATMENT: seek medical attention.

Malaria People used to think malaria was caused by breathing polluted air (hence the name, from Italian for "bad air"). We now know that the disease is caused by a parasitic protozoa carried by female mosquitoes. Four parasite species cause malaria. The *plasmodium vivax* species is the most common, and rarely fatal. *Plasmodium falciparum,* on the other hand, which accounts for only a small percentage of infections, can be deadly within hours. Keep in mind that even with prophylaxis, infection is still possible.

SYMPTOMS: chills and headache, followed by high fever, headache, nausea, diarrhea, stiffness, aching joints, brown urine, exhaustion, mental haziness and delirium. These symptoms, characterized by alternating hot and cold spells, usually recur in waves every two to three days.

TREATMENT: seek medical attention, even if a prophylaxis is being used.

■ Diseases of Sanitation

Cholera Luckily, attacks of this acute intestinal infection are often mild and easily treated. To minimize your chances of catching it, avoid contaminated food and water.

SYMPTOMS: sudden acute diarrhea, vomiting, extreme weakness and muscle cramps.

TREATMENT: stay hydrated to offset effects of diarrhea, seek medical attention. *(Tetracyclene, two 250mg pills , 4 times a day)*

Dysentery usually follows a bad bout of travelers' diarrhea, and comes in two forms. Bacillary or bacterial dysentery is highly-contagious but short-lived and will usually go away in a week. Amoebic dysentery, even though it is characterized by less severe symptoms, is more serious and can cause long-term damage. A stool analysis is necessary to determine the cause of the diarrhea.

SYMPTOMS: bloody diarrhea, stomach pain, headache (both types), fever, vomiting (bacillary only).

TREATMENT: immediate medical attention for prescribed antibiotics. *(Bacillary dysentery: tetracyclene, one 250mg capsule, 4 times a day for 7-10 days)*

Giardia (Giardiasis) is caused by ingesting an intestinal parasite through contaminated water or food, and occurs around the world.

SYMPTOMS: severe digestive system distress, diarrhea, fatigue and weight loss.

TREATMENT: eat, drink and rest as much as possible. *(Metronidazole or Flagyl, one 250mg pill, three times a day for five days)*

Hepatitis A (Infectious Hepatitis) is a disease which attacks the liver. It is transmitted through improper hygiene, contaminated food or sexual contact and is especially dangerous for pregnant women.

SYMPTOMS: nausea, headache, fever, vomiting and loss of appetite. Eventually, dark-colored urine, light-colored stool, a pain on the right side of the body near the liver. A yellowish tint to the skin and/or eyes may develop.

TREATMENT: rest, drink lots of fluids. Seek medical attention immediately.

Typhoid Fever is a dangerous infection of the stomach and intestines, transmitted through contaminated food or water. Immunization provides only limited protection.

SYMPTOMS: typhoid fever progresses through a detectable pattern beginning with flu-like symptoms—headache, sore throat, occasional diarrhea and vomiting, all during the first week. Fever rises while pulse rate drops. During the second week, trembling, delirium, weakness and weight loss set in and pink spots may appear on the body.

TREATMENT: drink lots of liquids, seek medical attention immediately.

▪ Other Health Concerns

AIDS Unless you plan to indulge in intravenous drug use overseas, the greatest risk of contracting AIDS is through sexual contact or a tainted blood transfusion. Therefore don't share needles, and if you plan to exchange bodily fluids with anyone whose sexual history you aren't sure of, use a condom.

SYMPTOMS: fatigue, chills, fever, sudden weight loss, white or dark spots on the skin (usually the face), a persistent dry cough, constant diarrhea.

TREATMENT: none.

Leeches However disgusting they may be, leeches don't transmit disease and their bite is painless. Always check for these after passing through bodies of water and damp forests. If you get one, don't panic and don't yank it off. Apply insect repellent, salt, lemon juice or vinegar, or burn it with a lit cigarette. Cover the cut with a band-aid and rub on some antibiotic ointment.

Ticks Check for ticks after passing through dry vegetation. It's important to get both the tick's body and head, which can remain behind and cause infection. To get rid of one, apply alcohol, Vaseline or oil. Or light a match, blow it out, and apply it to the tick.

Rabies If you are bitten by an animal that is acting strangely, whether overly friendly or foaming at the mouth, there's a chance you could contract this horrific disease. Treatment for rabies must begin before the first symptoms appear, because once rabies takes hold there is nothing that can be done to save your life.

SYMPTOMS: restlessness, irritability, inability to eat or drink, foaming at the mouth, insanity. Symptoms may take from 10 days to two years to appear.

TREATMENT: wash the wound thoroughly with soap and water but don't close it up. If possible, capture or kill the animal for testing. Seek medical attention immediately.

Transfusions Much of the blood supply in developing countries has not been screened for AIDS. If you find yourself or someone you know in a situation where a blood transfusion is required, first make sure a transfusion is absolutely necessary; in some cases, colloid or crystal plasma expanders can be used instead of blood transfusions. If a transfusion is imminent, try at all costs to insure that the blood has been screened for the HIV virus, even if it means moving to a different hospital in another country. Evacuation to your home country is an expensive but potentially life-saving alternative.

■ **Other Medical Resources**

Air Ambulance This Miami-based service can provide emergency evacuation to the US. *(Tel 305/525-5538)*

Herchmer Medical Consultants can prepare a health concern update customized to any travel plans. It usually takes about two months and costs around $15. *(Tel 800/336-8334)*

Travel Health Fax will send you a free index of 229 countries, from which you can choose a complete health report on any one for $10 each. *(Tel 800/777-7751)*

Immunization Alert is a computerized service which offers up-to-date travel and health information for more than 200 countries. Information on up to four countries costs $40; each additional country is $15. *(PO Box 406, 93 Timber Drive, Storrs CT 06268)*

The International Association for Medical Assistance to Travelers (IAMAT) seems almost too good to be true. For nothing at all (or a small donation), IAMAT will send you comprehensive pamphlets on many diseases. They also enclose a list of English-speaking doctors in almost every country around the world (including two in El Salvador), all of whom have agreed to a fixed-fee schedule and 24-hour availability. *(417 Center Street, Lewiston, NY 14092; tel 716/754-4883)*

Intermedic also has an international network of English-speaking doctors. *(777 Third Avenue, New York, NY 10017; tel 212/486-8900)*

Medic Alert supplies engraved bracelets and wallet cards for people with serious medical problems like allergies or diabetes. *(PO Box 1009, Turlock, CA 95381; tel 209/668-3333)*

Traveling Healthy is a bimonthly newsletter available for $29 a year, and a sample copy is $4. *(108-48 70th Road, Forest Hills, NY 11375; 718/268-7290)*

The US Center for Disease Control in Atlanta offers the International Travelers' Hotline (tel 404/332-4559; fax 404/332-4565), which provides continuously-updated information on health and disease issues around the world, including risk areas and treatments. Free information can be faxed to you. The Center also publishes *Health Information for International Travel*, an in-depth handbook on worldwide health and information risks, which is available for $6. *(Superintendent of Documents, US Government Printing Office, Washington DC 20402; tel 202/783-3238)*

The US Department of State's Citizens' Emergency Center can provide written and recorded travel advisories on most locations around the world. As a last resort, they also can arrange emergency medical help and/or evacuation. *(Bureau of Consular Affairs, Room 4811, NS, US Department of State, Washington DC 20520; tel 202/647-5225)*

■ **Books on Healthy Traveling**
International Travel Health Guide by Stuart R. Rose, M.D. *(Travel Medicine, Inc., 351 Pleasant Street, Suite 312, Northampton, MA 01060; tel 800/872-8633)*
The Medical Guide for Third World Travelers by Marc Robin and Bradford Dessery *(K-W Publications, 11532 Alkaid Drive, San Diego, CA 92126-1370; tel 619/566-6489; $16.95)*
The Pocket Doctor: Your Ticket to Good Health While Traveling by Stephen Bezruchka, M.D. *(The Mountaineers, 1011 SW Klickitat Way, Suite 107, Seattle, WA 98134; tel 800/553-4453)*
Staying Healthy in Asia, Africa and Latin America by Dirk Schroeder *(Volunteers in Asia Press, PO Box 4543, Stanford, CA 94305)* This is our personal favorite.
Travelers' Medical Resource by William Forgey, M.D. *(ICS Books, Inc., 1370 East 86th Place, Merrillville, IN 46410; tel 800/541-7323)*
Where There Is No Doctor by David Werner *(The Hesperian Foundation, PO Box 1692, Palo Alto, CA 94302)*

Money

■ **Currency**. The *colon* or *"peso"* equals 100 *centavos,* and is circulated in ¢5, ¢10, ¢25, and ¢100 notes. *Centavos* are available in 5, 10, 25 and 50-*centavo* coins.
Since the government initiated a free-market exchange system in 1990, a handful of *casas de cambio* (exchange houses) have sprung up to compete with banks.

■ **Exchanging money**. Plan on carrying your money in US dollars—it's as simple as that. Any bank in the country will exchange cash US dollars for *colones.* Travelers' checks in other currencies are accepted in few places. Other Central American currencies and dollars can be exchanged on the black market and at borders, but know the rate before you do this.
  Travelers' checks are difficult to change everywhere in El Salvador, but you stand a better chance if you carry your receipt and passport with you. If you stop by American Express' office in San Salvador, they will stamp your checks and send you to the bank upstairs for a quick and easy exchange.
  El Salvador has a **black market** for exchanging money, but since the rates are no higher than they are in banks, the only time you should change money this way is when banks are closed. Again, only US dollars work, preferably cash.
  Rates for exchanging money vary from place to place, and travelers' checks get the highest rate. *Casas de cambio* and banks offer the best rates, while hotels are the worst—they occasionally won't let you exchange money at all unless you're a paying guest.

Exchange Rates (1994)		
¢8.7	=	1US$
¢6.25	=	1A$
¢6.4	=	1C$
¢5.2	=	1DM
¢13.2	=	1UK£

BASICS

■ **Carrying money**. Despite the difficulty of exchanging them, you should carry most of your money in **travelers' checks**. American Express is the most recognized brand, and they have an office in San Salvador. Though travelers' checks are replaceable, you should safeguard them like cash since a refund center may be far away or closed when you need it. Also, carry a copy of your receipts, a list of refund centers and the phone numbers of refund centers and the home office, in case you have an emergency and need to call collect. Small denominations are best, because that way you're less likely to get stuck with unspent *colones* and because Salvadoran banks don't charge commission on exchanges.

Travelers also need to carry some **US dollars cash** with them. You'll need them if you get stuck in a town that won't accept your travelers' checks or otherwise find yourself in a situation where travelers' checks won't do. Again, small denominations are best.

Credit cards are accepted at most big restaurants and stores in the major cities and are the best form of back-up funds. There's a problem with credit card numbers being "borrowed," though, so get in the habit of calling collect back to your credit card company every now and then to check the status of your account and to make sure that all charges on it are yours. If you plan to drive a car, most credit cards will cover the cost of insurance and eliminate the need for a cash deposit.

■ **Getting money**. There are various convenient and inexpensive ways to get money while abroad. However you decide to handle your finances, plan in advance by speaking with your credit card company, and be sure to carry at least one copy of a list of telephone numbers and addresses that you'll need as you go.

American Express cards are worth getting for their travel benefits alone. Cardholders can cash a personal check for $1,000 every 21 days at American Express offices worldwide ($5,000 with a gold card). The fee for getting checks this way is one percent of the value of the checks you're buying. There's an American Express office in San Salvador (see San Salvador).

Some other **credit cards** will let you withdraw funds on the card, but most charge interest starting the day money is withdrawn. Check with your credit card company before you leave and find out how and where you can get money issued to you.

If you plan to use a credit card abroad and you'll be away for longer than a month, you'll have to deal with the monthly statement. With an American Express card, you can pay off your statement at any of its offices abroad. With other credit cards, you should be able to make a payment in advance and draw upon the funds as you use the card. The other option is to have someone at home handle everything. Whatever you do, stay in regular contact with your credit card company (most accept collect calls from abroad) and anyone else involved in keeping your finances straight.

Direct money transfers are generally the most expensive way to get money while abroad. In addition to its regular cardholder and traveler check services, American Express also has a Moneygram service that will transfer cash in ten minutes between any two of its offices, or from American Express in the US to a branch of some Salvadoran banks. The fee is based on how much you transfer, although it will usually be more expensive than cashing a personal check for cardholders. Call American Express collect for details (tel 303/980-3340; in the US 800/926-9400).

Foreign banks will also transfer money to Salvadoran banks. Do this only as a last resort, since your local bank won't likely have much experience transferring money to El Salvador. If you decide to do this, first go to the receiving bank to get all the details, then call home. Ask what currency the money will be issued in, what will be the rate of exchange and how long the process takes. Even if you try to clear up everything in advance, the process could still take weeks for any of a number of beautiful bureaucratic reasons.

Finally, US citizens have an emergency service (for jail or medical reasons only) and can have money issued to them by a consulate or embassy. Call the US State Department for information (tel 202/647-5225).

■ **Spending Money**. Bargaining is expected in many small purchases. It takes skill and patience—merchants or fruit sellers aren't your enemies, but they want to sell something for a high price just as much as you want to buy it for a low price. Don't let yourself be ripped off; just remember to keep things in perspective.

Speak with a few people selling the same thing first, and learn what a fair value should be. Playing vendors off against each other often gets prices down fast ("but that woman said she'd sell it to me for ten!"). Also, know when to bargain. In some places, like the market or with vendors selling goods on the street (except food), you're expected to bargain. In other places, like hotels in the off-season, your chances of getting a better price this way are smaller. Cooked food prices are generally non-negotiable.

■ **Costs**. El Salvador can be an inexpensive place to travel—if you have to, you can get by on $10 or less per day. But you don't win a prize for living on the cheap, and a hot shower or dinner at a nice restaurant can turn a bad day around. Hotel prices (in dollars) start in the single digits, but $10 is about the minimum you'll pay for a clean room with a private bath. Food on the street is very inexpensive, usually less than $2 per meal. Restaurants charge about half what a comparable place would charge in the US. Beers cost about $1 per bottle, and Cokes—available everywhere—are about $0.50 each. Public transportation is the best deal in El Salvador—the longest ride across the country will never cost more than $3, and most bus fares are under $1. Prices also vary from region to region. The east is slightly more expensive than the west, although La Unión is inexpensive. San Salvador, of course, is the most expensive place in the country.

Mail

Sending and receiving mail in El Salvador is an imperfect science. To ensure that your letter or package arrives, you probably won't want to use the regular postal service, but then again, you're going to have to pay much more.

■ **Sending Mail**. When deciding how to send something, consider what it's worth and how much you're willing to pay to get it where it's going. The regular postal system is inefficient, to say the least. There's even a slight chance that someone will go through your letter or

package. Allow two weeks for a regular letter to arrive in El Salvador, and a little less for one to be sent home.

If you are going to send a package from the post office, bring it there opened but in its packaging and ready to be closed, so customs can inspect it. If it's important, consider using one of the private courier services. EMS has an office in the main post office and Urgente Express has a good reputation (see San Salvador). They will deliver letters both to and from El Salvador, as well as between some other Central American countries.

Sending a letter outside of the country through the post office costs about $0.30. Packages cost more and take longer. Most courier services start at $5 for a letter and charge according to weight for packages, starting at $5-$10 for one pound.

■ **Receiving Mail**. To receive letters in El Salvador, you can either use the general delivery/poste restante system or have American Express hold your mail (see San Salvador). (It's best to send send general delivery/poste restante letters to San Salvador.) For either of these two options, use dull stamps, underline your family name on everything and make sure the sender puts only your name—no "Mr." or "Mrs." which might confuse the person filing the letters. For general delivery/poste restante mail, write clearly in this format:

> [Your name]
> Lista de Correos
> Correo Central
> [City], El Salvador
> Centroamérica

Telephones

Antel is the Salvadoran national telephone company, and has offices in every town. In spite of Antel's omnipresence (or perhaps because of its monopoly), the telephone system isn't perfect—Salvadorans will tell of having to wait two years to have a phone installed in their house. Calls outside of the country, though, are usually no problem. El Salvador's international country code is 503.

An Extra Digit

The Salvadoran phone numbering system was recently changed—one digit was added to the beginning of every telephone number to make a total of seven digits. If you come across an old six-digit number, add one of the following digits in front to get the new number. For example, in San Salvador 26-9987 becomes 226-9987.

■ **San Salvador City**	**2**	
■ **Western El Salvador**	**4**	(Sonsonate, Ahuachapán, Santa Ana)
■ **Central El Salvador**	**3**	(Chalatenango, La Libertad, San Salvador, Cabañas, Cuscatlán, San Vicente)
■ **Eastern El Salvador**	**6**	(Usulután, San Miguel, Morazán, La Unión)

Public phones require a coin for **domestic calls**. The coin system in the country was recently changed, and most street phones only take the older, bigger coins. Twenty-five *centavos* will let you call anywhere in the country for three to four minutes, and a one-*colon* coin gives you 15 minutes. Antel offices will also place a domestic call for you for the same price as using a street phone. It's more time-consuming to call at an Antel office, but at least the phones always work.

You have two choices for **overseas calls**. Antel offices charge about $3 per minute. Dial-direct services to the US, which can be made either from street phones or from Antel, charge an operator fee of about $2.50 plus about $1 per minute. These services also place collect calls, and AT&T answers with bilingual operators who can help you out if you're in a bind.

USA Direct-Dial Numbers

Call these numbers from any phone (no money is required) to speak to an operator:

AT&T	190
Sprint	191
MCI	195

Getting Around

■ **Buses**. El Salvador's buses are cheap, reliable and eye-catching. Whether you're traveling within a city or between cities, you'll be mixing with the masses, gazing out through colorful murals and speeding along at an alarming clip. And don't even consider standing out in the middle of any road in the country a moment longer than you absolutely have to, since these babies push their horns and engines to the limit but treat their brakes like fine china.

El Salvador is where old school buses go to die, although many of them seem to be doing quite well and are usually packed with passengers. Most Salvadorans travel on buses which get incredibly crowded and uncomfortable during peak hours. The government subsidizes the purchase of fuel for the bus system, so drivers are interested in getting as many passengers to squeeze on as they possibly can. Have your money ready.

Buses between cities offer a good panorama of the country. Life zooms by, but some of the same volcanoes sit on the horizon without moving for what seems like the entire trip. On the longer rides, stick your luggage somewhere secure and within sight. Vendors line the streets at transit points selling fruit and drinks. Some of the routes between major cities have express buses, which take less time than regular buses.

Recipe for a Salvadoran Bus

1. Take one old US school bus.
2. Paint up like a Beatles cartoon.
3. Write name of girlfriend on windshield and patron saint on side.
4. Add air horn and crazy driver, mix well.
5. Start engine and don't stop for anything.

You'll sometimes find that it saves time to take two buses to a

BASICS

destination by switching at a transit point. Some non-commercial towns, like San Francisco Gotera in Morazán department, don't have many regular routes, so switching buses is the most convenient way to get there.

You can cross into neighboring countries by taking a local bus to the border, walking across and then taking another bus on the other side, or you can take an international bus from El Salvador to a neighboring country that brings you across the border. International direct buses are usually more comfortable and eliminate the need to search for transport on the other side. You will have to wait for everyone on your bus to clear customs, though, and that may take some time.

Domestic buses depart regularly—usually every few minutes between major cities and less frequently for smaller towns. They run from around 5am until dark, when service stops. It's usually easy to flag a bus down, and they'll even stop for you in the middle of traffic (wave to the cars that line up behind as you step on board).

Estaciónes (bus stations) are located in the centers of major towns, except in San Salvador where three are scattered on the outskirts of town. Bus stations are dirty, unsafe places there aren't great for hanging around. Taxis that sit inside bus

Driving in El Salvador

- Look out for cows in the road, especially at night.
- Beware of bus drivers—they don't slow down to let you pass. And, if you try to pass and they're coming in the opposite direction, they sometimes speed up.
- Expect that every inch of the road you can't see at that very moment is filled with potholes, because as often as not it is.
- Check your oil, water and tires regularly.
- Always carry a supply of water, available at gas stations.
- Night driving can be harrowing. There are never lights on the road and rarely passing cars. This is also the time you're most at risk for being stopped and robbed. Don't drive at night if your car isn't working well or if you spook easily.
- People expect to pay a *colon* or two if you give them a lift—brighten their day by saying no thanks.
- With only two lanes on most roads, passing is dangerous. Learn to wave in—start waving your arm wildly on the passenger side to signal the person you are passing to slow down and let you pass. It feels ridiculous at first, but it just might save your life.
- Honk in advance when you pass through a town; children and animals often linger alongside roads.
- Drivers often disregard traffic lights, a habit learned during the war when cars were attacked at stoplights. So, be extra sure that cross traffic is stopped before moving on a green light.
- Many minor roads are impassable without a 4x4, and nobody for kilometers will have a phone. Don't bite off more than you can chew. Know when to turn around.
- Make sure you can see far ahead in the oncoming lane when passing. Don't pass behind another car.
- Most importantly, drive slowly enough so that you can avoid anything unexpected without going off the road.

stations and wait for passengers usually charge more than taxis which are passing out front.

■ **Taxis**. Salvadoran taxis are also inexpensive and reliable, if dilapidated. None have meters, so agree on a price before you leave the curb. Taxis are available in Santa Ana, San Miguel and San Salvador. In Santa Ana and San Miguel, don't pay more than $1.75 for a ride. In San Salvador, prices are a little higher, but you shouldn't pay more than $2.30 for a ride across town, and less for a shorter trip.

■ **Driving**. Driving your own car in El Salvador has some advantages

Car Rental Agencies

There are four main car rental agenciees in San Salvador. You'll find some smaller operators in the phone book, too, but be careful, since some of their cars are unreliable.

AVIS
43a Av Sur #137
Tel 224-2623

Bargain
79a Av Sur #6
Col La Mascota
Tel 223-1668

Hertz
C Los Andes #16
Col Miramont
226-8099

Dollar
Av Roosevelt #3119
Tel 224-4385

and disadvantages, but it definitely will change your experience of the country, for better and worse. Potholes rather than people may be your biggest memory and if you don't make a special effort to get out of your car, the only Salvadorans you'll meet will be the people who fill your tank.

With your own car you can stop where you want to take photos, turn on a whim down unexplored detours and travel to remote places that buses rarely see. With your bags in the trunk and your map in the back seat, pickpockets can't threaten you and somehow you'll always find a road to where you're going. But rental fees, gas and insurance make it expensive to travel by car and border crossing can be time-consuming and frustrating. You'll be in real trouble if the car dies kilometers from the nearest service station; El Salvador is not a place where you want to get stranded.

Tips on Renting a Car

● To get a good price, contact the rental agency as far in advance as possible.
● Small rental-car agencies are cheaper, but many of their vehicles are unreliable—no deal is worth the hassle of being stuck in the middle of nowhere.
● Your credit card should cover the cost of insurance, and you can use it in place of a security deposit.
● Longer rental schedules are cheaper.
● Pick-up trucks are cheap, durable and not as big a target for thieves.
● Get unlimited mileage or you'll be limited to the city.
● Make sure the tires are almost new. Don't risk a flat.
● Make sure the spare fits correctly by trying it out before you leave.
● Get the phone number of someone to call in case of an emergency. Even with this number, don't expect that they'll pay much attention to you if you get stuck, though. They have your security deposit slip, so you're on own your own as far as they are concerned.
● On the road, don't take any chances. If something sounds funny, return the car immediately.

The streets of the capital and most major cities are decent, but that changes quickly once you leave town. Parts of the Panamerican and Coastal Highways are in complete disrepair, and most minor roads are nothing but dirt and rocks, even though they're marked on maps with a big black line. In cities, look out for open manholes and bottomless potholes.

Foreign drivers in El Salvador are required to carry their licenses with them, although it wouldn't hurt to bring an international drivers' license too. Make sure your insurance applies for driving outside your own country. You won't have any problems finding gas, since even the smallest towns have gas stations that sell both diesel and unleaded fuel. Car repair shops litter all the main roads, especially at the entrance to towns, and don't charge much. Make sure the mechanic knows what to fix and establish what it will cost before he starts.

■ **Car Rental**. Renting a car eliminates some but not all of the problems you'd have with your own car. Rentals can be a cheap way to go if you're traveling in a group and you have arranged a deal in advance. Also, rental cars eliminate the hassle of bringing your car across the border and through customs.

■ **Motorcycles**. If you plan to take your motorcycle through El Salvador, the rainy season is not the time to do it. Look out for crazy drivers and make sure you can repair everything yourself.

■ **Bicycles**. Although bicycle racing is popular in El Salvador and there are many cyclists on the road, we don't recommend it; Salvadoran drivers aren't known for their willingness to share the road. Also, bad roads and rain can make leg-powered travel nearly impossible.

 ■ **Hitchhiking**. Hitching is a way of life in rural El Salvador, where truck drivers cover costs by giving lifts to peasants along the way. Buses pass so frequently along major roads, though, that hitching is usually unnecessary. Remember, like anywhere in the world, you're always taking a big gamble by hopping into a stranger's vehicle. If you get a ride in the back of a pick-up, offer to pay one or two *colones* for gas when the ride is over.

Accommodations

You shouldn't expect to pay very much—or get very much, for that matter—for lodging in El Salvador, except for a handful of first-rate hotels in San Salvador and some surprises in smaller towns. Throughout the country. though, you will be able to find a passable room with a private  shower for less than $10. The lone exception is for the adventurous few who find their own spot on a secluded beach—at times the country's finest accommodations of all.

Places to stay in El Salvador have various names. Hotels are usually, but not always, the best. Other titles like *posada, pensión, hospedaje* and *casa de huéspedes* are for places which can be good, bad or somewhere in between. Motels, which charge by the hour, are the exception—try to avoid them.

Salvadorans expect to vacation with their entire family and to sleep with everyone in a single room, so rates are occasionally bloated on the assumption that you'll squeeze in a few more people. Learn to live without hot water, because none but

Top: Temporary bridge, Puente Cuscatlán
Bottom Wharf, La Libertad

Top: *Guitarrista,* Playas Negras
Bottom: Political graffiti

the best hotels and the odd mountain town will have it. A sleeping bag and toilet paper are prerequisites for living on the cheap. Always ask to see a room first, since quality varies from one door to the next. Make sure that the sheets are clean, and ask for a fan if your room doesn't have one already.

Food & Drink

Salvadoran food is inexpensive, simple, occasionally unhealthy and sometimes delicious. *Pupusas* are the Salvadoran mainstay, although fast-food restaurants make hamburgers and pizza a competitive second. The country has tons of fresh, exotic fruit, its own soda and a few domestic beers. In the larger cities there are enough restaurants to satisfy any taste.

Lunch is the biggest meal of the day and can cost anywhere from about $1.50 on the street to a lot more in the capital's most exclusive restaurants. It's usually worth tracking down a restaurant instead of settling for street food, since restaurants can be inexpensive and the food is usually better (and better for you). Even the country's smallest towns have restaurants, and they're usually pretty good.

■ **Local Cuisine**. El Salvador has a variety of dishes and drinks, some traditional and others imported. The *plato típico*, served everywhere, consists of a cup of refried beans, a spoonful of cream, a fried plantain and a few cornmeal tortillas. *Mariscada* is a common cream-based seafood soup. It's usually best and freshest near the coast, naturally, but can be found just about anywhere. La Pema in Santa Rosa de Lima serves the Mother of all *Mariscadas,* the one by which all others are judged.

Pupusas, the most distinctive Salvadoran food, are small, thick *tortillas* filled with soft, white cheese. They're often fried, and are great hot off the skillet. A special version of *pupusas,* made from rice, is sold in the town of Olocuilta (see Olocuilta). You'll probably want to put some *cortido de repollo*—pickled and chopped cabbage and carrots, often in a jar on the table—on top of your *pupusas* to add some crunch and cool them down, followed by a sprinkle of chili sauce to heat them back up. You also have a choice of what goes inside: *chicharrón* (fried pork rinds); *queso* (cheese); *frijoles* (beans); or *revuelta* (everything). *Tamales* are made from cornmeal and margarine boiled in a large leaf. They're deliciously doughy when made well, and can come with chicken or beef inside. Vendors sell them hot on the street for about $0.10.

■ **Restaurants**. There's every type and quality of restaurant in El Salvador. Decent restaurants are often not much more expensive than little holes in the wall. Crowds are usually a tip-off that a place serves good food, so head out to eat lunch at the same time as the rest of the country—around noon.

El Salvador, and especially San Salvador, is filled with US fast-food chains; there sometimes seems to be a Pizza Hut on every corner, and sometimes two. A McDonald's occupies a beautiful building two blocks from the central plaza and

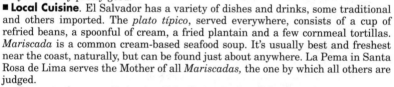

BASICS

Salvadoran Recipes

Pupusas

> *Masa* (a finely-ground corn meal available at many specialty food stores)
> Soft white cheese, such as mozzarella
> Tabasco sauce

Mix the *masa* with water and form the resulting dough into two thin *tortillas,* each about five inches in diameter and ½ inch thick. Place the cheese in the center of one *tortilla* and place the other on top, pressing the edges together to seal the filling inside. Place in a hot pan or on a griddle with a dash of vegetable oil and cook evenly on both sides. Serve with tabasco sauce and *curtido de repollo* (see below). Other fillings can be substituted for cheese, including cooked beans and meat.

Curtido de Repollo (Chopped cabbage in vinegar)

> One cabbage
> Vinegar
> Carrot, onion
> Oregano, salt, chili pepper

Slice the cabbage and vegetables into small strips, place in vinegar and add oregano, salt and chili pepper to taste. Allow the mixture to soak for approximately six hours before serving with *pupusas.*

Sopa de Frijoles Rojos o Negros (Red or Black Bean Soup)

> Red or black beans
> Water
> Onion
> Garlic, salt

After checking through the beans to remove any twigs or dirt, soak them in water overnight, wash them off and place in a pot of boiling water. Add the onion, garlic and salt, then cook until they are soft. Yucca or a ham bone may also be added to the soup for additional flavor. Best when served with fried rice.

Horchata

> Rice
> Milk, water, ice
> Sugar, nutmeg, cinnamon

Toast uncooked rice (two teaspoons per glass, about 3/4 cup per pitcher) in an un-oiled pan until slightly brown but not burnt. Grind up into a powder, using a food processor if you have one. Add sugar, nutmeg and cinnamon to taste. Mix in milk and water to fill glass or pitcher (two parts milk to one part water). Serve iced.

Burger King, Dunkin' Donuts and Wendy's are buying up some of the best real estate around. A few local fast-food chains, like Biggest, Sir Pizza and Toto's Pizza, thrive nationwide. Fried chicken is very popular, and Pollo Campero does it right by Salvadoran standards. You'll see many Salvadorans flying to the US carrying big boxes of drumsticks and thighs with them, at the request (or demand) of their families.

■ **Markets & Vendors**. Markets have the freshest fruit, which is the way to go if you have something to carry them in and can wash them off. The best fruit is available early in the day. Shop around for the best prices and buy in bulk.

Otherwise, the food stalls in the market serve up tasty—but not necessarily healthy—food. If you're going to eat there, or even at a restaurant, take a look around to see if it is clean. Also, ask a few people who work at the market where the best place to eat inside is; one or two places always have the best reputation.

■ **Fruit**. El Salvador's markets offer an amazing variety of fruit, including some you've never seen before—guaranteed. Many tasty fruits are also sold, sliced and bagged, on the street. *Mamei* is a fleshy orange fruit about eight inches long, and tastes tart like an apricot. A *zapote* is round, about three inches around with a brown peel and tastes like a fruity sweet potato. *Jocotes* are grape-sized fruit with a red or green peel, orange flesh and a big seed. You're supposed to bite through the peel into the fleshy inside, which tastes a little like a mango when the fruit is ripe (when the peel is orange to red).

■ **Drinks**. El Salvador has a large selection of native drinks for such a small country, including beer, liquor, soda and a surprisingly-refreshing beverage made out of milk, rice and cinnamon called *horchata*. Four brands of beer—Pilsner, Suprema, Regia and Golden Light—are produced domestically. Pilsner is most popular and has a vaguely Bohemian flavor, Golden Light tastes like water and Regia comes in big brown bottles popular with teenagers.

Aguardiente is a liquor produced by the government, distributed at *expendios* (government-licensed liquor stores) in almost every little town. This stuff is made from sugar cane, tastes vaguely like rum and could strip paint. Tres Puentes is the national brand, Muñeco is made in San Salvador and Unidas is from Santa Ana, but they're all basically the same cheap firewater. Alcoholic *chicha* is made of ground cornmeal, fermented and mixed with brown sugar. It's been consumed for thousands of years—they found traces of it at San Andrés—and it's still going strong.

Sometimes soda seems more plentiful than purified water. Coca-Cola does an amazing job of shipping the magic liquid to towns that helicopters couldn't even locate. For some reason Pepsi is scarce, except in Pizza Huts and Texaco Starmarts. Kolachampán, the "national soda," is an incredibly sweet concoction that Salvadorans love but many foreigners can't seem to develop a taste for. A few other smaller brands are passable, including Tropical's cream soda.

Mineral water is for sale across the country, including gas stations and supermarkets. It's a good idea to carry a bottle around with you, since the tap water can make you sick (see Health). Coffee, of course, is everywhere and is usually first-rate, even at tiny *cafeterías*.

■ **Vegetarian Food**. There are a handful of vegetarian restaurants in San Salvador and one in Santa Ana. Many peasants survive on beans, rice and tortillas since meat is too expensive, which makes a majority of Salvadorans default vegetarians anyway. Be warned that beans are often cooked in lard.

Media

■ **Newspapers**. The Salvadoran press, historically very right-wing, has begun to spread its boundaries. Compared with the period during the civil war when the press was clearly under the grip of the military, Salvadoran newspapers are experiencing something of a liberal Renaissance, although they still have a long way to go. *La Prensa Gráfica*, El Salvador's biggest daily, is very conservative but good for daily news events and goings-on, and includes

BASICS

Shortwave Frequencies

Time	Frequency (kHz)
BBC	
5-8am	15220
8-10:15am	17840
4-6:30pm	15070
5-9:30pm	12095
6-9:39pm	9915
6:30-8:30pm	9590
8pm-12:30am	5975
11pm-12:30am	9640
Voice Of America	
6-8pm	11740
6-8:30pm	5995, 9775
	9815, 11580
9-10pm	6130, 9455
Christian Science Monitor	
6pm-12am	13760
6-10am	13760

entertainment listings. Close on its heels is *El Diario de Hoy*, just as popular and even more conservative. *El Mundo* and *El Diario Latino* are smaller papers that come out in the afternoon, and both have a more moderate stance. *Primera Plana* is a left-leaning weekly that caters to a younger audience. The *El Salvador News-Gazette* is a free bilingual weekly with a good entertainment section.

■ **Radio**. Radio Venceremos (100.5 MHz) has evolved from the government-targeted, clandestine voice of the FMLN into one more Top-40 moneymaker. The morning news at 7am is good, though, with occasional interviews of political and entertainment hot-shots. The station still has an FMLN slant but political ties are slowly being severed.

Out & Around

■ **Hiking, Camping and Climbing**. For such a small, densely-populated country, El Salvador has a respectable range of places to enjoy the outdoors. Montecristo and Cerro Verde are the two most obvious spots, but there are also great trails and views near Apaneca, Metapán, and Santiago de María. Any large volcano, particularly those near big cities, is good for a day's climb, with spectacular views almost guaranteed. Plenty of options even further off the beaten path, like hiking in the hilly regions of Morazán and Ahuachapán departments, await the more adventurous. If you're going to go hiking, drop by the Instituto Geográfico in San Salvador before you leave to purchase a good map of the area (see San Salvador).

■ **On the Water**. El Salvador has some superb beaches and, if you come at the right time, you'll find some pristine and deserted sections of coast. El Espino, El Icacal and El Cuco are all great beaches. Fishing villages line much of the coastline, and for a reasonable price you can hop aboard for a roller-coaster ride on the waves or bargain for a lift to a nearby destination. Take a trip from Playitas to the islands in the Gulf of Fonseca, crash into the waves off of Playa San Marcelino or explore the quiet inlet near Barrio Santiago in a dugout canoe.

■ **Surfing**. It's hard to believe a country only 260 kilometers long has some world-class waves, but El Salvador does. Most breaks are concentrated near La Libertad, with a few more good spots in either direction.

The surf season lasts roughly from late February until November. Things are less active between November and February, but offshore winds can still create good waves during that period. In general, the waves are usually one to two-meter right breaks. Often they'll climb to three meters, and occasionally as high as five. *(Surfing information courtesy of Surfer Publications, publishers of The Surf Report, a small magazine on surfing destinations all over the world. For information on subscribing or ordering back issues or a more complete report on surfing in El Salvador, write to: The Surf Report, PO Box 1028, Dana Point, CA 92629; tel 714/496-5922 ext 3030)*

El Salvador's Best Breaks

Western Spots
- Playa Barra de Santiago to Acajutla
- Playa Los Cóbanos
- El Zonte

Near La Libertad
- El Zunzal
- Playa Conchalío
- The Point (La Libertad)
- La Paz (La Libertad)
- Playa San Diego

Eastern Spots
- Playa El Cuco
- Playa Las Tunas

■ **In Town**. A handful of cultural centers and galleries in the capital host art exhibits, plays and other events. Movie theaters in the larger cities show American films dubbed in Spanish (small-town theaters tend toward skin flicks and low-budget action-adventure movies). There are many options in San Salvador to enjoy live Latin or club music, provided you have the clothes and the cash, while La Luna and a few smaller cafés in the capital are considerably more relaxed and inexpensive. The national theaters in San Salvador, Santa Ana and San Miguel host concerts occasionally. If you'd rather relax at night, try the main plaza in a small town like Conchagua, where people gather to flirt, discuss the day's events and watch the stars come out.

Shopping

The *artesanos* of El Salvador produce a number of crafts that make good gifts or souvenirs. Hammocks, most from the small village of **Concepción Quetzaltepeque** in Chalatenango department, are intricately woven and come in many different materials and designs. They make good traveling companions, especially if you plan to camp out on the beach. The best ones are available in the town, although it is a full day's trip from the capital.

Small wooden boxes and other pieces from **La Palma** in northern Chalatenango department are El Salvador's most recognizable craft. The wooden pieces are painted with simple, childlike designs of the Salvadoran countryside in bright colors, and then lacquered. Any shop that sells Salvadoran crafts—in or out of El Salvador—will invariably include pieces from La Palma.

The western town of **Nahuizalco** is known for its wicker furniture. These pieces take an incredibly long time to make, and would be great souvenirs if only they weren't so hard to take home.

Ilobasco produces painted ceramics that are exported throughout Central America. Although some of the work is rather rudimentary, the ceramics studios make the city an interesting place to visit.

San Sebastián in San Vicente department has an outdated cottage industry that once produced the country's best textiles on big wooden looms. Now, you'll find more Chinese imports lining store shelves in El Salvador than textiles from San Sebastián, so there's not much reason to visit the city.

Leather goods are another great souvenir of El Salvador. Sergio Acevedos in **Santa Ana** will make you the sharpest, most comfortable pair of cowboy boots you've ever worn. Other stores and craftsmen throughout the country sell leather belts, saddles, handbags, wallets and shoes.

San Salvador is a good place to buy the country's best crafts. Hammocks are sold near the central plaza by peasants who travel from Concepción Quetzaltepeque. Numerous galleries sell Salvadoran arts and crafts, including some styles you won't find anywhere else. Two crafts markets outside the city center have a good selection of every type of Salvadoran handicraft, although prices are higher there (see San Salvador).

San Salvador

San Salvador Then

In many ways the history of San Salvador is the history of El Salvador. The city's anguishes, disappointments, high hopes, promises and occasional blessings mirror the experiences of the entire country. The grimy downtown streets and posh residential neighborhoods of the capital are as much a reflection of El Salvador as they are a reflection of its capital.

■ **Founding.** The Pipil capital of Cuscatlán, established in 1054, was the first major city settled in the vicinity of present-day San Salvador. This indigenous nucleus, situated in the nearby Zalcuatitán Valley, was wealthy and powerful.

The arrival of the Spanish quickly brought the prosperity of the Pipil culture to an end. Pedro Alvarado attacked the city when he entered El Salvador in 1524, but was soon defeated. He returned just as quickly to mount a second campaign against the Cuscatlecos, but soon realized that the only way to defeat the Pipils would be to establish a colony in the area.

Toward the end of March 1525, Gonzalo de Alvarado established the villa of San Salvador near Cuscatlán, naming it in honor of Christ, Divino Salvador del Mundo (Divine Savior of the World). Within a year, however, the new town was burned to the ground during a surprise Pipil uprising. The few Spanish who survived fled to Guatemala.

The Alvarado family's history with San Salvador wasn't through yet, though. In 1528, Jorge de Alvarado, in charge of the campaign to settle El Salvador in the absence of his brother Pedro, sent their cousin Diego to re-found the villa of San Salvador in its present-day location. Soon local tribes were subdued, and many settlers moved back into the area. San Salvador was declared a city in 1546, with the Parque Libertad, Iglesia El Rosario and El Cabildo (town hall) constituting the center of town.

SAN SALVADOR

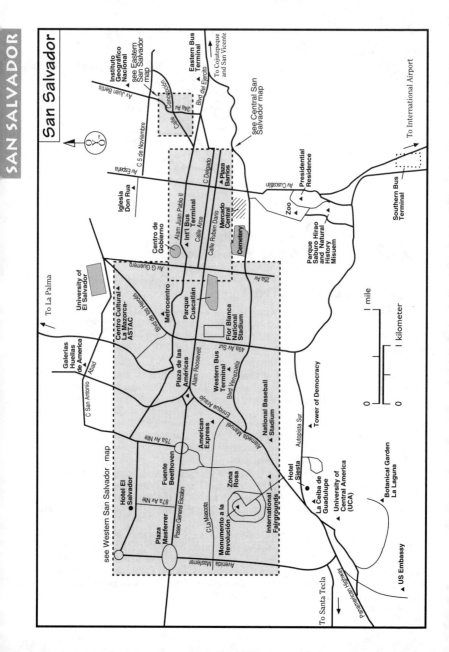

San Salvador

■ **Independence.** In 1811, Father José Delgado sounded the call for Central American independence from San Salvador. Early in the morning of November 5, church bells rang out across the city to show that the struggle had begun. When news reached San Salvador in 1821 that the revolution had been a success, the streets filled with celebrations. Loyalist Spanish forces from neighboring countries were completely subdued in 1835, and San Salvador was declared capital of the short-lived Central American Republic. The city became El Salvador's capital when the republic collapsed four years later.

San Salvador expanded quickly from the 19th century into the 20th. Telephones and electricity arrived by the 1880s, and the nearby San Salvador Volcano erupted repeatedly over the years. In 1940, about 100,000 people lived in the capital. Fifty years later the figure stood at one million, due in large part to an influx of *campesinos* from the impoverished and war-ravaged countryside.

■ **Recent History.** During the early part of the war, the capital escaped much of the fighting, but in August 1981, the FMLN dynamited eight nearby power stations and left the city without power for ten days. Aside from the psychological effects of a countryside engulfed in war, though, the capital didn't suffer much direct damage during the first half of the 1980s.

Citizens of the capital tried to go on with their lives as usual, but the effects of the war couldn't be ignored. A ten o'clock curfew was imposed and strictly enforced; the Church documented hundreds of cases of people who were killed after being caught violating the curfew. San Salvador's social rhythms were changed as well. Hotels started offering "taps to taps" deals, in which guests who didn't want to venture out after dark paid one price for dinner, dancing and a room for the night. Some people braved the danger and lingered outside in the evenings, to jog, stroll or hold hands.

■ **Earthquake.** This uneasy peace was shattered on October 10, 1986, when an earthquake measuring 7.5 on the Richter scale destroyed buildings throughout the city and closed down most businesses. Hotels and office buildings collapsed, trapping and burying hundreds. The US embassy, the Ministry of Planning and the old Gran Hotel San Salvador were all leveled or badly damaged. Four of six major hospitals were damaged along with thousands of homes, mostly in impoverished neighborhoods where the houses were poorly constructed.

The death toll rose into the hundreds, with tens of thousands injured and hundreds of thousands left homeless. The Salvadoran government appealed to the international community for assistance as it struggled to find adequate sources of water, food and medicine. The army, meanwhile, concerned itself more with staving off a possible guerrilla attack than helping out with the rescue effort, and it declared the city center a restricted zone. Helicopters and army trucks patrolled the streets to prevent the guerrillas from taking advantage of the chaos. In response, the FMLN declared a cease-fire in the capital during the emergency.

Today, the effects of the earthquake are still evident. Some buildings, like the Metropolitan Cathedral and the original National Library, are just now being repaired while other buildings, like the National Museum, remain closed due to damage from the earthquake. The tall black Torre Democracía (Tower of Democracy) on Autopista Sur near La UCA is still missing dozens of windows from the quake and later fighting.

■ **Fighting Reaches the Capital.** The FMLN succeeded in bringing the war to San Salvador in 1989. The rebels' original plans entailed simultaneous attacks on Usulután, San Miguel, Zacatecoluca, Santa Ana and San Salvador in an effort to instigate a popular uprising. They attacked on the eve of a holiday, when many soldiers were scheduled for weekend leave. The army found out ahead of time, however, canceled the leave and placed its units on alert.

As a result, the attacks on Santa Ana, Zacatecoluca and Usulután failed, and only San Miguel and San Salvador were jeopardized. In San Salvador, the guerrillas uncharacteristically stormed wealthy neighborhoods to tempt the army into bombing the homes of its major supporters, since earlier in the war the government had bombed poor neighborhoods occupied by the FMLN. President Cristiani's house in Colonia Escalón was one of the first attacked by the rebels.

The army didn't take the bait, however, and contented itself with driving the guerrillas out of the city slowly rather than trying to crush them outright. Only 200 soldiers were sent to fight and, when they failed, the army resorted to strategic air strikes. Although some wealthy residents later complained of air attacks on their neighborhoods, the northern and western sections of San Salvador suffered minimal damage during the occupation.

Though the guerrillas controlled as much as ten percent of the city at one point, they were driven out in part because they missed an opportunity to attack the Salvadoran Air Force at the nearby Ilopango airport. Also, San Salvador's population proved to be less than thrilled by the guerrillas' attempt to initiate a general uprising. City residents simply wanted the guerrillas to leave and to take the fighting elsewhere. In all, about 700 people died in the fighting in San Salvador, including almost 100 civilians. Two thousand people were wounded, half of them civilians, and emergency shelters were packed with more than 2,500 refugees.

San Salvador Now

The geographic, economic and political heart of El Salvador is probably the dirtiest, most crowded and most dangerous place in the country, but it also offers things that you won't find anywhere else. With a little patience, you can find almost anything in San Salvador, and since you can't really avoid the capital anyway, you might as well make the best of it.

Most of the tremors that hit the area come courtesy of the San Salvador Volcano which towers to the west, though the political and sociological earthquakes are all homemade. It's reassuring to know that this concrete jungle is only 30 minutes from the beaches near La Libertad and the shores of nearby Lago de Ilopango, both or which are good places to escape to if you're in the city for a while.

San Salvador is Central America's most densely-populated city, with an amazing 500,000 residents by official estimate. When everyone in the middle-class suburbs and ragged shantytowns that surround the city are added in, however, the numbers probably climb above 1,500,000.

People from all over the country come to the capital in search of work. Now that the war is over, many have moved back to the countryside, but unemployment in the city is still high. People get by, though, and you'll find vendors hawking everything imaginable on most street corners.

First impressions of San Salvador aren't usually positive. The pollution, the noise, the chaos and the crowds can be overwhelming at times. Crime is a problem,

Swinging in San Salvador

What the Pipils knew as Zalcuatitán, or "Valley of the Feathered Serpent," the Spanish renamed Valle de las Hamacas, or "Valley of the Hammocks." The more accurate (if less poetic) name came from the observation that the area swings like a hammock every time an earthquake or volcano strikes. San Salvador was first flattened by an earthquake in 1575, and averaged two or more each century for the next 300 years.

Soon after San Salvador was declared the capital of El Salvador, the quake of 1854 destroyed most of the city's buildings and stirred debate about whether the government should move its capital to a more stable location. In the end, the government decided to rebuild in the same area, although it restricted building height to two stories. Even though buildings have been constructed taller than that since then, Salvadorans have learned that in the swinging confines of their capital, shorter buildings are safer buildings.

especially downtown near the Plaza Barrios. You won't see many people out on the streets at night, which is unsettling in such a major city. Sometimes the city can be incredibly frustrating—try to stay calm when you find out that traffic is backed up for ten blocks because workmen are repairing a pothole in the busiest intersection of the city during rush hour. Even the more exclusive western neighborhoods, although clean, are more sterile than inviting. Colonia San Benito, for example, has high walls, wide, empty streets and few people in sight besides guards.

On the other hand, San Salvador is handily located right in the center of the country, within a day's travel of anywhere and conveniently close to the international airport. The city is packed with hotels, from five stars to no stars. You'll find almost every type of restaurant you could imagine here, including *pupuserías* and $20-a-plate gourmet eateries with piano bars and crystal glassware. San Salvador offers the best—some would say only—nightlife in the country, with many places worth checking out after hours. Museums and galleries are good for quiet Sunday afternoons, and there are usually games being played in the city's various stadiums. You can even go hiking nearby, either along the paths of the botanical garden at La Caldera or on the slopes of the San Salvador Volcano (see Santa Tecla).

On the whole, although San Salvador's crowds, crime and pollution may make you tense, you'll find there's plenty to do. The city is a convenient base from which to explore the country and will keep you occupied for days—whether you want it to or not.

Orientation

San Salvador can be a confusing concrete jungle at times. It does have enough of an order, though, that if you take a moment to learn what makes it tick—which way numbers go, what major roads cross and leave the city and where the major landmarks are situated—you'll find that getting around isn't too difficult after all.

■ **Streets and Avenues.** San Salvador's streets are laid out in a somewhat logical fashion; the only real problem is that many of the city's main roads keep switching names every few dozen blocks. Like most Salvadoran cities, San Salvador has

SAN SALVADOR

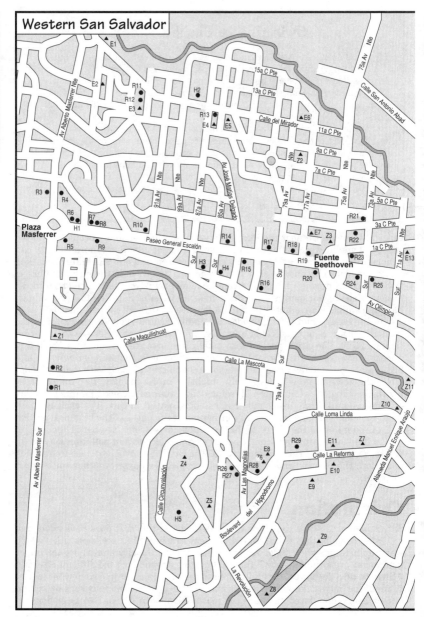

Western San Salvador

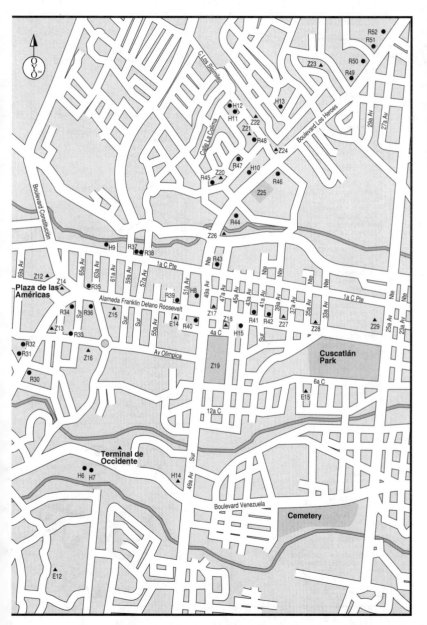

SAN SALVADOR

ACCOMMODATIONS ●

H1 Suky Apart-Hotel
H2 Hotel El Salvador
H3 Hotel Terraza
H4 Hotel Ramada Inn
H5 Hotel Presidente
H6 Hotel Roma
H7 Hotel Pasadena
H8 Hotel Occidental
H9 Novo Apart-Hotel
H10 Hotel Camino Real
H11 Hotel Good Luck
H12 Hotel Happy House
H13 Ximena's Guest House
H14 Hotel Valencia
H15 Hotel Alameda

FOOD & DRINK ●

R1 El Chalán
R2 Restaurant Del Arbol/El Arbol del Diós
R3 Kalpatarú
R4 Cardisi's ice cream
R5 Burger King
R6 Daruma, Nestor's Argentinean Restaurant
R7 Fonda del Sol
R8 La Taverna del Vino, Abordo
R9 La Pampa Argentina
R10 China Town
R11 El Rosal
R12 Kamakura
R13 Sambuca
R14 Beto's
R15 La Diligencia
R16 La Piccola Trattoria
R17 Panes con Pavo
R18 Jau Sin
R19 El Bodegón
R20 Las Carnitas de Don Carlos
R21 Restaurant China Inn
R22 Gino's Pizza
R23 Chela's Steak House
R24 Wendy's
R25 Sir Pizza
R26 La Madeira
R27 Restaurant Dynasty
R28 La Basilea
R29 Pizza Hut
R30 Pizza Boom
R31 Sao Yin
R32 Toto's Pizza
R33 Pronto Gourmet
R34 Burger King
R35 Pizza Hut
R36 Pops Ice Cream
R37 Tacomex
R38 Chel's Restaurant and Bar
R39 Restaurant München
R40 China Palace
R41 La Fuente de Salud
R42 Cafe de Don Pedro
R43 China de Oro
R44 Pueblo Viejo
R45 Restaurant Chantilly
R46 Restaurant Doña Mercedes
R47 Restaurant Metro-Canchas
R48 Restaurant El Carbonero
R49 Pupusería Margot
R50 El Corral Steakhouse
R51 Las Antorchas
R52 Villa Fiesta

OTHER ▲

Z1 Genesis 7 Curiosidades
Z2 Las Columnas Centro de Artes
Z3 Cines Gemelos Beethoven
Z4 Monumento a la Revolución
Z5 Galería 1-2-3
Z6 Bookmark's
Z7 Plaza San Benito
Z8 International Fairgrounds
Z9 Mercado Nacional de Artesanías
Z10 Bigith Supermarket
Z11 American Express office
Z12 TACA Airlines headquarters, Cines Caribe
Z13 Deluxe Theater
Z14 El Salvador del Mundo
Z15 American Airlines office
Z16 El Laberinto Gallery
Z17 Esso Automarket
Z18 Laundromat
Z19 Flor Blanca National Stadium
Z20 Hertz
Z21 Artesanias de La Palma
Z22 Laundromat
Z23 La Luna Nightclub
Z24 El Mundo Feliz Amusement Park
Z25 Metrocentro/Continental Airlines office
Z26 Metrosur shopping center
Z27 Artisans of El Salvador store
Z28 Military Compound
Z29 Hospital

EMBASSIES ▲

E1 Colombia
E2 Chile
E3 Venezuela
E4 Israel
E5 Mexico
E6 Argentina
E7 Ecuador
E8 Brazil
E9 Canada
E10 Uruguay
E11 Spain
E12 Panama
E13 Nicaragua
E14 Costa Rica/Peru
E15 Honduras Consulate

avenidas (avenues) which run north to south. Avenida Cuscatlán/España is the main avenue, and consequently it has two different names; one each for its northern and southern halves. Even-numbered *avenidas* increase east of Avenida Cuscatlán/España. West of Avenida Cuscatlán/España, *avenidas* are numbered with increasing odd numbers. The unofficial outer *avenidas* of San Salvador are Avenida Masferrer to the west and the Terminal Occidente to the east, and 49a Avenida divides the city roughly in half.

Likewise, *calles* (streets) run east to west. Calle Delgado/Arce divides all even (to the south) and odd (to the north) *calles*. The unofficial northern and southern limits of the city are Autopista Sur to the south and Calle San Antonio Abad to the north. The busiest *calle* has three different names: it starts out as Calle Rubén Darío in the city center, then changes to Alameda Franklin Delano Roosevelt near 25a Av as it heads west, and finally becomes Paseo General Escalón as it passes the Plaza de las Américas heading towards the Plaza Masferrer. Calle Delgado/Arce, one block north of Calle Darío/Alameda FDR/Paseo Escalón, is named Delgado in the city center, and changes to Calle Arce as it passes Avenida Cuscatlán/España heading west.

Really, it's simple once you get the hang of it. Avenida Cuscatlán/España and Calle Delgado/Arce bisect the city, meeting one block north of the Plaza Barrios in the heart of the city. Paseo General Escalón with its nice houses, Boulevard de los Héroes with its restaurants, nightlife and malls and Avenida Juan Pablo II in front of the Centro de Gobierno are the city's other main roads.

■ **Leaving San Salvador.** Many roads lead out of San Salvador in every direction. Leading out of the city to the north is 24a Av/Calle Concepción, which heads first to Apopa and then on to the departments of Cuscatlán and Cabañas. The Boulevard del Ejército runs east out of the city and joins the Panamerican Highway, before continuing on to San Vicente. Avenida Cuscatlán (which turns into Avenida de los Diplomáticos) and 49a Av head southeast out of the city towards the airport and the Costa del Sol.

You'll find another route south if you're heading west and you make a left (to the south) at the Plaza de las Américas and El Salvador del Mundo, toward Santa Tecla along Alameda Manuel Enrique Araujo. Once you leave the city you can either turn off to the south toward La Libertad or continue to the west to Santa Tecla.

■ **Landmarks.** If you ever get lost, you won't travel far before bumping into one of these, so its' a good idea to know where some of them are. On the Western San Salvador map, west to east along the Paseo Escalón you'll find the Plaza Masferrer, the Fuente Beethoven and the Plaza de las Américas with the statue of El Salvador del Mundo. Metrocentro is north a few blocks on 49a Av/Blvd de los Héroes, and the Zona Rosa restaurant and nightlife district is tucked in between Paseo Escalón and Alameda Araujo to the southwest.

The Central San Salvador map contains most of the major sites of the city, with the Metropolitan Cathedral, National Palace, National Library, National Theater and central market squeezed within two blocks of the Plaza Barrios. The Centro de Gobierno is north off of Alameda Juan Pablo II. A handful of budget hotels and poorer sections of the city are contained in the eastern map. The full San Salvador map lists a few more sites not shown in the other maps, including the University of El Salvador in the north, the zoo and presidential palace to the south and the University of Central America (La UCA) to the southwest.

IN THE NEWS

Gang Trouble

Gang violence in cities like Los Angeles and New York has spurred the US government to deport many of its worst offenders back to their native countries. For some Salvadorans with a history of violence and arrests, that means a return trip to El Salvador.

This forced repatriation is difficult both for the deportees and for their country. El Salvador isn't equipped to deal with gangs, and the deportees find that life back in their native country isn't so easy. To ease the transition, many of the members do what comes naturally to them to survive: they form new gangs in El Salvador.

Many young Salvadorans view gang members with a mixture of fear, awe and admiration. With their foreign clothes and confident swagger, gang members are easily able to find recruits among the country's undereducated and unemployed youth. As Salvadoran gangs become larger and their tactics more violent, the cycle of violence begun to the north gradually returns home.

■ **Bus Terminals.** The Terminal de Occidente (western terminal) on Boulevard Venezuela is south of the Plaza de las Américas. The Terminal de Oriente (eastern terminal) is on the Boulevard del Ejército on the north side of the notoriously congested Plaza Arce. A big factory sits like a fort between the terminal and Boulevard del Ejército. The Terminal del Sur is south of the center in the suburb of San Marcos. Three international bus stops are scattered around town, with one at the Terminal Occidente, another across from the Centro de Gobierno and the last next to the Hotel San Carlos (see Central San Salvador map).

■ **Neighborhoods.** The small streets around Paseo General Escalón west of the Plaza de las Américas and Colonia San Benito near the Zona Rosa are filled with some of the city's nicest houses. Here, empty streets are lined with trees, flowers, high walls, security cameras and barbed wire. Less wealthy areas of San Salvador, especially near the Terminal Oriente and around the central market, can be dangerous.

Inexpensive restaurants are scattered throughout central San Salvador, while more pricey ones sit along the Paseo General Escalón and in the Zona Rosa. Others, including many steak houses and restaurants with nightly entertainment, are set along the Boulevard de los Héroes. You'll find inexpensive and medium-priced hotels in the center and in the east, while the most expensive hotels, including the Hotel El Salvador and the Camino Real, are scattered throughout the city.

Accommodations

Luxury Hotels

Hotel El Salvador The poshest hotel in El Salvador just got better, thanks to an $8 million renovation. All the rooms in the new tower have top-rate facilities, with electronic key cards and the country's only fire extinguisher system that meets US standards. Many rooms have great views of the San Salvador Volcano and all have original Salvadoran art on the walls. The racquet club across the street offers guests tennis, squash and racquetball courts. *(Tel 298-5444, fax*

223-2901; 78 rooms $80, 190 rooms in new tower $130 and $150, two suites $400, all with private bath, hot water, AC, TV, phone; laundry; pool; 1pm checkout; parking; four restaurants, bar)

Hotel Presidente   Hopefully this recently-privatized luxury hotel will start showing the results of its new life sometime soon. For now, it still feels like a government-run bureaucracy, which it once was; they charge you for the bottled water in your room. Nice view out over the pool, though. (Zona Rosa, near Monumento de la Revolución; tel 279-4444, 226 rooms S $100, D $118, 18 suites $253; all with private baths, hot water, AC, TV, phone; laundry; 2pm checkout; 3 restaurants, bar)

Westin Camino Real   Same class as the Hotel El Salvador, just a bit older, although many rooms and furnishings are new. This is where most foreigners hung their hats during the civil war. Since then, businessmen have replaced journalists. You can enjoy live music at the bar every night, and mariachi music and a buffet by the pool on Wednesday and Friday evenings. (Opposite Metrocentro; tel 279-3888; 102 normal rooms $100, 102 deluxe rooms $130, all with private baths, hot water, AC, TV, phone; laundry; pool; 2pm checkout; restaurant, café,bar)

Hotel Siesta   This small luxury hotel next to the Ceiba de Guadalupe has a small pool with an interesting fountain. It's pleasant, but for what they're asking you'd expect a little more. (Panamerican Highway to Santa Tecla; tel 278-5266; 51 rooms, S $83, D $90, all with private baths, hot water; laundry; pool; 1pm checkout; parking; restaurant, bar)

Hotels in Western San Salvador

Hotel Occidental   This homey place looks like...somebody's home, with patio, courtyard, knickknacks on the shelves and pictures on the walls. The rooms are spacious and clean with large bathrooms. A good deal. (49a Av Nte #171, between 1a C Pte and Alam Roosevelt; tel 223-7715; 5S $9.20 with shared bath, 5D $17.25 with private bath, TV, all have fan; 24hr checkout)

Ximena's Guest House   A tired-looking little house with decent facilities. Check out the "green room" with its weird underwater light. Lisa de Carmona, the American owner, runs a Spanish language school here, which includes a room and 20 hours of instruction for $75 per week (call for info). The restaurant serves light food and is for guests only. Breakfast is around $1.70. (C San Salvador #52; tel 225-9268; 15 rooms, S $10.35 with fan, $12 with private bath, D $10.35 with fan, $15.50 with private bath; laundry; 2pm checkout; restaurant)

Suky Apart-Hotel   Fully-furnished apartments with small kitchens and full baths, for rent by the day or longer. (Pas Gen Escalón #5625, above Daruma restaurant; tel 279-4009; 10D $66, all with private baths, hot water, kitchen, cable TV; laundry; 2pm checkout)

Hotel Terraza   This place is getting an overhaul, which will hopefully send its dated facilities the way of the dinosaurs—the old section looks like a glorified student dormitory. The clean carpets and pool are a start, though. (Pas Gen Escalón and 85a Av Sur; tel 279-1680; 80S $74, D $80, all with private baths, hot water; laundry; pool; 1pm checkout)

SAN SALVADOR

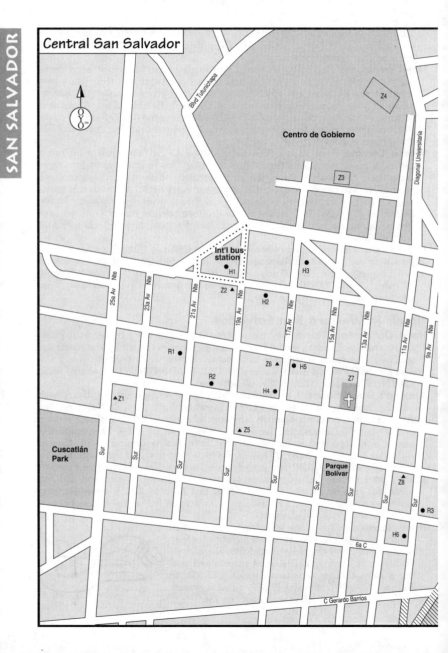

Central San Salvador

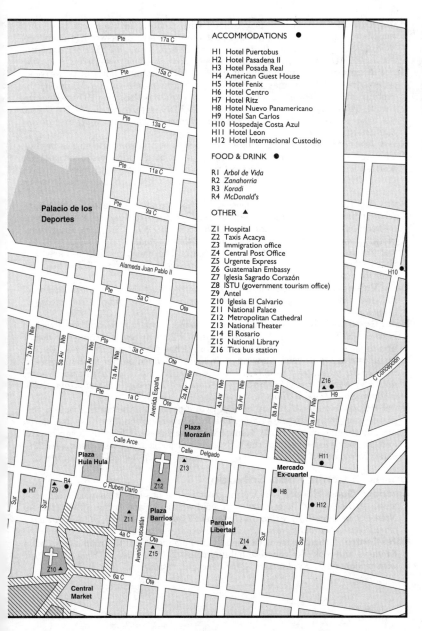

SAN SALVADOR

ACCOMMODATIONS ●

H1 Hotel Puertobus
H2 Hotel Pasadena II
H3 Hotel Posada Real
H4 American Guest House
H5 Hotel Fenix
H6 Hotel Centro
H7 Hotel Ritz
H8 Hotel Nuevo Panamericano
H9 Hotel San Carlos
H10 Hospedaje Costa Azul
H11 Hotel Leon
H12 Hotel Internacional Custodio

FOOD & DRINK ●

R1 *Arbol de Vida*
R2 *Zanahorria*
R3 *Koradi*
R4 *McDonald's*

OTHER ▲

Z1 Hospital
Z2 Taxis Acacya
Z3 Immigration office
Z4 Central Post Office
Z5 Urgente Express
Z6 Guatemalan Embassy
Z7 Iglesia Sagrado Corazón
Z8 ISTU (government tourism office)
Z9 Antel
Z10 Iglesia El Calvario
Z11 National Palace
Z12 Metropolitan Cathedral
Z13 National Theater
Z14 El Rosario
Z15 National Library
Z16 Tica bus station

Hotel Ramada Inn A high-priced hotel with modern facilities that have that back-home feel but can't quite get past an oppressive dark-wood atmosphere. *(85a Av Sur; tel 279-1700; 23 rooms S $65, D $75, T $81, all with private bath, hot water, AC, TV, telephone; laundry; pool; 2pm checkout; restaurant, bar, café)*

Hotel Alameda The management at this old, crumbling hotel is secretive—where does all the money from the high-priced rooms go? La Mansion, the restaurant next door, is also run by the hotel and has the same 1970s-style furniture. *(Alam Roosevelt and 43a Av; tel 279-0299; 110 rooms, S $57.50, D $63, all with private bath, hot water; laundry; pool; 2pm checkout; restaurant 6:30am-10:30pm, bar)*

Novo Apart-Hotel A decent long-term place to stay if someone else is paying. The staff is very helpful and the sculptures out by the kidney-shaped pool are worth a look. Hammocks swing next to the pleasant grassy courtyard. *(Tel 279-0099; 50 rooms, S $47.50, D $57.50 or $1,200 per month, all with private baths, hot water, AC, kitchenettes; 1pm checkout)*

Hotel Pasadena Not much to look at but the management does its best with what it has. The sheets are clean, at least. *(Boulevard Venezuela #3093, near western bus terminal; tel 223-7905; 10S $5.75, 6D $9.20, all have fans, hammocks, some with private baths; laundry; 24hr checkout)*

Hotel Roma Very basic, but a good bargain. The checkout time is early, but they're flexible. *(Tel 224-0256; 8S $4.60, $5.75 with private bath, 6D $6.90, most have fans; laundry, 8am checkout)*

Hotel Valencia Grimy and damp. *(Intersection of Blvd Venezuela and 49a Av; tel 223-1521, 87S $5.75, 4D $9.20, most with private bath; laundry; 11am checkout; comedor)*

Hotel Good Luck A Chinese family runs this big, spotless hotel and the attached restaurant. The rooms are large and clean, if a little pricey, and there's a washer and dryer to do your laundry. The restaurant has a lunch special for $1.15 that includes chicken or beef, chow mein and rice. It's open earlier for hotel guests. *(Av Los Sisimiles; tel 226-8287; 19 rooms S/D $23, T $31, all with private bath, fan, TV, +$8.60 for AC; laundry; restaurant Mon-Sat 11:30am-3pm, 5:30-9:30pm, Sun 11:30am-3pm)*

Hotel Happy House A step up in quality and price from the bargain hotels, this place seems to live up to its name. The little green garden, furniture and stereo are out of some happy 1970s home. The management is friendly (even happy) and the rooms are large, but the beds and bathrooms aren't very clean. *(Tel 226-6866; 15 rooms S $18, D $22, all with private bath; 2pm checkout; restaurant)*

Hotels in Central San Salvador

American Guest House This weird, groovy place has the atmosphere and odor of life at the turn of the century, with gold wallpaper and antique TVs. *(17a Av Nte #119, between C Arce and 1a C Pte; tel 271-0224; 2S $17.25, 9D $20, all with private bath, hot water; laundry; 2pm checkout; restaurant)*

Hotel Centro A clean place with friendly management, but the rooms don't have windows and look like concrete holding cells. *(Tel 271-5045, 21S/D $13.80, all with private bath, TV; laundry; 24hr checkout, restaurant)*

Hotel Fenix A big, dark place that actually looks like a hotel—check out the high ceiling in the entranceway and the steep winding central staircase. The pleasant lady who runs things will show you upstairs to your wood-paneled room and its ancient TV. *(Tel 271-1269; $6.90 per person with shared bath, D $11.50 with shared bath, S/D $17.25 with private bath, all have fans, color TV, hot water, laundry; noon checkout, restaurant)*

Hotel Pasadena II This clean, inexpensive hotel surrounds a tiny concrete courtyard. *(Tel 221-4786; 11S $6.25, 5D $10.35, all with private bath, fan; 11am checkout)*

Love Under the Volcano

Time passes. Towering *ceiba* trees grow from seedlings and fall to the ground. Young children become parents, grandparents and then pass away. But Cipitín is still beautiful. His eyes are still black, his skin is the color of cinnamon and he carries a sweet-smelling stick so he can leap over streams.

Time passes, but the son of the Siguanaba remains forever ten years old, his eternal youth a gift of the gods. Always elusive, he steals about, hiding among the foliage and playing among the petals of wild irises.

Cipitín is the god of young love. They say the young women of the town always go, in the chill of the early dawn, to leave him flowers so he will play on the banks of the river. From high in the treetops he spies on them, and when a girl passed below he shakes flowers free from the branches.

But you should know that Cipitín already has a sweetheart—a girl, small and beautiful, just like him. Her name is Tenáncin.

One day Cipitín had fallen asleep on the petal of a large flower. Tenáncin was wandering in the forest picking tiny flowers when she lost her way. Running, lost, she stumbled through the brambles and came to the flower where Cipitín was sleeping. She saw him.

The rustling of the bushes awakened Cipitín, and he fled leaping over the bushes.

He ran from flower to flower, singing sweetly. Tenáncin followed him. After a long time, Cipitín came to a rock on the side of a volcano. Tenáncin's feet and hands were scratched and bleeding from the thorns.

Cipitín touched the rock with a *shilca* and a door of moss gave way. Holding hands, the two entered—first Cipitín, then Tenáncin. The moss door closed behind them.

And Tenáncin was never seen again.

Her father searched the forest and hills, and several days later died from the pain caused by the loss. They say the cavern where Cipitín and Tenáncin disappeared is on the Sihuatepeque Volcano in the department of San Vicente.

Time has passed. The world has changed, rivers have run dry and mountains have been born. Yet the son of the Siguanaba remains forever ten years old. It's not unusual for him to perch on an iris or hide in the treetops, spying on the girls that laugh down by the river.

—Salvadoran Folk Tale

SAN SALVADOR

Eastern San Salvador

H1
Municipal Market
H2
H3
H4
H7
Calle Concepción
H5
H8
24a Avenida
H6
To Avenida Independencia

ACCOMMODATIONS ●

H1 Hospedaje Centro American
H2 Hotel Cuscatlán
H3 Hotel Yucatán
H4 Hospedaje Emperador
H5 Hotel Imperial
H6 Hospedaje Figueroa
H7 Hospedaje Santa Rosa
H8 Hospedaje Izalco

Hotel Posada Real Completely unremarkable. Clean, bare and cheap. *(Tel 271-5710; 4S $5.75c1D $10.35, all with fan, shared bath; laundry; 24hr checkout)*

Hotel Puertobus On the second floor over the Puertobus terminal, this hotel is spotless, convenient, impersonal, and outrageously over-priced. Take a cab across town for something one-quarter the price. *(Puertobus terminal; tel 221-1000; 7S $40, 20D $45, 7T $50, all with private bath, hot water, TV, phone, AC; checkout 2pm)*

Hotel Ritz Decent for the 60s but outdated and overpriced for the 90s. Everything here, from the bedclothes to the furniture (and more alarmingly, the elevator), looks old. *(Tel 222-0033; 6S $30, 24D $35.60, 22T $42, all with private baths, hot water; laundry; pool; parking; 2pm checkout; restaurant)*

Hotel Internacional Custodio Reasonably new, simple and clean. *(10a Av Sur #509 and C Delgado; tel 222-5698; 8S $5.75 with shared bath, $6.90 with private bath, 5D $9.20 with private bath; laundry; 1pm checkout)*

Hotel San Carlos The rooms are a little old and basic but a good deal for the price. Doña Rivera, the owner, runs a tight ship. *(C Concepción #121; tel 222-8975; 27 rooms $6.50 per person; laundry; 12pm checkout)*

Hotel Nuevo Panamericano Well-run and comfortable, but a little pricey for the quality of the rooms. You can change money downstairs. *(Tel 222-2959; 27 rooms $8.80 with private bath, fan, +$2.85 for TV, AC, additional bed; laundry; 12pm checkout, parking)*

Hotel Leon Not as nice as the San Carlos or as comfy as the Panamericano, but cheaper than either. *(C Delgado #621; tel 222-0951; 38 rooms $4/$5.25/$6.90 for 1/2/3 people without fan, +$1 for fan, +$2 to be on first floor; laundry; 12pm checkout; parking)*

Hospedaje Costa Azul A new building with simple, clean rooms. Much better than the dives around it. *(11 rooms $5.75 per person, all with private baths; 2pm checkout)*

Hotels in Eastern San Salvador

Probably setting some kind of record, seven budget hotels cram one block of Calle Concepción near the eastern bus terminal. There's also a collection of ratty *hospedajes* at the intersection of 14a Av Nte and 9a C Ote, near the much nicer Hospedaje Costa Azul (see above and Central San Salvador map).

Hospedaje Centroamericano A purely functional temporary residence that's not so clean but is a good deal. Catch a game of pool next door at Oscar's Billiards. *(C Concepción #837; tel 276-6689; 10S $2.30 with shared bath, $4 for two people; 7D $5.75 with private bath, fan, $8.75 for three people; laundry; 9am checkout)*

Hospedaje Rosita Because it's close to the market, this *hospedaje* is usually full with a regular clientele of vendors, so you might feel like you're intruding on a family of sorts. Quiet and clean. *(10 rooms $1.70, all with shared bath; 7am checkout)*

Hospedaje Figueroa Sofas, hammocks and flowering bushes give this place a comfy atmosphere. The rooms are clean and completely bare, and they lock the doors at 10pm. *(Tel 222-1541; 4S $2.85, 17D $4.60, 5D with private bath and fan $6.90)*

Hospedaje Emperador The only thing unusual about this place is the funny smell in the bathrooms. The liquor store/*comedor* Rosita next door fills this place with other, more tempting aromas. *(Tel 222-7572, 10 S/D rooms $4.60 with shared bath, $6.90 for three people, 13 rooms with private bath, AC $5.75, $8.05 for three people, +$2 for TV; 24hr checkout)*

Hotel Imperial Big, old run-down rooms are nonetheless a good bargain. *(Tel 222-5159; 13 rooms $4 per person with shared bath, 25 rooms $5.75 per person with private bath; laundry; 2pm checkout; restaurant)*

Hotel Yucatán Run by a friendly family that enjoys talking with foreigners. *(Tel 221-2585, 11S $2.85 with private bath, 9D $5.75 with private bath, less for shared bath; 2pm checkout; parking)*

Hotel Cuscatlán Dark, overpriced for the area and smells like a wet rug. *(Tel 222-3298; 10S $6.90, 25D $8.05, all with private bath, TV; 12pm checkout)*

Hospedaje Izalco A big place that extends back off the street forever. $2.30 more will get you cable TV. *(Tel 221-7214; 49D $8.05, 14 rooms with fan $9.30, all with private bath, TV; laundry; 1pm checkout; parking)*

Hospedaje Santa Rosa Clean enough, and a better deal than the Izalco. Grab a beer with the locals next door at Ara's Beer or a bite at the Comedor Centroamerica in front. *(Tel 222-9290; 1 room $2.30 with shared bath, 14 rooms $2.85 per person with private bath, all with fan; 12pm checkout; parking)*

Food & Drink

(Refer to Western San Salvador and Full San Salvador maps for locations.)

On Paseo General Escalón

Nestor's Argentinean Restaurant Rough wooden tables packed on two floors and wooden banisters make this little *rancho* a nice place to dig into some red meat, which is about all they serve. The *chorizo*, 8oz of beef, costs $4. *(Plaza Masferrer; 11am-3pm, 6-10pm)*

Daruma This Japanese restaurant in the same complex as the Suky Hotel is about as close as El Salvador will get to Japan, apart from some financial aid packages to fix bridges. A few Japanese paintings and a small *sushi* bar say it all. *Sushi* dishes run around $9.20. *(Next to Nestor's, 12-3pm, 6-11pm)*

Kalpataru Enjoy the famous coffee with a view out over Avenida Masferrer at this vegetarian restaurant up above a small health-food store. The lunch buffet runs about $5.75, and the salad bar goes for half that. Natural fruit juices and daily specials are served. For dessert, go across the street to Cardisi's for ice cream. *(7-8:30am, 12-3pm, 3-9:30pm)*

La Pampa Argentina An Argentinean grill that would be right at home on the *pampa*, aside from the waiters in tuxedos. The rough wood theme is carried over from sign to ceiling to walls, tables and benches. The special, *pamperito mixto* for $10.35, includes 6oz of grilled, mixed beef and shrimp. (This is one of two La Pampas in San Salvador.) *(Pas Gen Escalón; Mon-Thurs 12-2:30pm, 6-10:30pm, Fri-Sat until 11pm, Sun 12-3:30pm, 6-9:30pm)*

Fonda del Sol A formal restaurant made to look like a house, with pewter plates, exotic (but real) flowers and a small wine cellar on the wall to the right. Try the delectable *Corvina Fonda del Sol* (a fish filet with asparagus and cheese) for $10.90. *(Pas Gen Escalón, across from La Pampa Argentina; 12-3pm, 7pm-12am)*

La Taverna del Vino This dark, romantic little corner seems out of place on Escalón. The woodwork is decorated with carved wine bottles, and the cellar offers wines from California, Spain, Chile, France, Italy and Portugal. Bottles run around $17.25, and a few vintages are available by the glass for around $2.30. Top it off with a cheese fondue for $4-$7.50. *(Pas Gen Escalón; 6pm-12am)*

El Bodegón Formal, formal, formal with wooden tables out of some museum and a management too uptight to make this place enjoyable. The *paella valencia*, a Spanish rice dish with chicken and shrimp, costs $8.05. Other plates are $11.50 and up. *(Paseo Escalón and 77a Av Nte; Mon-Sat 12-3pm, 6-11pm)*

Jau Sin In a big old house with a few Chinese wooden dividers and wooden chandeliers. *Chow mein* costs $4 and seafood is $5.75 and up. *(Tues-Sun 12-3pm, 6-11pm)*

Panes Con Pavo Grab a big turkey sandwich for $1.70 at this simple cafeteria that's always packed with people. *(Col Escalón and 79a Av Nte; 12-10pm)*

Beto's Hanging nautical artifacts give this seafood and pasta joint a slightly salty air, but can't hide the steep prices. Grab a beer and a $5.75 seafood cocktail and kick back under the big red awning. *(Mon-Thurs 11:30am-10:30pm, Fri-Sat until 11:30pm, Sun until 10pm)*

La Diligencia Candlelight and the murmur of voices fill this restaurant decorated with stained glass windows and staffed by friendly waiters. Meat dishes start at $10.35. *(7am-11pm)*

Las Carnitas de Don Carlos Stylish but traditional, overlooking the Plaza Beethoven. There's a big oven in the center to grill the dishes, which are served by waiters in colorful outfits. Munchies like tacos and *fajitas* are $2.85-$5.75, and more substantial plates are $8-$12.65. *(6am-11:30pm)*

Café de Don Pedro At 3am, this 24-hour open-air restaurant that looks like a 1950s drive-up will be the only place open. It has a wide-open, everyone-knows-everyone feel, with a varied menu that includes everything from inexpensive omelettes and soups to *filet mignon* for $6.90. Six bottles of beer in a bucket of ice will run you $4.80. Musical trios roam with guitars and accordions every evening until the wee hours of the morning.

Restaurant München German down to the faded posters on the walls and the *umlauts* on the menu. Dig into a German würst, starting at $4, and wash it down with a Heineken for $2.30. *(Col Roosevelt, Mon-Sat 11am-12pm)*

China Palace Mao Zedong would feel at home here—he's dead and so is the atmosphere. The large menu includes many inexpensive dishes. *(Between 51a and 53a Av; Weds-Mon, 12-2pm, 6-10pm)*

La Fuente de Salud A vegetarian cafeteria popular with the lunch crowd. A plate of food at the "fountain of health" includes rice, *tortas* and strange-tasting soy beef and costs $1.60. A big fruit salad is $0.70. *(Condominio Roosevelt #2218, N side of Alam Roosevelt between 41a and 43a Av Nte; Sun-Fri)*

La Piccola Trattoria Well-done Italian atmosphere with folksy accordion music, subdued lighting, an indoor fountain and gracious service. The food, though, is only so-so. Pasta dishes are $4.60, seafood is more expensive. *(81 Av Sur #131, one block south of Col Escalón; Mon-Sat 11am-3pm, 6pm-1am)*

Near the Zona Rosa

La Madeira One of the most attractive and elegant restaurants in El Salvador, set in a gorgeous rust-colored Spanish-style house built in the 1950s. The whole place is very well-done, from the meticulously-landscaped outdoor patio to the pottery and art on the walls. It's so classy that even the bar has a name (La Seramouche) and the menu is written in three different languages. Entrees are $11.50-$17.25, lobster $25.85, *sopa de consommé* $4. *(12-3pm, 6:30-11:30pm)*

Restaurant Dynasty Red neon borders the walls above the tall black screen at this swank Chinese restaurant. You can enjoy a $11.50 sweet and sour shrimp plate inside or outside on the terrace overlooking the Zona Rosa. *(Next to La Madera, in the Zona Rosa; 11:30am-3pm)*

La Basilea A comfortable restaurant set on the second floor overlooking the Zona Rosa. Two parrots look out from their cages on the edge of the lushly-bordered patio. Paintings by Salvadoran and international artists are for sale in the one-room gallery in the back room. Vegetarian and pasta dishes fill the menu, with the special *corvina almandine* (sea bass) at $7.50. *(Centro Commercial La Basilea, Zona Rosa; 11am-11pm)*

On Boulevard de los Héroes

Pueblo Viejo Rusted rifles and old photos on the stucco walls give this restaurant an old-world feel in every respect but the price. This place can get loud for such a nice restaurant, especially when soccer games are shown on the big screen TV. Sixteen ounces of *churrasco* cost $8.60. The big colorful painting on the wall is of Apaneca. *(Metrosur; 6:30am-11:30pm, Thurs-Sat until 1am)*

Las Antorchas Over 100 rough wood tables fill this steak house which hosts live *salsa* and *merengue* groups on weekends for a $2.30 cover. *Tacos* are $2.05 and other dishes are around $3.45. *(6pm-2am)*

Pupusería Margot One of the biggest *pupuserías* you'll ever see, run by a woman who owns another Pupusería Margot in Santa Tecla. *(Noon-10pm)*

Villa Fiesta The food here is really an afterthought to the drinks and weekend nightlife. The five plates they serve average around $8 each, while beers and drinks cost $1.15-$3.45. The cover to dance is $2.85 on Thurs and $5.75 on Saturday. *(Blvd Los Héroes; Weds-Sat 6pm-late)*

El Corral Steak House Yet another steak house, but at least the waiters here wear cowboy outfits. You can find live music almost every night of the week, from Latin to rock. After 8pm on Friday and Saturday the cover to dance is $2.85. Grilled plates run $2.30-$6.90. *(Mon-Weds 11:30am-11pm, Thurs until 12:30am, Fri-Sat until 1am)*

Other Restaurants

Kamakura This Japanese restaurant welcomes you with sliding wooden doors and offers a small *sushi* bar serving authentic raw fish for $1.70-$2.30 a piece. Prices for plates like *tempura* and *sashimi* start at $8.60 and go way, way up. The Japanese woman who owns Kamakura learned her Spanish back in Japan, then came here to open a restaurant. *(93a Av Nte #617, half block from C El Mirador; Mon-Sat 12-3pm, 6-10:30pm)*

Sambuca Vincenzo Belvito owned a few restaurants in Dallas before he came to San Salvador with his girlfriend and turned this house into an Italian bistro. He has done a great job, too, and prepares all the food himself, including pizzas baked over a stone fire. The homemade rolls and *calzones* are delicious and moderately priced. *(85a Av Nte #643 and C El Mirador, one block from Hotel El Salvador; 8am-3pm, 6pm-12am)*

Restaurant Del Arbol Located in the same building as Fernando Llort's Galería del Arbol (see Entertainment), this restaurant is set tastefully in the back rooms, near a courtyard and next to a patio. Llort's art fills the walls. Heft the painted brass menu and treat yourself to a delicious bowl of black bean soup for $4, or an entree for $8.05-$11.50. The Kahlua flan for $3.45 is tasty, too. Happy hour is on Wednesday from 6:30 to 7:30pm and offers half price drinks, music and free munchies. *(Final C La Mascota and Av Masferrer, take bus 101d; Mon-Thurs 12-10pm, Fri-Sat 12-11pm)*

El Chalán This recently opened Peruvian restaurant is run by a Peruvian couple who serve up a seafood-heavy menu, including *ceviche* for $5.75. Try the special dessert "La Negrita," made with black corn brought from... you guessed it, Peru, for $1.70. *(Av Masferrer #5; 11:30am-3:30pm, Mon-Sat 6:30-9:30pm)*

El Rosal In a corner house above a pewter store, this informal Italian restaurant is packed with simple wooden tables. *Lasagna tres quesos* (three-cheese lasagna) is $5.75, and spaghetti with meat sauce goes for $4.10. *(93a Av and C del Mirador; 12-9pm)*

Pronto Gourmet Wines, spices and other goodies from all over line the wooden shelves of this gourmet deli. They serve cold cuts, cheese and hot dishes for $4.60 and up. *(Mon-Sat 8am-10pm, Sun 10am-3pm)*

Chela's Steak House A tastefully decorated nook near the Fuente Beethoven specializing in meat and seafood. The walls are covered with an interesting collection of menus from all around the world. Steak *pimienta* (pepper steak) costs $11.50. *(12pm-12am)*

Chino de Oro It may not look like much, but this little restaurant has some of the best Chinese food in the city. Ask what the fresh fish of the day is, then order it breaded and fried—it'll melt in your mouth. Big bowls of soup are almost a meal in themselves. *(11am-10pm)*

Sao Yin Even though the food here is mediocre at best, the atmosphere is intriguing. It has the nostalgic feel of an old Chinese temple, once grand but lately fallen into disrepair in spite of the decorated columns and fountain outside. Now, half the menu is karaoke selections. The economy plate is $1.60, while regular entrees are overpriced at $4.60. *(Carretera Santa Tecla #1066)*

Sights

Monuments

El Salvador del Mundo (West San Salvador map) The national symbol of El Salvador—Christ on top of the globe—stands tall in the Plaza de las Américas. The original version of this famous monument was sculpted in 1777 by a Franciscan, Silvestre García. This one was erected in 1990. *(Plaza de las Américas, Alam Roosevelt and 65a Av)*

Monumento de la Revolución (Full San Salvador map) The entrance to the wealthy neighborhood of San Benito is the unlikely location of this towering image made out of a mosaic of colored stones. The naked Orwellian figure with its arms thrown upwards and head back is an impressive sight, making the monument look a little like a place to perform ritual sacrifice at night. It was supposedly erected to commemorate the "revolutionary movement of 1948," but it could just as easily have been built to commemorate recent events instead. *(Plaza de la Revolución, Col San Benito)*

Parks

Zoo (Full San Salvador map) Home to hundreds of different kinds of animals, this zoo is often packed with families on weekends. *(South from center on Av Cuscatlán, then west on C Modelo to end; take city bus 2; tel 270-0828; Tues-Sun 9am-5pm; children $0.10, adults $0.15)*

Parque Saburo Hirao/Natural History Museum (Full San Salvador map) If the zoo isn't enough to entertain the little tykes, follow the signs half a block south to the Parque Saburo Hirao. This children's park has playgrounds and an adult area where parents can watch their kids. Inside the park is the small Natural History Museum, with a few exhibits on different kinds of plants, animals and the sciences. *(350m south of zoo; city bus 2; Weds-Sun 9am-4pm; admission $0.10)*

La Laguna Botanical Garden (Full San Salvador map) Escape the hubbub of the capital to spend an afternoon wandering along the cool, quiet paths of La Laguna. Located at the bottom of the crater of an extinct volcano, the garden shelters hundreds of different plants and flowers from around the world. *(Take city bus 101c, 101d or 42 towards Santa Tecla, garden is to the south of the road leading back toward San Salvador, get off at the sign, walk 1km downhill to park; tel 223-7584; Tues-Sun 9am-5pm; admission $0.25 per person)*

Churches

Metropolitan Cathedral (Central San Salvador map) This huge chunk of concrete is in many ways a metaphor for the country: lots of promise but still in need of repair. It was built to replace a wooden church that burned down in 1951, only to be badly damaged itself in the 1956 earthquake. Shortly before his death, Archbishop Romero declared that Church funds would not be used to rebuild the cathedral until more pressing needs, like feeding people, were satisfied first.

Romero was killed in 1980, and it was on the steps of the cathedral that civilians were filmed being gunned down by the army during his funeral. The cathedral remains one of the most striking reminders of El Salvador's troubled past. It's still being repaired and is closed to visitors. *(Plaza Gerardo Barrios)*

Iglesia Don Rua (Full San Salvador map) A short distance from the city center stands the largest functioning church in the city. The plain white and yellow walls contrast with two levels of ornate stained glass. One series of windows tell the story of Don Bosco, a 19th-century Italian saint known throughout El Salvador for his work with children. There's a painting of him to the right of the altar. Directly overhead in front of the altar are four triangular mosaics of Ezekiel, Daniel, Isaiah and Jeremiah. If you can wrangle permission to climb the huge bell tower, the view of the city and the valley can't be beat. *(5a Av and 25a C)*

La Ceiba de Guadalupe (Full San Salvador map) The prettiest church in the capital sits a stone's throw away from the fumes and horns of the Panamerican Highway on the road to Santa Tecla. But pass through the intricately carved wooden doors on the blinding white exterior, and the highway sounds quickly fade. Inside, you'll find an incredible wood ceiling, paintings of the Virgin and angels over the altar, and interesting round stained glass windows that rotate to let in outside air. *(Panamerican Highway towards Santa Tecla, next to La UCA)*

■ Other Interesting Churches

Iglesia El Rosario Father José Delgado, the father of Central American independence, is buried here. *(6a Av between 2a and 4a C Pte, facing Plaza Libertad)*

Iglesia El Calvario *(End of 6a C Pte, one block from Av Cuscatlán)*

Iglesia Sagrado Corazón *(C Arce and 13a Av Nte)*

Other Sights

National Palace (Central San Salvador map) The entrance to this grand old building is flanked by statues of Christopher Columbus and Queen Isabel, donated in 1924 by the king of Spain. Formerly the presidential residence, the palace has since fallen into disrepair and is currently undergoing a (relative) whirlwind of restoration. The old tile floors, plaster columns and black iron grillwork surrounding the expansive, tree-filled courtyard inside come from another era, as do the old carved wooden doorways and cracked marble staircases.

The National Archives are stored in the basement and contain documents that date back to the 1600s. During the war, documents were collected from city halls across the country to protect them from the guerrillas. The palace is closed to the public, but you might be able to sweet-talk the guard at the door on the south side of the building into letting you take a peek around. *(West of Plaza Gerardo Barrios)*

National Theater (Central San Salvador map) An ornate opera house seems as out of place in the middle of downtown San Salvador as a nine-hole golf course, but go a block east of the Metropolitan Cathedral and you'll find this 80-year-old building filled with plush red seats and marble floors. Thick carpeting and ornate scrollwork muffle the traffic noises and make you feel as if you've stepped into another century. There are different rooms representing various art styles and the bathrooms are probably the nicest in the city. The chandeliers are from Austria and a famous 230 square-meter mural covers the ceiling. Some rooms still show damage from the 1986 earthquake.

Theatrical productions and poetry readings are presented here from time to time, and the National Orchestra plays about every two weeks for $2.85. All the seats in the three levels are the same price, but the second floor gives you the best angle over the stage. The box office opens shortly before showtime. (See Entertainment for ticket information.) *(1 block east of Metropolitan Cathedral; see Entertainment for ticket information)*

National Library (Central San Salvador map) Relocated in 1993, the National Library continues to suffer the effects of the 1986 earthquake that destroyed 40 percent of its collection. Today, this monolith seems sadly empty inside the huge building formerly occupied by a bank. The first floor houses the reference section and international works. Up the broken escalator on the second floor are Salvadoran and Central American books and the card catalog. There's also a large painting upstairs which depicts all the past presidents of El Salvador, life-size, up to Cristiani. *(South of Plaza Gerardo Barrios; tel 222-9181; 7:30am-5:30pm)*

Universidad de Centroamerica (Full San Salvador map) The shaded campus at the UCA ("La UCA") is a good place to relax and meet Salvadoran college students. There's a decent bookstore, an eatery with food resembling what you'd find at US college campuses and plenty of stores outside the doors to the campus that make a brisk business out of photocopying textbooks and notes. *(Behind Ceiba de La Guadalupe, at the end of bus route 101 specially marked for UCA)*

Shopping

Mercado Central (Central San Salvador map) This huge market surrounding the Iglesia El Calvario is a mob scene by 6am. Come early to get the freshest fruit, but the armadillo skins and used clothing are available all day long. You'll notice some vendors selling neat bundles of medicinal herbs. Ask them what each is for and you'll be amazed at the home-made remedies that are available for every conceivable ailment. *(Between 10a and 12a C Pte, C Gerardo Barrios and 5a Av Sur)*

Mercado Nacional de Artesanías (Full San Salvador map) Every type of Salvadoran craft is available here, although at about a 50 percent markup from what they sell for where they're made. Goodies from Guatemala and other Central American countries are also for sale. *(Next to internacional fairgrounds, Panamerican Highway south; 9am-6pm)*

Mercado Ex-Cuartel (Central San Salvador map) Salvadoran crafts, among other things, are available here. Prices are generally lower than in the Mercado Nacional de Artesanías. *(Between C Delgado and 1a C Ote, 8a and 10a Av Sur)*

SAN SALVADOR

Señora Luck

Two types of lottery tickets are sold on nearly every street corner in El Salvador. You scratch the silver tickets to see if you've won instantly. The others, on white paper with a row of numbers, give you a shot at the weekly national lottery. Tickets cost between $0.60 and $0.80.

Metrocentro & Metrosur (Western San Salvador map) These US-style shopping malls are among the largest in Central America. Inside are supermarkets, clothing stores, restaurants, banks, a post office, Antel and *casas de cambio*. Prices are high, though. *(Blvd de los Héroes)*

Genesis 7 Curiosidades (Western San Salvador map) This small shop sells a quirky selection of crafts and knickknacks from all over Central America. You can browse through paper flowers, wood carvings and new-age literature, or rent a compact disc. Check out the bead curtains made of dried seeds. *(Mon-Sat 8:30am-7:30pm)*

Entertainment

Nightlife

The **Boulevard de los Héroes** is the closest place to the center of the city to grab a bite, tie one on and hit the dance floor. Restaurants along the Boulevard range from cheap to expensive, but it's the pricier ones that have music at night. Las Antorchas, El Corral Steak House and Villa Fiesta all have live music on weekends for a modest cover.

The **Zona Rosa** is San Salvador's most popular place for late-night entertainment. This collection of open-air restaurants, chic clothing stores, cafes and ritzy discos spreads out in Colonia San Benito at the intersection of Boulevard del Hipódromo and Calle La Reforma. If you feel like dancing, come well-dressed and expect to pay a $5.75-$8.60 cover. Mario's is a popular club, along with El Búho and the Underground Discotec.

Colonia Escalón is a good destination for an evening's entertainment. Near the Parque Beethoven, at Colonia Escalón and 75a Avenida, there are a few discos,

restaurants and movie theaters.

At the end of Escalón at the intersection with Avenida Masferrer, you'll find the **Plaza Masferrer**, a mellower alternative to the high-priced, exclusive nightclubs at the Zona Rosa and Boulevard de los Héroes. Cafés, cheap food and drink stands are down side streets around the plaza, and *mariachi* bands make their musical rounds until the wee hours of the morning. Best of all, it's free.

■ Clubs

La Luna (Western San Salvador map) A group of artists turned this house into a nightspot to give people a place to come, relax and enjoy the arts. Set in the middle of a residential neighborhood, its painted walls and hip, college-age-and-up crowd make it look straight out of Greenwich Village. Nightly music ranges from Latin to jazz to rock. During the day there are yoga lessons, film screenings, poetry readings and even modern dance performances. Come by and grab a schedule at the front door. An attached store called El Ropero sells left-leaning reading material, clothing and jewelry. Entry is free before 7pm, and about $2.30 per person after that. *(C Berlín #204 and #228, two blocks from Blvd de los Héroes; tel 225-5054; 4:20pm-2am)*

Cultural Events

Check in the **El Salvador News-Gazette** for weekly updates on plays, movies and art exhibits.

■ Cultural Centers

Centro Cultural La Mazorca—ASTAC (Full San Salvador map) Look for the bright murals on the front wall of the building, then come inside for a photography exhibit or educational video. The small store next door, La Cosecha, sells handicrafts. Call for their current schedule. *(C San Antonio Abad #1447; tel 226-5219; Mon-Fri 8am-6pm, Sat 8am-12pm)*

Las Columnas Centro de Arte/Academia de Teatro y Arte "William Shakespeare" (Western San Salvador map) Offers theater, art and music productions and courses for children and adults. Schedules are posted on the door. *(9a C Pte #4036, between 77a and 79a Av Nte)*

Also, **Yuri Omar Ben-Iosef** is a very friendly authority on cultural events in El Salvador. He's a tour guide who speaks nine languages, so no matter where you're from he'll be able to point you in the right direction. He has information on productions at the Teatro Nacional and Teatro Presidente in San Salvador, the Teatro Nacional in Santa Ana and the Teatro de San Miguel, and he can help you buy tickets. *(Tel 273-3056, 221-6350)*

Museums and Galleries

Galería El Arbol del Díos (Western San Salvador map) You'll recognize this gallery, in the same building as the Restaurant del Arbol (see Food & Drink), by Fernando Llort's distinctive childlike figures on the white front wall. A pricey gift shop sells Salvadoran crafts, and the gallery sells hundreds of Llort's colorful, cubist originals and prints that make some of the most beautiful, if expensive, souvenirs from El Salvador. A 20x30cm print sells for $58-$115 and originals start in the hundreds. If you have any money left, stop off for a bite at the Restaurant del Arbol next door. *(Mon-Thurs 12-10pm, Fri-Sat 12-11pm)*

Galería Huellas de América Everything at the gallery "Footprints of America" is made out of finely-worked cow and snake skin. Crafts are made on the premises, so ask to take a peek in back to see how it's done. *(Mon-Fri 9am-9pm)*

Galería 1-2-3 Features works by artists from throughout Central America. *(Av La Capilla #258, Col San Benito; tel 223-1624; Mon-Fri 8:30am-12:30pm, 2:30-6pm, Sun 8:30am-12:30pm)*

El Laberinto *(Av Olímpica #3341; tel 223-1115; Mon-Fri 9am-12:30pm, 3-6:30pm, Sat 9am-1pm)*

Festivals

■ **The August Festivals.** The Fiestas Agostinas began in the 16th century with a simple parade. By the 18th century they had grown, thanks to the sponsorship of local aristocrats. A wooden image of El Salvador del Mundo, El Salvador's patron saint, was carved and carried through the town. Soon images were carved for each of the city's patron saints. Today, when the float bearing the image of El Salvador del Mundo passes, everyone kneels. On the last day of the festival, a carved image of Christ is carried through the city in front of enormous crowds.

Buses

Urban Buses

San Salvador city buses are numbered under 100, except 101 which goes to Santa Tecla. All cost about $0.10, except buses that go outside the city proper. Microbuses also run roughly the same routes—albeit much more quickly—and cost the same amount.

■ **Major Destinations: National University (3, 9, 30)** from central market and Metrocentro; **(33b)** from eastern San Salvador. **Planes de Renderos (12pr, 12mc)** from central market. **Lago de Ilopango and Turicentro Apulo (15)** from central San Salvador ("Wula Wula" bus stop). **Panchimalco (17p, 17r)** from central market. **Ciudad Merliot toward Santa Tecla (42)**. **La UCA (44)** from Metrocentro. **Plaza Masferrer (52)** from Metrocentro. **US embassy and Santa Tecla (101)** from city center past Plaza de Las Américas.

■ **Major Departure Points: Western bus terminal (4cd)** to northeastern San Salvador; **(28)** to Plaza Libertad; **(34)** to the Zona Rosa or central market; **(42)** toward Ciudad Merliot and Santa Tecla. **Eastern bus terminal (5, 21)** to southern San Salvador; **(7)** to Plaza de las Américas via C Arce; **(8)** to southwestern San Salvador; **(23, 24)** to north-central San Salvador; **(29)** to Metrocentro. **Southern Bus Terminal (Ruta A)** to central San Salvador. **Central San Salvador market (6)** to north-central San Salvador; **(16)** to western San Salvador, then north to C San Antonio Abad; **(20)** to northeastern San Salvador; **(30)** to Metrocentro and National University; **(34)** to western bus terminal and the Zona Rosa. **Plaza Masferrer (Ruta A)** to southern bus terminal. **Metrocentro (29)** to eastern bus terminal; **(30)** to central market and National University; **(44)** to La UCA; **(52)** to Plaza Masferrer; **(Ruta B)** to Centro de Gobierno. **Centro de Gobierno (31)** to southeastern San Salvador; **(Ruta B)** to Metrocentro. **Zona Rosa (34)** to western bus terminal and central market.

Eastern Bus Terminal

Berlín (303), 6, 11am, 1, 3pm, 109km, 2hr 30min. **Chalatenango (125)**, every 10 min until 6pm, 69km, 2hr 20min. **El Poy (119)**, every 30 min until 3:30pm, 90km, 3hr 30min. **Ilobasco (111)**, every 10 min until 7pm, 54km, 1hr 30min. **La Palma (119)**, every 30 min until 3:30pm, 81km, 3hr. **La Unión (304)**, every 30 min until 3:40pm, 183km, 4hr. **Lolotique (442)**, 10:45am, 130km, 3hr 30min. **San Francisco Gotera (305)**, 6:40am, 12:30, 2:40pm, 197km, 4hr. **San Miguel (301)**, every 10 min until 5:10pm, 136km, 3hr. Direct is 2hr 30min. **San Sebastián (110)**, every 20 min until 6pm, 50km, 1hr 30min. **San Vicente (116)**, every 10 min until 8pm, 58km, 1hr

Top: Buses, San Salvador
Bottom Crafts shop, La Palma

Top: FMLN museum, Perquín
Bottom: Model guerrilla camp, FMLN museum, Perquín

30min. **Santa Rosa de Lima (306)**, every 15 min until 3:20pm, 176km, 4hr. **Santiago de María (302)**, 6, 7am, 4pm, 118km, 3hr. **Sensuntepeque (112)**, every 15 min until 5pm, 80km, 2hr 15min. **Suchitoto (129)**, every 25 min until 6:30pm, 44km, 1hr 30min. **Usulután (302)**, every 10 min until 4:15pm, 122km, 2hr 30min.

Western Bus Terminal

Acajutla (207), every 10 min until 6:50pm, 81km, 2hr. **Ahuachapán (202)**, every 5 min until 6:30pm, 100km, 2hr 20min. **Apaneca (206a)**, 5pm, 91km, 2hr 30min. **Chalchuapa (456)**, every 10 min until 6:20pm, 78km, 1hr 10min. **Juayúa (206)**, 2, 3, 4pm, 81km, 2hr 30min. **La Hachadura (498)**, 128km, 3hr. **San Antonio del Monte (206b)**, every 10 min until 6pm, 68km, 1hr 30min. **San Cristóbal (498)**, every 10 min until 6pm, 93km, 2hr. **San Juan Opico (108)**, every 10 min until 6:45pm, 40km, 1hr 10min. **Santa Ana (201)**, every 5 min until 6:40pm, 63km, 1hr 30min. **Sonsonate (205)**, every 5 min until 6:30pm, 65km, 1hr 30min.

Southern Bus Terminal

Costa del Sol (494), every 20 min until 6:30pm, 60km, 1hr 30min. **La Herradura (134)**, every hour until 6pm, 60km, 1hr 30min. Near Costa del Sol. **La Libertad (166)**, 7, 9:20am, 12, 2pm, 32km, 1hr 45min. **Puerto el Triunfo (185)**, every 3 hours until 2:10pm, 107km, 2hr 30min. **Usulután (302)**, every 10 min until 4:30pm, 112km, 2hr 30min. **Zacatecoluca (133)**, every 10 min until 7pm, 55km, 1hr 20min.

International Buses

■ **From the Western Terminal: Mermex** sends buses to Guatemala. Until the bridge at Chinameca is fixed, this bus will cross the border at San Cristóbal. **Guatemala City**, 4:15am and 8:30am, 5hr, $4.65. **El Condo** sends buses to the Mexican border at Tecunumán and Talisman via Sonsonate and La Hachadura **Mexican Border**, 7am-9pm, 9hr, $10.

■ **Quality** has daily buses leaving for Guatemala and Honduras from the Hotel Siesta and the Hotel Presidente. The buses leave from the Hotel Siesta, then pass the Hotel Presidente. *(Condominio Balám Quitzé, Local 4b; tel 279-4166)* **Tegucigalpa**, 12:45/1pm, $30. **Guatemala City**, 6:15am/6:30am, 3:15/3:30pm, $22.

■ **Puerto Bus** sends buses to Guatemala, Honduras and the Mexican border. Same-day ticket purchases only. *(Alam Juan Pablo II and 19a Av Nte, near Centro Gobierno; tel 222-2158)* **Guatemala** every 30-45min from 3:30-11am, every hour 11am-5pm daily, $5, 5hr 30min. **Honduras**, 6am, 1pm daily. $15, 6hr 30min. **Mexican border**, until 11:30am, $10.35, 10hr.

■ **Cruceros del Golfo** is in the same building as Puerto Bus, and sends two buses a day to Tegucigalpa. *(Alam Juan Pablo II and 19a Av Nte, near Centro Gobierno)* **Tegucigalpa**, 6am, 1pm, $16.

■ **Comfort Line** leaves for Guatemala from the Hotel El Salvador. *(89a Av Nte and 11a C Pte; tel 279-3382)* **Guatemala City**, 8am, 2pm, $22.

■ **Tica Bus** runs buses to most Central American countries. You can buy tickets here during the office hours. Buses pass by the office shortly before departure. *(Next to Hotel San Carlos on C Concepción; tel 222-4808; Mon-Fri 9am-12pm, 2-7pm, Sat 9am-12pm)* **Guatemala City**, 6am, 7hr, $8. **Tegucigalpa**, 5:30am, 10hr, $15. **Managua**, 5:30am, 13hr, $35. **San José**, 5:30am, 24hr, $50. Stops for the night in Nicaragua. **Panama**, 5:30am, 40hr, $75. Stops in Nicaragua, Costa Rica.

Details

■ **American Express** *(Centro Commercial La Mascota, local #1; tel 279-3844; Mon-Fri 8am-12pm, 2-5pm, Sat 8-10am)*.
■ **Courier Services: Urgente Express** *(C Rubén Darío #1056 and 19a Av Sur, Edif Bolívar #2-1; Tel 221-0487; in the US 800/262-1389)*. **Leon Express** *(Alam Roosevelt #2613, between 49a and 51a Av Sur, tel 224-3005, 224-3026)*.
■ **Emergency Numbers (PNC):** 121.
■ **English-Language Bookstores: Bookmarks** has a moderate selection of English novels, and magazines. No travel guides, though. *(Centro Commercial Basilea; Mon-Sat 9am-7pm, Sun 10am-6pm)*.
■ **English-Language Church Services:** Union Church of San Salvador has "Expatriate Christian Services" on Sunday 9:30am, Bible Study, choir, Sunday school. *(Final C #4, Col La Mascota; Pastor Ray Hollis 223-5505)*. Jewish Temple services in Hebrew, Fridays at 6:30pm. *(Blvd Del Hipódromo #626 in front of Finata; Tel 223-6124)*. Father Dennis Hand gives Catholic mass in English Saturday at 5pm at the Church of the Holy Innocent, Antiguo Cuscatlán.
■ **Groups/Associations: American Women's Association** *(Tel 224-5217)*
■ **Hospitals:** The best hospital in the country is the **Hospital de Diagnostico** *(21 C Pte, in front of the old US embassy; tel 226-5111, 226-8878)*. Ask your embassy for recommendations of other hospitals for specialized treatment.
■ **Immigration Office:** The immigration office in the Centro de Gobierno will handle visa extensions and other questions, although you might have to wait a while in line. *(Centro de Gobierno, Federal Building, Mon-Fri 8am-4pm; tel 221-2111)*.
■ **Laundry:** San Salvador has more than its share of dry cleaners, but a few laundromats also let you wash clothes by the load: **Lavandería Lavapronto** *(Av Los Sisimiles #2924, Col Miramonte, one block from Hotel Camino Real)*. **Lavandería Exclusiva** *(Av Rio Amazonas #11, near Jardines de Guadalupe)*.
■ **Mail:** The **central post office** is in a sketchy area just north of the Centro Gobierno, east of the Parque Infantíl and the Palacio de los Deportes. There's another branch at Metrocentro. *(Mon-Fri 8am-5pm, Sat 8am-12pm)*.
■ **Maps:** The **Instituto Geográfico Nacional** is the place to pick up all maps of El Salvador, especially if you plan to go hiking or will be in the country for a while and need a good map to get around. Prices are $4.60 and up. *(Av Juan Bertris #79 in Ciudad Delgado, looks like a big fortress on the right,with "IGN" painted on the outside; tel 276-5900; Mon-Fri 8am-12:30pm, 1-4pm)*.
■ **Phones: Antel** has offices in the Centro Gobierno *(Mon-Fri 8am-12pm, 1-4pm)*, on C Rubén Darío and 5a Av Sur *(Mon-Fri 6am-10pm)* and at the Torre Roble in Metrocentro *(Mon-Fri 8am-12pm, 1-4pm)*.

■ **Tourist Information:** The **Salvadoran Institute of Tourism** (ISTU) can provide you with xeroxed packets of information about traveling in El Salvador. A lot of it is fluff, but the people who work there are nice. There's also an ISTU office at the airport *(C Rubén Darío #619, between 9a and 11a Av Sur; Tel 222-8000; Mon-Fri 8am-4pm)*.

■ **Spanish-Language Bookstores: Ercilla** *(4a Av Nte #119, around the corner from the National Theater)* **La UCA bookstore** *(Dissal Av España #344 and 5a C Ote)*. **Excito** *(Av Juan Pablo II, Centro Comercial Juan Pablo II, local 305a)*.

Near San Salvador
Food & Drink

A few fancy restaurants take advantage of the view over the city from the hills to the south.

Restaurant Bella Vista This formal restaurant has an amazing view of the city, best in the early evening. It's decorated inside with some impressive cut-glass scenes made from photos of El Salvador in the 1920s. The "Pretty View" Restaurant, around since 1945, was handed over to Ana Palomo, the current manager, and her sister Lorena by their parents. Dishes start at $14. *(On the road to Planes de Renderos, km6; tel 370-0144; Tues-Fri noon-3pm, 6-10pm, Sat noon-midnight, Sun noon-8pm)*

Restaurant Placita Grill This fancy little restaurant is set around a small family room with a great view of San Salvador. The menu is amusing—check out the Bellena Rellena de Camarones ("Whale Stuffed with Shrimp," 1,000,000 *colones*) and find out why they're closed on Mondays. A New York steak is $5.75, chicken tacos cost $2.20. *(On the road to Planes de Renderos, km6.5; Tues-Sun 12-3pm, 6-9:30pm)*

El Cordoba This small white house, up a steep hill, is an informal restaurant with yet another wide vista of San Salvador, the San Salvador Volcano and Santa Tecla. The owner, Evelyn de Castro, decided to open a restaurant when everyone who enjoyed the view from her café told her that they would be interested in coming there for dinner. It's filled with young people late in the week, enjoying the all-you-can-eat shrimp on Thursday for $6. *(On the road to Planes de Renderos, km7, up a steep rocky road to the right, look for the sign; Sun-Wed 11am-9pm, Thurs-Sat 11am-11pm)*

Sights

Parque Balboa This large municipal park 12 kilometers south of San Salvador sits high up in the Planes de Renderos district. It's a popular day trip from the city, but is covered with trash. A handful of private *pupuserías* and outdoor cafés cater to Salvadorans on a romantic (if dirty) getaway. The football field sees some heavy use. *(Bus 12 'Mil Cumbres' from the Mercado Central in San Salvador to Planes de Renderos and Puerto del Diablo, every 15 min until 7pm)*

Puerto del Diablo An enormous boulder split in half here long ago, leaving behind a curious formation known as the "Devil's Door" at the summit of Cerro Chulo. There's a great view of the coast from the top of these two boulders, 14 kilometers south of San Salvador. The Lago de Ilopango is visible to the left and the San Vicente Volcano sits straight ahead. You can see the red roofs of Panchimalco at the foot of the precipice.

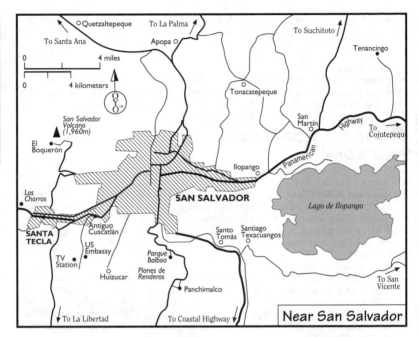

Near San Salvador

During the civil war Puerto del Diablo's beauty was marred by death squads who dumped the bodies of their victims over the edge. Now the only thing that's dumped here is trash; the trail to the top is littered with 25 years of bottle caps. It begins at a clearing between the two large rocks off to the right. *(Bus 12 'Mil Cumbres' from the Mercado Central in San Salvador to Planes de Renderos and Puerto del Diablo, every 15 min until 7pm)*

Los Chorros   It's a turicentro, and it's near San Salvador, but it's still surprisingly pleasant. Four pools are filled by water cascading down thickly-vegetated slopes—almost like a Hawaiian jungle paradise, except for the crowds. The highest pool seems to have the cleanest water, and the entire turicentro is surrounded by ferns, flowers and dripping moss. If you didn't bring a picnic you can grab a bite at one of the small *comedores* at the bottom.

If you come during the week, Los Chorros is cleaner and less crowded, great for an afternoon dip. Whenever you come, bring flip-flops for the changing rooms and leave your valuables somewhere else, since there's nowhere to put them; the changing rooms will only hold your clothing. Smaller side paths up the mountain may look tempting, but we advise against it—robberies have been reported there. *(18km west of San Salvador, on the Panamerican Highway west of Santa Tecla; bus 79 from San Salvador from 11a Av Sur and C Rubén Darío toward Lourdes, every 10 min; 7am-5pm; $0.60 per person; changing rooms 8am-noon, 2-5pm)*

Panchimalco

Nahuat, "Place of Shields and Banners"
Pop. 33,500
17km from San Salvador

Panchimalco Then

According to legend, a natural catastrophe in the 11th century forced people living in the Planes de Renderos, which today looks out over the city of San Salvador, to seek refuge in what is now Panchimalco. In recent years, archeological evidence has surfaced which confirms that there actually was a migration to Panchimalco at that time, and that the town's population quickly expanded across two square kilometers in the aftermath.

During the Spanish invasion, Panchimalco earned the alternate translation of its name: "The Fort." The concave shape of the land around the city provided a natural barrier which allowed the inhabitants to stave off attacks by Spanish troops longer than most other indigenous villages.

Panchimalco Now

A dusty, quiet town, Panchimalco's location in a geological concavity leaves it surrounded by towering mountains on all sides. It's within five kilometers of the Planes de Renderos and beside the Parque Balboa, with the Puerto del Diablo visible to the north. Pigs, dogs and children compete for space and attention along the hilly cobblestone streets, while other youngsters play ball in front of the old white church.

Panchimalco is still inhabited by many Pancho Indians, descendants of the Pipils who take pains to distinguish their culture from that of mainstream El Salvador. There's not much going on here except the festivals in May and September, but Panchimalco still makes for an interesting side trip from San Salvador.

Sights

Colonial Church of Santa Cruz Panchimalco This national monument built in 1725 lost three arched gables and an organ to the 1854 earthquake that destroyed much of San Salvador. The altar and the carved ceiling above it are worth a peek, and the room to the right houses some of the holy icons (including one depicting the burial of Jesus—notice His indigenous features) that are carried around during the town's festivals.

Details

■ **Buses: San Salvador (17)**, every 15 min until 6pm, 17km, 40min. A microbus also leaves for Panchimalco from the southern side of the Central Market in San Salvador, in front of the Banco Cuscatlán. It's also #17 and takes less time.
■ **Festivals: May 1-3 and September 12-14 (13)** Señor de la Santa Cruz de Roma. These famous festivals are best known for the Procesión de las Palmas on the second Sunday afternoon in May, in which the Virgin Mary is paraded through the streets accompanied by large palm fronds. Both festivals are held in honor of the same saint, and used to be a much bigger affair. Today, with help from ISTU,

the fairs are more general entertainment than indigenous festival, and the one in May is larger. Both feature the sale of traditional weavings and pottery, along with dances, music, speeches, marathons and fireworks. **December 23-25 (24)** Nacimiento del Niño Jesús.

IN THE NEWS

Life Under Fire

The densely-wooded slopes of the Guazapa Volcano, 24 kilometers north of San Salvador, once teemed with guerrillas. The FMLN controlled the 1,370-meter volcano for most of the war, and set up a successful community that survived and even prospered during the fighting.

In spite of the government army's occasional presence at the top of Guazapa, where they maintained a base, the FMLN controlled the slopes throughout the 1980s. The army declared the volcano a "free-fire zone," which meant that soldiers could shoot at anything that moved. Government jets bombed the volcano continuously and were rumored to have used napalm and phosphorous on occasion to flush out the rebels.

During quieter periods, though, the daily life of the Guazapa guerrillas took on an almost comfortable pattern. Every morning, male and female troops lined up to sing the FMLN anthem to keep up morale. During the day the guerrillas went about their daily chores like the rest of the country. Farms were tended and extra food was traded for supplies. The rebels also ran makeshift hospitals in their camps, often with help from politically-neutral Quaker doctors. Children learned the basics in rebel schools, 40 of which operated in or around Guazapa. The curriculum was a little unusual, though, since in addition to learning spelling and mathematics children had to learn how to survive air raids.

Guazapa was 20 percent female, so the roles of men and women were different than in most Salvadoran communities. Female guerrillas grudgingly appreciated men who washed their own clothes, although they grumbled that the men "didn't make their own tortillas, yet."

At night, the atmosphere was a little more relaxed. Troops gathered around the fire as *guitarristas* strummed away and sang songs in celebration of the revolution. Lyrics ridiculed the government and praised fallen comrades. ("At least when a guerrilla dies," the rebels would say, "he knows his friends will write a song about him.") Radio Venceremos and Radio Faribundo Martí brought static-filled news of battles, including numbers of casualties inflicted and weapons seized.

At any moment on any given day, the stillness could be shattered by the roar of jets overhead or a battalion of advancing government soldiers. Today, parts of the mountain that were denuded by government bombs are still visible in the distance.

Lago de Ilopango

Nahuat, "Goddess of Maize"
16 km from San Salvador

The placid Lago de Ilopango straddles the borders of the provinces of San Salvador, La Paz and Cuscatlán, and is surrounded by volcanoes and mountains. This volcanic lake is the country's largest and one of El Salvador's most popular tourist sites, especially since it's so close to the capital. Dramatic cliffs overlook the green waters of the lake and in the early morning mist the area resembles a scene from a traditional Chinese painting.

Accommodations

Hotel Vista Lago The private cabins are nothing fancy and the facilities are a little run down, but the view from up here is spectacular. The restaurant sits out on the ridge overlooking the lake, and has entrees for $3.45-$8.60. *(Carretera Apulo km12.5; tel 295-0532; 13S cabins $13.80, 19D cabins $16.24, all with private baths, hot water, AC; laundry; 10am checkout; restaurant Tues-Sun 9am-5pm, bar)*

Recreation

Club Salvadoreño This sprawling club at the end of the road around Lago de Ilopango boasts one of the few golf courses within easy reach of the capital. Palm trees dot the posh, manicured facilities, next to rows of polished cars and small private boats. If golf isn't your game (even for only $11.50 a round), there are also tennis courts, pools, a soccer field and a volleyball court. Choose among two restaurants and two bars, and if you want to stay the night, five 6-person *cabañas* are available for $7.50 each. For membership info, call the central office in San Salvador at 225-1634 or 225-1654. *(At end of lake road; Weds-Sun 8am-4pm, Thurs-Sun to 6pm; $2 per person to enter)*

Lago de Ilopango Region

To Cojutepeque

San Agustín

C. Roosevelt • Soyapango

Panamerican Highway

Apulo

Corinto

Eastern Bus Terminal

Blvd del Ejercito Nacional

Hotel Vista Lago

Club Salvadoreño

Turicentro Apulo

SAN SALVADOR

• Amatitán

Lago de Ilopango

Rio El Desagüe

N

To International Airport

Turicentro Apulo The closest *turicentro* to San Salvador is one of the most popular in the country, with large pools, tall trees and restaurants on the shore of the lake. It was remodeled after the war, and still looks like a war zone on weekends when the crowds pour in from San Salvador. The beach isn't breathtaking but local boatmen will take you for a trip around the lake if the price is right. Small boats that hold up to 10 people rent for about $6.90-$8 per hour, and three hours should be enough for a good tour. Fishing gear is occasionally included in the price. Some of the more attractive sights around the lake include Amatitán (a private part of the lake with extravagant houses), Rio El Desagüe to the east, Corinto (the cantón where the Club Salvadoreño is located), San Augustín and Cujuapa (cantóns).

Details

■ **Buses: San Salvador (15)**, every 15 min until 5pm, 16km, 55min. Leaves from the "Ula Ula" (or "Hula Hula," or "Wula Wula") bus stop in San Salvador near the Metropolitan Cathedral and Avenida España.

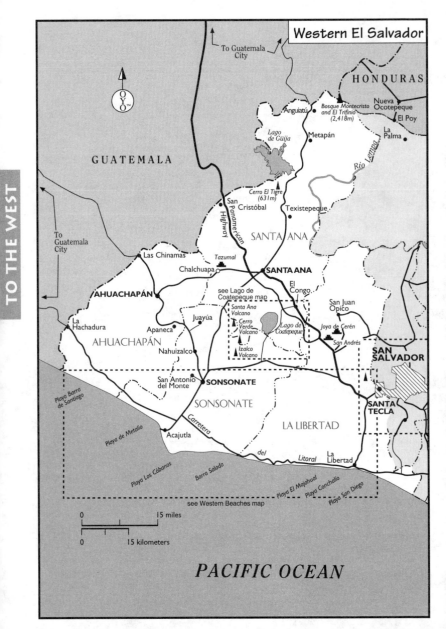

Western El Salvador

To Guatemala City

HONDURAS

Nueva Ocotepeque

El Poy

La Palma

Bosque Montecristo and El Trifinio (2,418m)

Anguiatú

Metapán

Lago de Güija

Río Lempa

GUATEMALA

Cerro El Tigre (631m)

San Cristóbal

Texistepeque

SANTA ANA

Pan American Highway

Las Chinamas

Tazumal

Chalchuapa

SANTA ANA

El Congo

To Guatemala City

AHUACHAPÁN

see Lago de Coatepeque map

Santa Ana Volcano

San Juan Opico

Joya de Cerén

La Hachadura

Apaneca

Juayúa

Cerro Verde Volcano

Lago de Coatepeque

San Andrés

SAN SALVADOR

AHUACHAPÁN

Nahuizalco

Izalco Volcano

San Antonio del Monte

SONSONATE

SANTA TECLA

Playa Barra de Santiago

SONSONATE

Carretera

LA LIBERTAD

Playa de Metalío

Acajutla

del

Litoral

La Libertad

Playa Los Cóbanos

Barra Salada

Playa El Majahual

Playa Conchalío

Playa San Diego

see Western Beaches map

0   15 miles

0   15 kilometers

PACIFIC OCEAN

To The West

Western El Salvador, with its beaches, forests, volcanoes and mountain towns, seems straight out of a tourist brochure. The region was spared much of the destruction of the civil war, so it's a good place to start your explorations outside the capital. Western El Salvador has some of the most dramatic volcanoes and mountains in the country, from Cerro Verde, Izalco and the Santa Ana Volcanoes, clustered near the Lago de Coatepeque, to the cloud forests of Montecristo in the northern reaches of Santa Ana department. In the other direction, flat coastal plains slide into the beaches of Santiago and Metalío.

The cities of the west are as diverse as its geography. The coffee city of Santa Ana, the second-largest city in the country, is one of the most enjoyable places to spend time in El Salvador, while the cloudy mountain towns of Juayúa and Apaneca are about the most relaxing.

Finally, the west is packed with things to do. Spend some time climbing the mountains near Lago de Coatepeque or hiking in the Montecristo Reserve. Splurge on a fine pair of boots in Santa Ana and strut like a real *vaquero* or explore the beaches and inlets south of Ahuachapán.

Despite Santa Ana's economic importance as the heart of El Salvador's coffee country, the FMLN was never able to gain a strong foothold in this cool, hilly department. However, they occasionally did disrupt the local economy. During the 1980s, guerrilla raids and labor disputes cut coffee production in half, repeatedly leaving thousands out of work for the duration of the three-month coffee harvest. Fighting from Chalatenango spilled over into northern Santa Ana department near Metapán. Rebel attacks in southern La Libertad in the mid-80s caused extensive damage and threatened to open a new theater of military action. Death squads, meanwhile, kept everybody terrified.

The sights of western El Salvador are close to the capital. A day's travelling, with or without a car, will get you anywhere and back to San Salvador if you leave early in the morning. The roads here are better than anywhere else in the country, although stretches of the Coastal Highway will still shorten your spine. Many buses run between San Salvador, Sonsonate and Santa Ana, and even small towns like Apaneca and Juayúa are easy to get to. Public transportation is more difficult to find along the Coastal Highway and north toward Montecristo.

Heavy rains douse the west from July to October, so don't be surprised if many dirt roads become impassable during that time. You can cross into Guatemala at La Hachadura and Las Chinamas in Ahuachapán department and at San Cristóbal (scheduled to be re-opened in 1995) and Anguiatú in Santa Ana department.

■ **Emergency Police Numbers (PNC): La Libertad department:** 328-1426. **Sonsonate department:** 451-0374. **Ahuachapán department:** 443-1681. **Santa Ana department:** 447-7900, 447-7832, 447-7907.

Santa Tecla
(Nueva San Salvador)

Pop. 87,000
12km from San Salvador

Santa Tecla Then

Santa Tecla, also known as Nueva San Salvador, is located next to San Salvador in the earthquake-prone Zalcuatitán Valley. By the 19th century, at least two quakes every 100 years led many people in the area to suggest that it might be better to relocate the Salvadoran capital to a more stable spot. It took the destructive quake of 1854, though, to convince the government to move, and the ranch of Santa Tecla was chosen as the new location. Somehow, though, the switch was never made, and San Salvador still "swings" every few decades.

Santa Tecla Now

Sandwiched between the San Salvador Volcano and the coastal mountain range in the Uliman Plain (from the Nahuat, meaning "place where rubber is harvested"), Santa Tecla is ringed by mountains that keep it cool. The Panamerican Highway bisects the city, carrying countless tractor-trailers right through the center of town. Towering palm trees fill a broad main plaza and a market chokes many streets, including the highway, in the center of town. Aside from many commercial centers and mini-malls, Santa Tecla is quiet, essentially just a glorified suburb of San Salvador. It does offer one of the few real bookstores in the country and some interesting places to eat. It also serves as the handiest departure point for climbing the San Salvador Volcano.

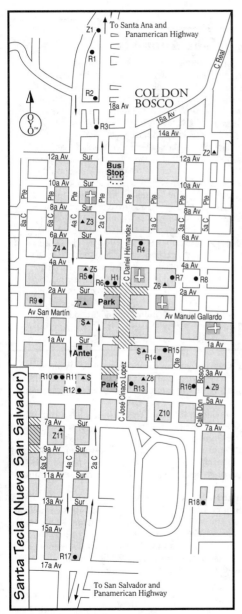

ACCOMMODATIONS   ●

H1 Hotel Tecleño

FOOD & DRINK   ●

R1   Mariscos Las Delicias
R2   Cusuco Con Feliz
R3   Pip's Carymar
R4   *Zantie Pizza*
R5   *Pizza Atto's*
R6   *Ice cream*
R7   Pizzería Italia
R8   *Pupusería*
R9   El Caminito Americano
R10 La Casona de Doña Maria
R11 *Restaurant OK*
R12 Elsy's Cakes
R13 *Toto's Pizza*
R14 *Cafetería Las Palmeras*
R15 *Cafetería Pupusas Tin*
R16 Nestor's Argentinean Restaurant
R17 Restaurant La Marea
R18 Restaurant La Cueva

OTHER   ▲

Z1   Shell gas station
Z2   Lavandería Colonial
Z3   Supermarket
Z4   FMLN sign
Z5   Clásicos Roxsil
Z6   Police
Z7   Shopping Center
Z8   Shopping Center
Z9   Club Tecleño
Z10 Crafts shop
Z11 Shell gas Station

Accommodations

Hotel Tecleño The only place in town is grubby, with fake flowers and patched paint walls. *(8S $5.75, 2D $9.20, all with TV, ceiling fans, +$2.30 for private bath; 24hr check-out; comedor)*

Food & Drink

Cusuco Con Feliz Enjoy a steaming bowl of *sopa de garrobo* (iguana soup) for $3.50 at the "Happy Armadillo"—that is, if you can hear yourself over the trucks rattling by on the Panamerican Highway right outside. Look for the colorful sign at the north end of town and dig the pop-out menu. The name comes

IN THE NEWS

The Big Adobe Anomaly

The US government has done its darndest to add a *de facto* tourist sight to otherwise drab San Salvador. The enormous new US embassy, just outside of town on the road to Santa Tecla, was incredibly expensive and is as secure as it looks. With the civil war now over, though, the embassy is something of an anomaly.

The embassy at Santa Elena replaced the older one in San Salvador that looked like a bunker and was frequently defaced with anti-US graffiti. During the 1986 San Salvador earthquake, the top three floors of the old embassy came crashing down, giving the US a legitimate excuse to construct a new one. Workers building the new embassy, however, had to contend with heavy combat between government and rebel forces.

The eight buildings of the new embassy are spaced out over a 26-acre lot and cover 26,000 square meters. All the buildings were designed to resemble Mayan architecture, so each is set at a different angle. The embassy can hold as many US employees as the US embassy in Brazil (with 150 million people versus El Salvador's five million). The end result looks like a huge *pueblo* redesigned to withstand a hydrogen bomb. In fact, the firm that constructed the embassy claims that it can withstand any kind of military action—except a nuclear attack.

The $80 million required to build the embassy was approved by the US Congress when the US was funding El Salvador to the tune of $600 million per year. Walls are eight feet thick, windows are sealed shut and bullet-proof and the corners of the outside walls have manned turrets, designed to allow return fire during an attack. If they haven't fixed it yet, there's also a row of bullet holes—only scars, actually—in the front guardhouse window.

from the unusual animals the owners buy from local *campesinos*. Whatever arrives, they cook up and serve hot. The owner claims it has become more difficult to find certain kinds of animals lately, so the menu isn't as interesting anymore. *(11am-9pm)*

El Caminito Americano An unremarkable fast-food restaurant with a red, white and blue star-studded sign out front. Dishes range from *platos tipicos* to Chinese food, $2.30-$3.50. *(Mon-Sat 10am-9pm)*

Mariscos Las Delicias A seafood restaurant packed with slick wooden tables and surrounded by an ivy-covered brick wall. The moderately-priced food is mediocre, at best. Music groups play on the small stage on Saturday nights. *(11am-11pm)*

Nestor's Argentinean Restaurant Satisfy your saturated-fat intake for a month with one of Nestor's legendary 16oz steaks. Then, see where it came from on one of the cow part charts on the walls. Beef dishes run from $2.85 to $7. *(11:30am-9pm, Sun 11:30-3pm, closed Mon)*

Pip's Carymar A large *pupusería*/restaurant/pastry shop with all the atmosphere (and noise) of a truck stop. A glass of *horchata* costs $0.50 and *pupusas* are served from 3:30pm on. Full plates are more expensive. *(8am-9pm)*

Pizzería Italia Enjoy a large cheese pizza for $4.60 in this festive place filled with music, beer posters and bright colors. Just so things don't get out of hand, though, there's a three-beer limit per person. *(Thurs-Tues 10am-2pm, 4-9pm)*

Restaurant La Casona de Doña María Open-air dining under a high ceiling or no ceiling at all. They serve chicken, seafood and the special *Churrasco a la Casona*, 8oz of beef with shrimp, costs $5. Look for the hanging wood sign next to the Restaurant OK. *(11:30am-9:30pm)*

Restaurant La Cueva This restaurant is one of the classier places in town, set up on the second floor over the owner's house. Meat and seafood dishes run $4.50-$7, while a big bowl of *mariscada* costs $7. Their special is a Cuban meat dish with cheese, onions, cilantro and a special tomato sauce, all for $2.85. *(Mon-Thurs 11am-9pm, Fri-Sat 11am-10:30pm)*

Restaurant La Marea A more expensive place overlooking the street. Cocktails cost about $3.50, and plates start at $3. Try the *Mariscada La Marea* for $6.25. *(Mon-Sat 9am-9pm)*

Hiking

San Salvador Volcano The crater of this looming giant is a beautiful place to hike and to view the surrounding landscape, including San Salvador, Santa Tecla, the San Vicente Volcano, the green waters of the Lago de Ilopango and the Puerto del Diablo. Quezaltepeque, as the San Salvador Volcano is also known, actually has two peaks. The higher peak, Pichaco (1,890m), is about three kilometers east of the lower peak, El Boquerón (The Big Mouth), that's good for a climb. The three kilometers around the lip of El Boquerón take a few hours to hike. The path down into the crater is about 500 meters long, but it's slow going and difficult. Inside the crater you'll find a second, smaller cone formed in the 1917 eruption that flattened most of San Salvador.

To get there, take bus 103 from Santa Tecla to the pueblo of Boquerón near the top of the volcano. From there, it's about one kilometer more to the rim. *(See Near San Salvador map; bus 103 to El Boquerón, every two hours)*

Details

■ **Bookstores: Clásicos Roxsil** The friendly López family—mother, father and two daughters—has been publishing books in El Salvador for 25 years, and runs one of the country's best bookstores to boot. They carry an extensive collection of Salvadoran authors and other Latin American and Spanish literature, as well as large and small color maps of El Salvador. Plus, they can order you almost anything from anywhere else in the country. Tell them you heard it here. *(Mon-Fri 8am-12:30pm, 2:30-6pm, Sat 8am-12pm)*

■ **Buses:** All the buses that leave San Salvador's western terminal pass through Santa Tecla on their way west (see San Salvador). Also, bus **101** runs between Santa Tecla and San Salvador, passing near El Salvador del Mundo.

"You know, let whoever wins, win. But let this war be over."

— Elderly man, overheard during a gun battle in his small town

| VOICES FROM THE WAR |

TO THE WEST

- ■ **Entertainment:** The local theater **"Adalberto Guirola"** hosts plays by local organizations from time to time.
- ■ **Festivals: September 13** Santa Tecla. **December 16-25 (24)** Natividad del Señor.
- ■ **Laundry:** Washing and drying a full load costs around $3.50 at either place, and can usually be done the same day if they're not too busy. **Lavandería Colonial** *(12a Av Nte, Mon-Sat 7-6pm, Sun 8:30-5pm).* **Zamper's Lavandería** *(C Merliot towards San Salvador; Mon-Sat 7am-6pm)*
- ■ **Sports: Club Tecleño** If you're going to be in the country for a while, you can use this private club's tennis courts, pools, basketballs court and restaurant for $35 per month, payable every three months. No short-term memberships and no guests. *(Tues-Sun 10am-9pm)*

San Andrés

32km from San Salvador

San Andres ●
Santa Tecla

These ancient ruins lie in the Zapotitán Valley to the west of San Salvador, in the middle of the beautiful, rolling countryside along the Panamerican Highway. The setting is as interesting as the ruins themselves, making San Andrés more enjoyable than educational.

The Maya, Aztec and Pipil all built their campfires here at one time or another. Evidence has been found that indicates that the region had been inhabited since 200 BC, although most construction occurred after 600 AD.

The ruins were first explored in 1940, but it wasn't until 1977 that a formal excavation was begun. Archeologists have found an abundance of painted pottery nearby along with two *metates* (stone implements used for grinding grains) which indicate that families once lived here.

The partially-unearthed ruins cover three and a half kilometers of what would otherwise be prime farmland in the department of La Libertad. The rest remains hidden under smooth, rolling grassland dotted with signs that warn against playing soccer on the site. Like Tazumal, the low step pyramids are mostly covered in smooth concrete, leaving little of the original structures visible.

One main tower and two smaller towers surround a main plaza area. The largest, a double-terraced pyramid with a staircase on its western side, is made mostly of blocks of compacted volcanic ash. A structure to the west may have been an altar for rituals performed by priests or nobles. (The sign at the far end of the site simply explains why that section of San Andrés is closed off.)

Since it's so close to the capital, San Andrés receives 150,000 visitors a year—enough to cause heavy traffic at times. The small museum next to the ruins is usually closed, and it only contains a few photographs with descriptions of the site in Spanish. There's also a small food stand.

San Andrés is more suited for a picnic than anything else. Come on a sunny weekday to avoid the crowds and to enjoy the stark, simple lines of the ruins and the surrounding scenery. To the east, you can watch clouds roll up the base of the San Salvador Volcano. *(Northwest of San Salvador on the Panamerican Highway, just past the Río Sucio and the military base with two tanks out front. Take any bus west from San Salvador towards Santa Ana and get off at the sign for San Andrés, then walk 200m down the dirt road to the ruins. Tues-Sun 9am-12pm, 2-5pm; free admission)*

IN THE NEWS

Cash From the North

Money sent from relatives working abroad has had a big impact on Salvadorans back home. While some families suffered through the war with barely the clothing on their backs, others prospered with funds sent to El Salvador from hardworking family members in the US.

Nearly one-third of all Salvadorans have relatives in the United States. The exodus north began in the late 1960s, when the first emigrants realized they could earn much more working in the United States.

Now, nearly $1 billion is sent from family members in the US to relatives in El Salvador each year—an amount greater than the value of all Salvadoran exports combined. Money travels back by couriers, who make the weekly trip in heavily-guarded convoys. A good day in a medium-sized city can mean receipts of nearly $25,000. Near Christmas, the amount increases to more than $100,000 in the same towns.

The war dampened the flow of funds, not only because so many people were leaving, but because few businesses wanted to risk carrying such large sums of money into the country.

Though the money sent back is the product of hard labor, the extra cash doesn't necessarily mean good things for El Salvador. The economy isn't benefitting much, since a generation of Salvadorans is learning to survive on the funds they receive rather than from the money they earn working local jobs. Nearly 80 percent of the money is spent on food, and little is reinvested in the country.

Families occasionally suffer from the situation as much as they benefit. Almost an entire generation, most aged 17-40, left in search of work abroad. Eldest sons, young husbands and hardworking housewives and mothers abandoned homes and tradition in search of a better life, but at the expense of their families. Schools closed for lack of students and marriages fell apart, sometimes from the strain of a long-distance separation and other times when the spouse abroad found someone new. In a few cases, the spouse left behind supported a lover who helped spend the money sent from abroad.

For many, however, the money has made life back in El Salvador better. Since many Salvadorans who emigrated had always scraped by with what little money was earned in the coffee fields, newfound wealth has conferred status on many people who once labored as peasants. Some use their money to buy luxuries like cars, furniture and stereos, while others repaired damage caused by the war or helped fund elaborate weddings in El Salvador.

Joya de Cerén

25km from San Salvador

Unlike most Central American ruins, which are the remains of fancy religious centers and royal residences, Joya de Cerén is the best-preserved domestic archeological site in the Americas. The ruins, near San Juan Opico, are spread over a small area and none are particularly stellar, but the site and the museum next door are both good places to learn what everyday life in El Salvador was like 1,500 years ago.

■ **Background.** The history of Joya de Cerén has been shaped by the volcanoes that loom (and loomed) menacingly on the horizon. The Ilopango Volcano, which stood where the Lago de Ilopango is today, erupted in 260 AD and smothered the surrounding Zapotitán valley under one meter of volcanic ash.

Over the next three centuries, people gradually drifted back into the area, bringing with them a complex culture which in many ways allowed them to live better than many Salvadorans do today. Archeological evidence indicates that Joya de Cerén's inhabitants ate deer and dog meat, corn, three varieties of beans, squash, chili peppers, cacao, avocados and nuts. Farmers fought erosion in their small cornfields with low soil ridges to divert water runoff, and houses were surrounded by vegetable, flower and fruit gardens. Residents traded with civilizations in Honduras, Guatemala and perhaps others as far away as Costa Rica.

But just as the region was completely resettled by the end of the 6th century, the Laguna Caldera Volcano erupted and buried part of the valley again, this time under three meters of ash. Though nobody could have possibly survived the eruption and the 1,000-degree ash that blanketed the area, no human remains have been found at the site, leading archeologists to theorize that the inhabitants had advance warning and left in time.

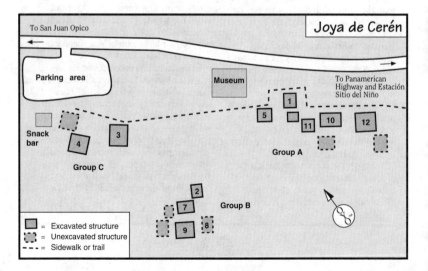

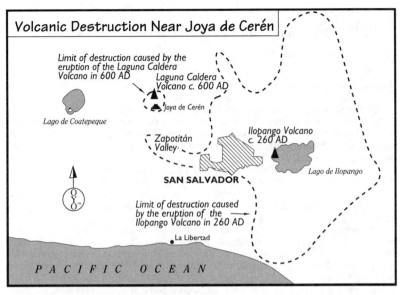

Volcanic Destruction Near Joya de Cerén

Limit of destruction caused by the
eruption of the Laguna Caldera
Volcano in 600 AD

Laguna Caldera
Volcano c. 600 AD

Joya de Cerén

Lago de Coatepeque

Zapotitán
Valley

Ilopango Volcano
c. 260 AD

SAN SALVADOR

Lago de Ilopango

Limit of destruction caused
by the eruption of the
Ilopango Volcano in 260 AD

La Libertad

PACIFIC OCEAN

TO THE WEST

At such extreme temperatures vegetable remains were instantly carbonized, preserving the plants that were part of the daily lives of Joya de Cerén's inhabitants. So much rock and dust accumulated, in fact—14 layers at last count—that the site became a small time capsule on the order of Pompeii in Italy.

The ruins were discovered in 1976 when a bulldozer clearing land for grain silos overturned part of an ancient wall. The discovery was initially ignored—the grain silos were constructed and still operate side by side with tourists and archeologists. In time, though, archeologists realized that something important was waiting just beneath the surface, and ground radar was used to locate other buildings deep beneath the clay and ash.

Dr. Payson Sheets, from the University of Colorado in the US, has supervised the excavation from the very beginning. He comes down every summer with a group of his students and conducts excavations for two months. His name is spoken with a certain tone of reverence in these parts.

■ **The Site.** The entire excavation is no more than 100 meters from end to end, and only two of the three groups of ruins (A and C) are open to the public. These sections are visible from the path, set back inside large steel enclosures to protect them from the weather and overzealous souvenir hunters. The walkway begins at group A and continues to group C. Group B can only be visited with special permission.

TO GET INVOLVED

If you're interested in participating in a dig, try contacting either Dr. Sheets at the University of Colorado at Boulder (Boulder, CO 80309) or María Isaura Arauz at Concultura, the Salvadoran organization that coordinates the digs (43a Av Sur and 12a C Pte, Col Flor Blanca; tel 271-0480).

> # "It is almost odd to die of natural causes in this country."
>
> — Salvadoran church leader, 1983

VOICES FROM THE WAR

All the buildings at the site were found lined up 30 degrees east of north, possibly to catch a cross-wind for ventilation. The houses were built on platforms of baked clay, with clay columns, walls, and thatched palm roofs. In group A, structures 10 and 12 were for shamanistic or communal use by healers or priests. They are distinctly shaped, with restricted access via a small doorway.

Structure 3 in group C is a community house, the largest (40 square meters) and best-preserved structure in the site. Two large vases were found here holding traces of *chicha,* an alcoholic drink consumed at group meetings. Structure 4, probably a house, contained a sleeping mat and plant seeds. Remains of henequen, cacao and guava trees were found nearby.

Archeologists were stumped by the shape of structure 7 in group B before figuring out it served as a steam bath, with solid mud walls lined with a bench and a small round hole in the domed ceiling. The ceiling is important in that it proves the indigenous inhabitants of the Americas already used the arch in construction before the Spanish arrived (it was previously thought that they had learned it from the Europeans). The bath was used for both medicinal and ceremonial purifications. Structure 9 is a warehouse.

Joya de Cerén's inhabitants left few things behind in their hasty departure. On the floor of one house researchers found a lump of hematite used to paint pottery. Some ceremonial pottery was also discovered, including a sculpture with an alligator head.

The museum next to the site is very well-done and clearly organized, with explanations of the history of the site in Spanish, examples of beautifully painted pottery and the fossilized footprint of an early resident. There are usually some enthusiastic young archeology students around—identified by their Joya de Cerén T-shirts—who will be glad to give you a free guided tour of the museum and site. A small cafeteria serves snacks and drinks.

There's a lot to learn here if archaeology is your thing. If, on the other hand, you prefer impressive masonry and lingering vistas, you'll probably be disappointed. You can't actually walk in and around the delicate ruins, since they are closed off

inside cages and below ground level. The museum is informative and is small enough so that you can take your time poring over the exhibits and still have time to visit the site. The whole thing can be done in about two hours. By bus, you might be able to squeeze Joya de Cerén and San Andrés into a long afternoon. The area is often packed with schoolchildren on field trips for the day. *(8km south of San Juan Opico, just north of steel bridge; take bus 108 from San Salvador to San Juan Opico, get off at "ruinas" stop; Tues-Sun 9am-4:30pm; admission free)*

Near Joya de Cerén

Estación Sitio del Niño This interesting place, once an old train station, is about two kilometers south of Joya de Cerén. Trains still pass but most of the station has been converted into a restaurant and gift shop run by an enthusiastic, friendly group of ladies. A functioning post office sits in front.

The station serves simple dishes and sells T-shirts, postcards, crafts and books about the ruins (available for much less in San Salvador). There are a few maps on the walls and you can flip through a 1989 Archeological Investigation Report by Sr. Joya himself, Dr. Sheets. A breakfast of *frijoles* and plantain costs $1.40, and a lunch of meat and rice with salad is $3.50. The fruit drinks are particularly refreshing on a hot summer day. Outside you can hire a skinny horse to ride to Joya de Cerén for about $5. The beautiful smile on the cover of this book belongs to Sulema Antonia Soriano, a young girl who lives near here—she's a local celebrity now. *(Right before the Kimberly-Clark paper factory on the road toward San Juan Opico, 100m west of the road; ask to be dropped off bus 108 at the Kimberley-Clark factory; 7:30am to 5pm)*

La Libertad

Pop. 36,000
32km from San Salvador

La Libertad Then

The port city of La Libertad is situated south of San Salvador in an area known to ancient tribes as "Oak Mountain." La Libertad was first used for international shipping in the 18th century, but didn't expand until the 19th century. In 1854, the city hosted the first steam boat ever to ply the coastal waters of El Salvador. Three years later, a multi-national force of 1,200 left from here to boot meddling US filibuster William Walker out of Nicaragua once and for all.

La Libertad Now

La Libertad is a commercial and fishing port somewhat smaller than Acajutla, and is a popular weekend beach getaway from San Salvador. Stores sell beach balls and practically every restaurant in town serves fresh seafood. The streets teem with all types of people, from wealthy weekenders from the capital to old expatriate surfers, with the town's notorious thieves keeping an eye on everyone. Every afternoon the city comes even more alive, as fishermen return to sell their catch on the wharf controlled by a handful of fishing cooperatives.

La Libertad isn't beautiful, but it certainly is happening. Stay here to travel to the surrounding beaches during the day or to cruise along the Coastal Highway and enjoy the view. The beach, where Oliver Stone filmed part of *Salvador,* is black with volcanic sand, and kids wander up and down it peddling shells. More shells are for sale on the wharf, where everybody gathers to ogle the day's catch and to watch the fishing boats being hauled up. *Pupusas* and fresh and dried fish are sold on the wharf.

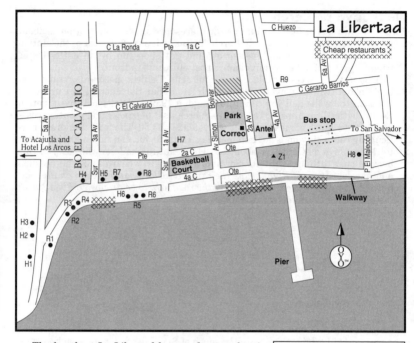

The beach at La Libertad has good waves but is too rocky. Besides, all the fishermen throw their fish guts and other junk right off the wharf. Other beaches a few kilometers in either direction are good, but the best surf is a few hundred meters to the right of the wharf on a rocky corner of the beach called Punta Roca.

Sights

Turicentro La Libertad The poor Antiguo Puerto de La Libertad (Old Port of La Libertad) has been converted into a *turicentro*. As usual, admission includes access to bathrooms and changing rooms. *(8am-5pm, $0.50 per person, clothing check 8am-2:30pm)*

Accommodations

El Malecón Don Lito Clean, jungle decor and a nice pool. The restaurant serves seafood dishes for $5-$10. Room prices double for 24 hours. *(Tel 335-3201; 16S $19.50, 4D $20.25, all with private bath, AC; restaurant)*

ACCOMMODATIONS ●

H1 Hacienda Don Rigo
H2 La Posada de Don Lito
H3 *Motel Rick*
H4 Hotel Rancho Blanco
H5 La Posada Familiar
H6 Hotel Amor y Paz
H7 Hotel Puerto Bello
H8 El Malecón Don Lito

FOOD & DRINK ●

R1 El Delfín
R2 Restaurant Punta Roca
R3 *El Nuevo Altamar*
R4 *La Fonda Española*
R5 *Sandra Restaurant*
R6 Restaurant El Viejo Alta Mar
R7 *Restaurant Los Amigos*
R8 *Restaurant Alta Mar*
R9 *Ice cream*

OTHER ▲

Z1 Turicentro La Libertad

La Posada de Don Lito Owned by guess who, so wave to him as you walk by. There's a restaurant across the street. Prices double for 24 hours. *(Tel 335-3166; 10 D $19.50 all with private bath, AC)*

Hacienda Don Rigo The third site in the Lito Empire. *(Tel 335-3166, 20D $17.25, $19.50 with AC, all with private bath)*

Hotel Amor y Paz The nice old owner of this place under construction on the main drag is pretty laid-back about specifics, so it may help to clarify the price up front. *(Attached to the restaurant Los Amigos; tel 335-3187; 4S, 7D, 1T $4.50-$7; laundry)*

Hotel Rancho Blanco Run-down rooms, and only one has AC, but wait until you try the *pescado deshuesado relleno con camarones* (fish stuffed with shrimp). *(Tel 335-3584; 1S, 1D, 2T $8-$17.25, doubles and triples with private bath; laundry; restaurant 8am-8pm)*

La Posada Familiar Simple, clean little rooms. The restaurant serves chicken for $1.75 and fish for $2.25 and up. *(Tel 335-3252; 8S 4D, $7-$11.50, some with private baths; 24hr checkout; laundry; restaurant)*

Hotel Puerto Bello The rooms in this hotel, squeezed into a 3-floor apartment, are too dark to tell if they're clean or not. If you do stay here, get a room with a good window and watch out for cockroaches. *(Tel 335-3013; 20S $5, 5D $9.25-$13.80, some with private bath, fans; laundry; 24hr checkout; bar)*

Hotel Los Arcos A clean pool and fountain, a courtyard set off from the road, and spacious, clean rooms—what more could you ask for? Better prices, maybe. Watch for the deer and geese behind the pool. The family rooms will fit six to eight people. Seafood soup in the restaurant is $7 and de-boned fish stuffed with shrimp will run you the same. *(Two kilometers west of La Libertad along Coastal Highway; tel 335-3490; 7S $20 with double bed, 7D $28.75, 4 family rooms $37.25 with 4 beds, refrigerator, all with private bath, TV, AC, phone; pool; 24hr checkout; restaurant 8am-8pm)*

Food & Drink

Restaurant El Viejo Alta Mar Enjoy shrimp or salad plates along the beach for $8-$11.50. *Mariscada* is their specialty, and costs around $7.

The Don of La Libertad

Don Lito is a controversial character around town. Give him credit for running some pretty spiffy, clean hotels that cater to El Salvador's emerging middle class. He'll roll every one of his r's describing to you how he engineered everything himself and built his mini-empire from scratch. Salvadorans flooded to La Libertad during the civil war in search of a psychological escape from the terror, and a night's stay at one of Don Lito's hotels was a good break. He also has a lot to do with the emergence of La Libertad as an international tourist attraction.

But to be fair, there aren't too many people around La Libertad who seem to like Don Lito. To some he's a scheister making extra bucks by charging a 12-hour rate that doubles for a full day. (He explains that his rates are competitive with hotels in Miami, where he has spent time.) He's also said to go to extremes to steal business from other businesses nearby. With other good hotels and restaurants nearby, you could probably do better.

Restaurant Punta Roca Probably the best place on the beach to have a beer and relax, on two floors with a nice view. Bob Rotherhan, a Miami native, runs the place. Bob came to La Libertad in 1974 and was the first in the area to open a restaurant. During the war, most of his business came from Salvadorans escaping from the city. *(10am-8pm)*

El Delfín A decent patio overlooks the waves. Manager Ricardo Guardado has been around for 11 years and likes to talk (in Spanish) about the local scene. A tasty lobster *reina* costs $9.25. *(7am-9pm)*

Details

■ **Buses: Playa San Diego, Playa Conchalío, Playa Majahual (80). San Salvador (102)**, every 10 min, 32km, 1hr 20min.
■ **Festivals: October 22-24 (23)** San Rafael and San Miguel. **December 7-8 (7)** Virgen de Concepción.

RHINA DE REY PRENDES

Señora Presidente?

R hina de Rey Prendes is an exception in Latin American politics, which traditionally has reserved its spotlight for men. Prendes first gained recognition when her husband was elected mayor of San Salvador, and her career began to take shape when she was appointed the country's Attorney General.

In 1994, Prendes became the first woman in the country's history to run for president, and spent six months on the campaign trail. At each of her stops Prendes asked for the support of Salvadoran women. At the same time, she was able to sway male votes by kicking off festivities with two female dancers who gyrated as bands played in the background.

Prendes raised $125,000 in her bid for the presidency, enough to run a solid campaign but less than she needed to compete with major party candidates. Although Armando Calderon Sol won the election, Prendes has paved the way for Salvadoran women to assume roles in the upper levels of their society from which they have been excluded.

Playa San Diego

Look for signs for the Villa San Diego or the Villa del Pacífico beach resort about five kilometers east of La Libertad off the Coastal Highway. A long stretch of white sand with soft waves, this beach is practically uninhabited during the week. Along the beach are a mixture of cheap eats and dream houses built by people who are never around to use them. Bamboo shack restaurants along the beach charge about $3.50 for a plate of fresh fish. Your best bet is to drive down and find a passage in between the brick walls to a nice section of the beach.

Accommodations

Las Cabañas de Don Lito The suites and cabins each hold two people. Prices double for 24 hrs. *(On the highway outside the entrance to the beach; tel 335-3216, 4 suites $23, 12 cabins $23, all with private baths)*

Villa San Diego Simple and clean but the common bathroom has a slight cockroach problem. Prices are for 12 hours and go up 30 percent on weekends. *(Tel 335-3320; 4S $17.25, 2D $25, all with private baths; laundry; bar)*

Villa del Pacífico The garden is pleasant but the management is rude and expects to charge foreigners double. *(About 100 meters off the road; 5 rooms $28.75)*

Hotel Paraíso Right off the road, with a small pool and garden. Seafood dishes at the restaurant are about $6. *(2D $18.50 with private bath; laundry; restaurant 8am-6pm)*

Details

■ **Buses: La Libertad (82)**, every 15 min until 6:20pm, 3km, 20min.

Western Beaches

Playa Conchalío

When the tide is low, Playa Conchalío is enormous—a nice place to relax in relative solitude. A kiosk at the entrance called "Champa Las Brisas" serves oysters, clams and beer. The beach in front is rocky, but 20 meters to the right is a sandy area backed with countless palm trees, with many more places to eat.

To get there turn left about three kilometers west of La Libertad, right after the Hotel Los Arcos. Make the first left onto a dirt road, turn right at Rancho Tabosa after about 100 meters, then go through the little neighborhood straight ahead to the beach. Or, tell the bus driver to let you off in front of the Hotel Los Arcos. From there it's a five or ten-minute walk.

Details

■ **Buses: La Libertad (80)**, every 10 min until 5:30pm, 3km, 20min.

Playa El Majahual

El Majahual is a grimy, active beach filled with Salvadorans looking for business or a good time. The beach here has soft, shiny black sand, medium waves and no rocks. As soon as you walk in you're mobbed by people begging you to stop at their hotel or *rancho*. Not surprisingly, the cheap accommodations and *comedores* seem to go on forever—look around, because some are better than others. People on the beach sell pony rides, coconuts and drinks.

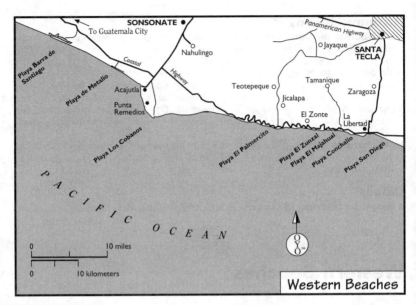

Western Beaches

Food & Drink

Numerous *comedores* serve fish, shrimp, chicken and meat. Most close around 10pm, but some are open all night. Try a *mariscada* for $4, or a fish plate for about $1.75.

Accommodations

Many *ranchos* offer food, parking, changing facilities and rooms for the night. Prices vary from $4.50 for a weeknight to $7 for a weekend night for a tiny room with a single bed and light. Bring bug repellent.

Hotel El Pacífico A juke box makes this place loud and lively. Most people just come here for the day, and no wonder—the rooms are stark and small, with just a bed, fan and table. Rates are for 12 hours. *(Along the road to beach; 45 rooms $7 with common bath, $8 with private bath; pool; restaurant)*

Hotel Solimar Turn left before the Hotel Pacífico, and go down the dirt road about 100 meters to find the hotel in a grassy enclosed area, with a small pool and so-so rooms. Again, usually just a day hangout, so the prices are for 12 hours only. Singles will fit two people. A seafood plate at the restaurant runs around $5. *(16S $7 for 12 hours, all with private bath; restaurant)*

Club Tecleño Lots of grass and breezes, coconut trees and benches. You need to get permission (in the form of a courtesy card) from the main office to use the private beach area. Or just drive in, since there's usually no one at the gate. To stay overnight, reservations are usually required about a week in advance. Small rooms fit four people, large rooms eight, and the restaurant serves breakfast and lunch. *(C Don Bosco 3-1, past El Majahual beach across from the Cerro Mar Resort; tel 328-3468, small room $5.75, large room $9.25, all with kitchen, private bath and furniture; restaurant)*

Details
■ **Buses: La Libertad (80)**, every 10 min until 6pm, 4km, 25min.

Playa El Palmarcito
Accommodations
Club Atami This stylish grassy resort with thatched huts, pools, and well-kept picnic areas is farther down the coast near Playa El Palmarcito. The view from the garden over the ocean is magnificent. This place makes a great secluded getaway, even if there isn't any service at night. If you'd like a room, reservations are necessary at the main office in San Salvador (69 Ave Sur #164 and Col Escalón; tel 223-9000). You can also spend the day here if you have a passport; just explain at the gate that you're a tourist. *(49km from La Libertad on Coastal Highway, near Playa El Palmarcito, take bus 192 from La Libertad; $5 per person per day, hut $2.25 with 4 hammocks, doubles and quads $15 per person per night, all with private bath; checkout 3pm; restaurant 8:30am-9pm)*

Details
■ **Buses: La Libertad (80)**, every 10 min until 6pm, 4km, 25min.

Playa Los Cóbanos
Fifteen kilometers south of Sonsonate near Acajutla lies Los Cóbanos, one of El Salvador's most popular beaches. The section right where the road ends is rocky and not too impressive, but wider, flatter expanses await a moderate walk in either direction. It will cost you $1.15 to park and $0.50 to enter through a private gate with a changing room and picnic tables.

Two hotels, the Solimar and the Mar de Plata, are available if you want to spend the night, but it's better to stay in Sonsonate and come here for the day. Many restaurants along the beach serve seafood, with typical fried fish dishes running $3.50-$5.75. Try a *camarones a la plancha* (a shrimp specialty served with salad, *tortillas* and *salsa)* for about $7. To the west of Playa Los Cóbanos is **Punta Remedios**, which is quieter and less developed. Ruby Express buses run to Sonsonate every hour and take about 30 minutes. A taxi to the city costs $4.50.

Acajutla

Nahuat, "Place of Tortoises and Sugar Cane"
81km from San Salvador
15km from Sonsonate

Acajutla is really only good as a jumping-off and supply point for travel to nearby beaches. The sea breeze usually keeps the city cool, but can't seem to blow away the atmosphere of sleaziness that pervades the streets. Acajutla isn't very pretty, and is more prone to bars and prostitutes than restaurants and hotels. The neighboring docks, the huge ships passing just offshore and the throngs of tourists that fill this place on weekends just add to the grimy feel of the town.

Accommodations

Hotel Miramar The only decent place in town, with a small pool and a seafood restaurant overlooking the beach. *(3 blocks from bus station, tel 542-3183, 12 rooms $7 with private bath; laundry; 10am checkout; pool; restaurant)*

Details

■ **Buses: San Salvador (205)**, 81km, 3hr. **Sonsonate (207)**, 15km, 45min.
■ **Festivals: October 23-24 (24)** San Rafael Archangel. During a special nighttime ceremony, an image of San Rafael is placed in a special *panga*, or canoe, decorated with flowers and lights. A procession of local fishermen follows the image from the new dock to the old dock, where mass is held.

Beaches West of Acajutla

The beaches at Metalío and Barra de Santiago lie along the undeveloped plains bordering the Coastal Highway as it heads towards the Guatemalan border. The shores here are less cluttered with private homes than usual, since Metalío and Santiago are less accessible and exotic than other beaches further east. Both beaches are perfect for lazing around in a hammock and doing...nothing.

The Coastal Highway to the Guatemalan border begins 15 kilometers south of Sonsonate, about three kilometers south of where the Coastal Highway leaves to the east toward La Libertad. The gravel road is wide but has more ruts than a riverbed, courtesy of the constant stream of tractor trailers carrying goods from the western border. One muddy river after another flows south towards the ocean under rough concrete bridges.

Playa de Metalío

Metalío is a quiet, narrow beach close to Acajutla. The grey sand here is a mixture of the black sand you find near the city and whiter sand from the other direction. The beach is lined with palm trees and continues off into the mist to the west. To the east you can see Acajutla—about as close as you'd want to be—which accounts for the trash that washes up on shore. Some of the lots along the shore are owned by fishermen who string out their nets between palm trees to dry, and drink stands line the road to the beach. Metalío isn't as fancy as other Salvadoran beaches, but it's a good day trip from Acajutla or Sonsonate.

To get there, turn left off the Coastal Highway ten kilometers from the Sonsonate-Acajutla road at the little town of Metalío (the first real cluster of buildings you'll pass). From there hop a microbus, hitch a ride or walk the two kilometers to the beach.

Barra de Santiago

Playa Barra de Santiago is the closest easily-accessible beach to the border with Guatemala. The long way there is, well, long, but if you don't have your own car there's an enjoyable little boat ride that can shorten your trip.

The beach at Barra de Santiago is fairly wide and completely empty from end to end, making it nicer than Metalío and worth the extra kilometers. You can string up a hammock between palm trees for the night and sack out; just be careful of your things (and yourself) out in the middle of nowhere. The best spots are at least a kilometer away from the small, run-down fishing village of Barra de Santiago. There are a few *comedores* in town, along with places to store your things while you're at the beach. Hire a fishing boat to explore the placid waters of the estuary for an afternoon, and take one back across to the Coastal Highway if that's how you arrived.

There are two ways to approach Barra de Santiago, depending upon how you're traveling. If you are driving, take a left off the Coastal Highway 24 kilometers past the turnoff for Metalío, right in front of a bridge painted with FMLN logos and across the street from a yellow sign for "Las Villas de Shasca."

The dirt road to the beach is lined with thick vegetation and filled with some impressive potholes. After a few kilometers it turns to the right while an even rougher road leads straight ahead to the ocean. Head to the right, and before long you'll pass the Villas de Shasca on the left with a huge yellow wall and gate. Further on are lots filled with evenly-spaced palm trees. The road ends after about ten kilometers at the village of Barra de Santiago in between the ocean and the El Zapote estuary.

If you're not driving, on the other hand, go farther down the Coastal Highway until you reach the sign for "Barra de Santiago," near a sharp turn-off back to the left and a big Coke emblem on a *pupusería*. This is the road to the estuary's boat launching area. Hitch a ride on a passing pickup seven or so kilometers to the shore of the estuary, where you can catch a small fishing boat across to the town of Barra de Santiago. The slow, pleasant ride in a dugout canoe takes 15 minutes and costs about $0.25 per person.

Details

■ **Buses: Ahuachapán (249, 285, 288, 503)**, every 45 min until 3pm, 108km, 3hr 30min. **La Hachadura/Guatemalan border (200, 249, 259, 503)**, every 10 min until 5pm, 23km, 30min. **San Salvador (200)**, 5 and 6:10am, 130km, 3hr. **Sonsonate (251, 259, 286, 429)**, every 10 min until 5:20pm, 65km, 1hr 30min.

Sonsonate

Nahuat, "400 Waters"
Pop. 85,000
65km from San Salvador

Sonsonate Then

Sonsonate sits near El Salvador's humid, fertile western coast with the Río Grande de Sonsonate passing through its center and continuing on to the coast. The area was densely populated by the Izalco Indians before the Spanish arrived. According to legend, the city was founded by Pedro de Alvarado in 1524 as he rolled into Cuscatlán from the west.

The region's importance during the 18th and 19th centuries hinged on its prosperous cacao and balsam plantations and its proximity to the port of Acajutla. In 1833, Sonsonate served as the seat of the congress of the Central American Federation.

Sonsonate Now

The *"Heroic y trabajador"* (heroic and hardworking) city of Sonsonate, according to the sign at the southern entrance, is a smaller, stickier, dirtier version of Santa Ana. The muggy coastal climate makes Sonsonate only bearable as a point of transit to El Salvador's western beaches and to the pleasant mountain towns of Apaneca and Juayúa to the north. There's also a problem with the local water supply that leaves the town dry from time to time.

> In the late 16th century, historian Juan López de Velasco wrote, "Sonsonate has many good vegetable and melon gardens, and good houses made of tile and adobe. The land is very fertile, especially for cacao, which is exported from the port of Acajutla three leagues hence."

Accommodations

Sonsonate has many small *hospedajes* and hotels, but most owners will give you a strange look if you ask to rent a room for the whole night (hint, hint).

Hotel Orbe The best lodging in town, which isn't saying too much. Clean but nothing special, with bare rooms and bathrooms that are a bit smelly. *(Tel 451-1416; 17S $7 with fan, 7D $10.50 with fan, 2D $13.80 with AC, all with private bath; parking; 10am checkout; cafetín)*

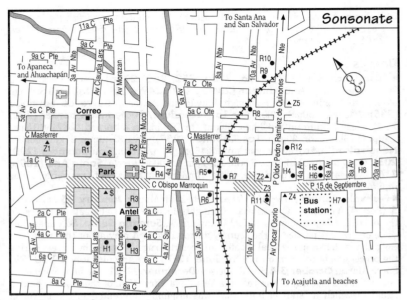

Food & Drink

Restaurant Bariloche A pleasant restaurant and tea house where people come after work to talk and eat around a sunny open patio. Typical food is served, with a *churrasco* costing $3.75. *(9am-9pm)*

Burger House El Centro A small local fast-food place where you can enjoy a cheeseburger for $0.75, or splurge on a steakburger for $1.40. *(10am-8pm)*

Burger House Plaza Looks like a nice Burger King inside with some seats outside on a patio. The fried chicken special, known as "Menu #2," will get you three pieces of chicken with potato, salad and bread for $2.30. *(10am-9pm)*

Restaurant La Terraza Similar to the Burger House Plaza with orange plastic chairs and more expensive food. The *plato mixto* for $6.25 includes meat, shrimp and fixins. *(10am-9:30pm)*

Restaurant Hi-Lay Green skylights give the back room of this Chinese restaurant an underwater feel. Chop suey is their best plate, for $2.30, but they don't have any vegetarian dishes. *(Mon-Fri 9pm-8pm, Sat-Sun 9am-9pm)*

ACCOMMODATIONS ●

H1 *Hospedaje New York Mini*
H2 Hotel Orbe
H3 *Hotel Santa Rosa*
H4 *Hospedaje El Brasil*
H5 *Hospedaje Rinconcito*
H6 *Hospedaje El Recreo*
H7 *Hotel Florida*
H8 *Hospedaje El Pacifico*

FOOD & DRINK ●

R1 Burger House El Centro
R2 *Pops Ice Cream/Pasteleria*
R3 Hi-Lay
R4 *Restaurant Bariloche*
R5 *Pasteleria*
R6 *Pops Ice Cream*
R7 *Pasteleria*
R8 *Panaderia El Angel*
R9 *Restaurant La Terraza*
R10 Burger House Plaza
R11 *Restaurant Island Club*
R12 Deli Pizza

OTHER ▲

Z1 Hospital
Z2 Los Leones (car repair)
Z3 Shell Station
Z4 Texaco Station
Z5 Shell Station

TO THE WEST

Deli Pizza A large cheese pizza here costs $8. They'll deliver a fresh pie by bicycle (but not all the way to the beach). *(Tel 451-0213; Mon-Fri 11am-2pm, 4-9pm, Sat-Sun 11am-9pm)*

Details

■ **Buses: Acajutla (207, 215a, 216a, 252, 260, 278a),** every 10 min until 7pm, 16km, 35min. **Ahuachapán (206a-c, 249, 249a, 269, 503),** until 6:30pm, 36km, 1hr 30min. All pass through Juayúa and Apaneca. **Barra de Santiago (285),** 7:45am, 4:30pm, 49km, 1hr. **La Hachadura/Guatemalan border (200, 259),** every 10 min until 6:30pm, 60km, 1hr 30min. **La Libertad (287),** 6:15am, 3:40pm, 76km, 2hr 30min. **Los Cóbanos (259),** until 3:40pm, 25km, 50min. **Nahuizalco (205a),** every hour until 3:45pm, 9km, 15min. **San Salvador (200, 205),** every 5 min until 6pm, 67km, 1hr 20min. 200 is *directo*. **Santa Ana (209b, 216),** every 40 min until 5:40pm, 40km, 1hr 40min. 209b is via Cerro Verde, 216 is *rápido*.

■ **Festivals: January 19-20 (19)** San Sebastián Mártir. **January 25-February 5 (Feb 4)** Virgen de Candelaría. Highlights include the Cabalgata Artística de Candelaría, a horse show in Rafael Campo park. **Semana Santa.** Sonsonate has some of the best parties in the country during Easter. A play about the tragedy of Golgotha is shown in the local theater, and colorful rugs decorate the streets during the procession of the Santo Entierro. **June 12-13** San Antonio. **July 29-30 (29)** Santa Marta. **October 3-4** San Francisco. **December 24-31** Nacimiento del Niño Jesús. On the last day of the year the Vela de la Vara (Vigil of the Staff) is held, a ritual in which a "staff of authority" was originally presented to the mayor of Sonsonate. Today the staff is presented to a "mayor" specially chosen for the night's festivities. Once located, the mayor is given ceremonial power to rule the city for a night. The new mayor's first order of business is always a command to capture everyone in town. Once captured, the citizens must *pasayuba bosu,* Nahuat for "pay the fine." Any money collected goes to charity. Citizens who refuse to pay the fine are threatened with being forced to smell a cow skull or a piece of cow manure.

San Antonio del Monte

Pop. 12,000
68km from San Salvador
3km from Sonsonate

San Antonio del Monte Then

In 1733 the Dominican friars of the convent of Santo Domingo built a hermitage just west of Sonsonate. Soon indigenous people and *mulattos,* attracted by the convent, built a small village around it. More and more people settled nearby, including many drawn by rumors that an image of San Antonio inside the church could perform miracles.

Top: San Francisco Gotera
BL: Two girls, Concepcíón Quetzaltepeque
BR: Coconut vendor, Costa del Sol

Top: Soccer game, San Salvador
BL: Grandparents with grandchild, near La Unión
BR: Young girl, near La Unión

San Antonio del Monte Now

The church that dominates the center of this small town is the most interesting thing about San Antonio del Monte. Vendors sell souvenirs and religious icons outside the church, giving the place the feel of a miniature holy Graceland. Sonsonate is almost within walking distance, so come here for a few

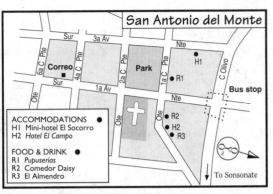

hours if you're interested in colonial churches. Or just spend an afternoon at one of the *comedores* facing the church, watching people come and go.

Accommodations

Mini-Hotel El Socorro All of these simple clean rooms come with a fan. They'll wash your clothes for a modest fee, too. *(Tel 451-2755; 6S $3.50, 4D $4.60, 3T $5.75, all with private bath; laundry; parking)*

Food & Drink

Comedor Daisy Strike up a conversation with Toña, the feisty owner of this small eatery—it's hard not to. She'll tell you all about her town as she makes you a grilled chicken plate for $1.70.

El Almendro A *comedor* popular with locals and pilgrims.

Sights

Iglesia San Antonio del Monte This colonial monolith was begun in 1841 and funded by contributions left by faithful pilgrims. It took two decades to complete, and replaced the original 13th-century church that had stood in the same spot. An overhead mural of Saint Anthony shows him in his deathbed surrounded by his disciples as angels wait to carry his soul away. Near the back of the church are hundreds of icons left by devotees. Worshippers leave these objects on top of the altar to ask the Saint for help or a favor, or to give thanks for a favor that has already been granted.

Details

■ **Buses: Sonsonate (53)**, 3km, 15min.
■ **Festivals: June 13** San Antonio del Monte. **August 22-26 (25)** Commercial Fiesta. During the traditional Baile de los Puros (Dance of the Cigars), two young women are selected to be the *madrinas*. Each dancer carries a tray full of cigars. In exchange for a cigar, spectators must dance with the *madrina* and put money into a little sack she carries in her blouse.

IN THE NEWS

Terror From the Left

Murder, kidnapping and the destruction of government targets were hallmarks of guerrilla strategy from the beginning of the war. Gradually, support for the FMLN dwindled as the rebels' list of killings and destruction approached that of the army.

In the 1970s, the loosely-organized guerrilla groups contented themselves with kidnapping the country's elite and using the ransom money to finance their growth. They soon became more violent, and in 1977 leftist forces killed the Salvadoran foreign minister after taking him hostage. By the end of the following year, both the chancellor of the National University and the former president of the National Congress had been gunned down by the rebels. During the 1978 elections the guerrillas bombed homes of right-wing politicians in an attempt to disrupt the voting process.

When the civil war began in the early 1980s, the rebels expanded the scope of their attacks. The old US embassy was covered with revolutionary graffiti, and bombed and shot at repeatedly. The FMLN kidnapped prominent Salvadoran industrialists and businessmen and killed the South African ambassador in a bid to express their participation in a "global struggle against repression."

In June 1983, the US embassy reported that 42 government soldiers had recently been captured and subsequently executed by the FMLN. Many of the bodies showed signs of having been tortured to death.

The FMLN also targeted small-town mayors in the mid-80s an attempt to influence local elections. Many houses and offices of government officials were set ablaze in the middle of the night, often destroying legal documents townspeople needed to vote in the process.

In rebel-controlled areas, villagers were pressured to collectivize their land, send their children to FMLN schools and encourage them to join the rebel army. As case after case of rebel harassment began to touch the lives of many Salvadorans, people who once sympathized with the left began to wonder whose side the FMLN was really on.

Caluco

Pop. 8,500
61km from San Salvador
8km from Sonsonate

The road to this town, about two kilometers off the road between San Salvador and Sonsonate, is lined with banana and coconut trees. A sleepiness pervades Caluco, as residents doze in hammocks in bamboo houses. Three nearby sights are more interesting than Caluco itself: the Atecozol *turicentro,* the swimming spot at El Balneario and the ruins of a colonial church on the edge of town. Find a room in Sonsonate and come here for a picnic at the church ruins or visit the nearby sights.

Sights

Turicentro Atecozol A statue of Atonatl, the Indian chieftain who shot an arrow into the leg of Pedro de Alvarado, overlooks six swimming pools filled with clean spring water. Dense vegetation surrounds this shady but somewhat dirty *turicentro,* with many small *comedores* serving snacks and drinks. If you don't want to use the free changing room, a small cabin where you can change and store your clothes runs $3.50 per day plus a $1.70 deposit. The urban bus 205 between Sonsonate and San Salvador can drop you off nearby. *(Two km north of Caluco; 8am-5pm, $0.60 per car, $0.60 per person)*

Colonial Church Ruins Dominican monks built this brick church in the 17th century on what was believed to have been an Indian worshiping site. The church was destroyed in the Santa Marta earthquake of 1773 when the Izalco Volcano erupted. Now the site is overgrown with weeds and surrounded by local shacks, but it still maintains an air of imposing dignity. Some decorations on the outside have survived the years. The view across fields and mountains from the far end of the church is beautiful, and makes this a great place to stop for lunch—bring your own. *(500 meters south of Caluco, look for the path up to the left by the archeological work sign)*

Balneario Agua Caliente Also known as the Balneario Shuteca, this glorified swimming hole isn't as large or as clean as Atecozol. A local river was dammed up to make a pool that is usually filled with Salvadoran children. The dishes used by the few *comedores* are washed in the river, so the food here probably isn't very sanitary. *(1km south of Caluco past the ruins of the colonial church; 8am-5pm; $0.10 per person, $0.25 per car)*

Details

■ **Buses: Sonsonate (205)**, 6km. **San Salvador (205)**, 65km.
■ **Festivals: June 23-29 (28)** San Pedro Apóstol.

Nahuizalco

Nahuat, "Four Izalcos"
Pop. 42,900
72km from San Salvador
9km from Sonsonate

Nahuizalco Then

Nahuizalco began as one of the strongest Pipil population centers in El Salvador, established long before the Spanish arrived. Two local legends relate how the town may have earned its name. First, a Franciscan priest reported in 1586 that the town had four times as many indigenous inhabitants as the town of Izalco. Also, four families from Izalco were said to have resettled here after Spanish forces swept through. Izalco remained predominantly indigenous well into the 20th century, although much of the population was decimated by government forces in *La Matanza* of 1932.

Nahuizalco Now

A dry, dusty town with a shell of a church, Nahuizalco still has one of the largest indigenous populations in the country, the massacre of 1932 notwithstanding. Many of the older women still wear the traditional one-piece wraparound skirts as they have for centuries.

The town's wicker crafts and furniture are really all that justify a trip from Sonsonate. Nahuizalco was famous for the beauty and durability of its woven goods as far back as the 19th century. Today many shops in the backs of stores turn out baskets, hats, tables, and chairs. Check carefully for bugs in wicker that hasn't been varnished.

Food & Drink

Ranchón Tío Alex   Carlos Calderón, a Los Angeles native, opened this place in 1994 and named it after his uncle. It is a family-style, outdoor restaurant with good music and no competition. Breakfast here is $1.70 and a plate of *tortillas* costs $4. *(9am-10pm)*

Sights

Casa de la Cultura You can watch craftspeople weave baskets and mats here. Tiny baskets cost $0.25 and small mats are $4.60. *(Across the street from park on the north edge of town; Mon-Fri 8am-12pm)*

Details

■ **Buses: Ahuachapán (249)**, every 15 min, 13km, 2 hr. **Sonsonate (530)**, every 5 min, 9km.

■ **Festivals: March or April (Thursday and Holy Friday)** Semana Santa. **June 20-25 (24)** San Juan Bautista. **November 2** Día de los Difuntos (Day of the Dead). Participants offer food to the dead in a candlelight procession that leads to the cemetery. **December 22-29 and January 3-7** Niño Jesús y los Reyes Magos.

Juayúa

Pop. 27,500
78km from San Salvador
17km from Sonsonate

Juayúa Then

In January 1986, a force of 100 rebels attacked Juayúa in an attempt to strengthen support for the FMLN in the west. Guerrillas bombed the bank, fired grenades at the town's civil defense headquarters and covered town walls with FMLN slogans.

Juayúa Now

The road to Juayúa winds past coffee plantations up into the hills of the Cordillera de las Apanecas (Apaneca Range) that surround the town to the north, east and west. Juayúa is a relaxed mountain village with plenty of fresh air and a church that's worth a visit. Flowers decorate a fountain in the main park, kept tidy by an active local government. There are some good opportunities for hiking and camping in the nearby mountains.

> Whoever maintains the Parque Unión in the center of town evidently means business. Sign warnings are sharp and to the point: "Don't throw trash," "Don't stand on the benches," "Don't cut the flowers," "Don't enter the garden," and most importantly, "Don't mistreat the plants."

Accommodations

El Típico This dark wood hotel, like an urban cabin, is surrounded by trees and flowers. Rooms are bare but clean. The restaurant serves a good beef dish for $3.45. *(12S $4.60, some with private bath, 3D $9.20, all with bath; checkout 9am; restaurant)*

Food & Drink

Oskar's A fast-food restaurant and pizzeria owned and run by Oskar. Sandwiches are $1.15, and a plate of meat, potatoes, salad and rice is $4. *(7:30am-11pm)*

Rincón Suizo Open only on weekends, this place sells sandwiches for $1.70-$2.30 and main dishes for $4.60-$6.90. A mini-market is next door. *(Sat-Sun 12-10pm)*

Juayúa Hot This clean fast-food joint usually opens in the late afternoon. If it looks closed, just knock and the owner will open up for you.

Juayúa

ACCOMMODATIONS ●
HI Hotel El Típico

FOOD & DRINK ●
R1 Restaurant Oscar's
R2 Pastelería "Festival"
R3 Restaurant Rincón Suizo
R4 Restaurant Juayúa Hot
R5 Pollo Rico

To Ahuachapán

9a Av · 7a Av

Bus Stop

To Apaneca

Antel

Av Daniel Cordón

Correo
C Mercedes Cáceres

5a Av · 3a Av · 1a Av

R1 ●
● R3

2a Av

Park

R2 ●

3a C
1a C
R5
2a C
H1 R4 ●
4a C

BO EL CARMEN

COL LA PROVIDENCIA

6a C

Pollo Rico Three dining rooms with high ceilings surround an airy courtyard garden, like a homey KFC. Chicken is $0.60 per piece and platters run $2.30. *(11am-8:30pm)*

Sights

Templo del Señor de Juayúa Red arches and crosses decorate the front of this church, built in 1957. An impressive nave is flanked by dark marble columns. Look behind the altar for the famous icon of the Black Christ of Juayúa, made by the same craftsman who created the Black Christ of Guatemala.

Climbing, Hiking and Swimming

There are some good hiking destinations in the mountains around Juayúa. The two most popular are the Cerro de Apaneca (1,800m) to the west and the Cerro de los Naranjos (1,950 m) to the northeast. Two mountain lakes are within a day's hike and are good places to swim and camp. Ask locals for detailed directions before heading off.

Laguna de las Ranas A lake near the summit of Cerro Buenos Aires. *(Take 1a Av Sur out of town to the north.)*

Laguna Verde The road towards Ahuachapán passes near Laguna Verde, which rests on the slopes of an extinct volcano of the same name. You can drive by 4x4 or take the two-hour walk.

Los Chorros de Calera Swimming holes here were created when the power company dammed up the natural springs. They make a nice half-day hike and picnic spot, as butterflies of every imaginable size and color fill the air. On the way there, notice the coffee fields on the facing hillside, with their characteristic line of bushes planted to break up the wind over the hillsides and to shade the coffee plants from the sun.

The first waterfall off to the right (watch your step!) is the highest but also the dirtiest, since women from town wash clothes in the river upstream. If you keep going the trail soon becomes slippery and narrow, so be careful. The second set of falls, with the Pollo Rico ad painted on the rock, comes into sight 50 meters later.

The third set, further down the path, is similar to the second. Finally, if you want to be totally secluded, the last set are the shallowest and prettiest and are a great place to kick off your shoes and relax. *(Take the dirt road east out of town and turn right where the road splits near the house. A few hundred meters after the split, follow a short, steep, gully that leads 100m down off to the right. At the end, you'll arrive at a dirt road and a foot bridge off to the right. If you're driving, the road winds around until it reaches the bridge. Take the path across the bridge through the white painted stone gate, then head for the sound of the falls.)*

Details

■ **Buses: Ahuachapán (249)**, every 30 min until 6pm, 24km, 1hr 15min. **San Salvador (206)**, one around 10 am, 78km, 3hr. **Sonsonate (64)**, every 30 min until 6pm, 17km, 1hr.

■ **Festivals: Jan 6-15 (15) Cristo Negro** Try, if you dare, the *elote loco* (crazy corn) sold during this festival. It's a local specialty made of tender corn with a stick through the middle, and is covered with mayonnaise, ketchup, mustard and cheese.

Ahuachapán

Pok'omáme, "City of Oak Houses"
Pop. 87,000
100km from San Salvador

Ahuachapán Then

Ahuachapán sits in the geothermally active western reaches of El Salvador, where hot springs, fumaroles and geysers fill the air with the smell of sulphur. It's El Salvador's westernmost city and is one of the oldest and most densely populated in the country.

Pok'omáme Indians founded the city around the 5th century, evidenced by the many ceramic artifacts found nearby. At the end of the 15th century, the Pipil Indians conquered Ahuachapán but the Pok'omáme culture survived. A Spanish visitor noted in 1549 that while the male inhabitants spoke the "rich, sweet, harmonious tongue" of their Pipil conquerors, the women still communicated in their native Pok'omáme language. The Pok'omáme name, which describes the huge oak trees that once covered the area, has survived through the ages.

In 1821, the Battle of Espino erupted two kilometers north of town and resulted in the first victory for the young Republic of El Salvador in its fight for independence from Spain. In 1860 and again in 1937, Ahuachapán was devastated by earthquakes. By the early 20th century, the city had established a reputation as a center for coffee production.

During the 1980s, the owners of enormous local estates struggled to oppose any measure of land reform. When the government moved to confiscate any land holdings over 1,200 acres as required by law, some local landowners responded by forming their own private armies to defend their turf. Many of these private armies were better equipped than the government's forces.

Ahuachapán Now

A clock tower overlooks the kiosk in the middle of the plaza near the beautiful white Iglesia Asunción. The palm-lined road north to the Guatemalan border at Las Chinamas passes a lush middle-class neighborhood full of gardens. The kiosk in the main park serves drinks and snacks.

For those entering El Salvador from the west, Ahuachapán is the best place to spend a few days getting accustomed to the country. It is more relaxed than Santa Ana (except around the bus station) and has some good, inexpensive hotels. It's also within reach of a few secluded beaches to the south.

Accommodations

Casa Blanca Boarding House Built in traditional Spanish style, this hotel is a great place to spend a few days outside of San Salvador. A grand entrance leads into a colorful interior decorated with antiques and an attractive wooden ceiling. Flowers and plants fill a center courtyard that encloses a small fountain. The attached restaurant serves breakfast, lunch and dinner. *(Tel 443-1505; 8D $17.25-$20, all with private bath, hot water; laundry; 24hr checkout; restaurant)*

Hotel San José This hotel is at least as old as the friendly man who keeps it clean. The gate is locked at 10pm; after that, ring the bell. *(Tel 443-1820; 12 rooms $9.25-$13.75, all with private bath, fan; laundry; 11am checkout)*

Gran Rancho Hotel Rooms here seem a bit dated, but at least each has a fan. Musical groups play on Sundays. Seafood or meat dishes at the restaurant cost $2.75-$4. Many microbuses to the border and elsewhere pass by here, on the road to Hotel El Parador. If you're looking for this place and you arrive at the old arch, you've gone too far. *(1km outside of town toward Las Chinamas; tel 443-1820; 3S, 2S, 3T, 2 apartments $4.60 per person, all with private bath; laundry; pool; restaurant)*

Hotel El Parador While Casa Blanca has to be Ahuachapán's sentimental favorite, only El Parador offers a crocodile in a cage on the premises. Brand-new, colonial style with a swimming pool. The restaurant serves all meals, and a seafood plate will cost you $4-$7. Any bus or pickup to Chinamas passes by here. *(2km outside of town, to the right of the old arch on the road to Chinamas, 100m past Pauly's Restaurant; tel 443-0331; 9S, 2D $25-$30, all with private bath, hot water, TV, AC; laundry; 1pm checkout; restaurant, bar)*

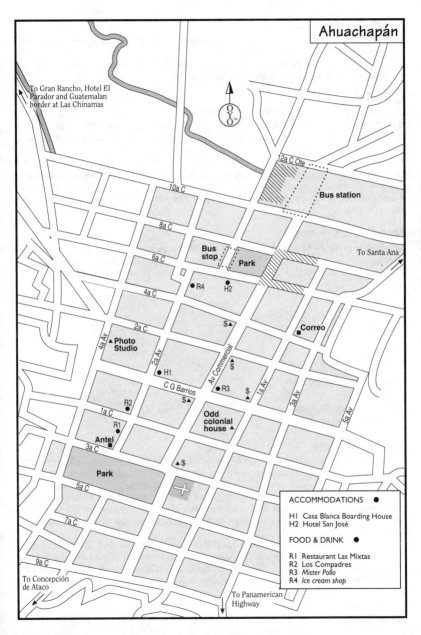

Ahuachapán

TO THE WEST

To Gran Rancho, Hotel El Parador and Guatemalan border at Las Chinamas

12a C Ote

Bus station

10a C

8a C

6a C

Bus stop

Park

To Santa Ana

4a C

● R4   ● H2

2a C

$▲

Correo

4a Av

▲ Photo Studio

2a Av

Av Commercial

▲
$

● H1

C G Barrios

● R3

$

1a Av

3a Av

5a Av

● R2

$▲

1a C

● R1

Odd colonial house ▲

Antel

3a C

▲ $

Park

5a C

7a C

9a C

To Concepción de Ataco

To Panamerican Highway

ACCOMMODATIONS ●

H1 Casa Blanca Boarding House
H2 Hotel San José

FOOD & DRINK ●

R1 Restaurant Las Mixtas
R2 Los Compadres
R3 Mister Pollo
R4 Ice cream shop

Food & Drink

Los Compadres Moderately-priced fast food such as hamburgers, pizza and sandwiches. A *típico de carne* is $2.25.

Las Mixtas A lively place that is packed at lunch. Pizza and sandwiches run $1 and up, and fruit juice choices are listed on the wall.

Details

■ **Buses: San Salvador (202, 204, 206),** until 8pm, 100km, 3hr 30min. **Santa Ana (210),** until 6pm, 40km, 2hr. **Sonsonate (249),** until 7pm, 55km, 2hr. When the Guatemalan border at Chinamas re-opens in 1995, buses and microbuses will once again run through there, every 10 min until 6pm, 30min.

■ **Festivals: February 5-14 (13)** Dulce Nombre de Jesús. Almost a mini-Olympics, with bicycle races, soccer matches, marathons, swimming, basketball, motocross and ping-pong.

■ **Sports: Soccer games** are played in the town stadium on Sundays, November through March.

Near Ahuachapán

Concepción de Ataco and the Cruz de Ataco A walk to this nearby town and mountain cross, about five kilometers south of Ahuachapán, takes about two hours in each direction. Along the way, you can take a dip in the rivers.

Apaneca

Nahuat, "River of the Wind"
Pop. 12,000
91km from San Salvador
15km from Sonsonate

Apaneca Now

Situated in the rolling hills of one of El Salvador's most important coffee-growing regions, Apaneca is clean and comfortable, the epitome of a quaint mountain town. Tiled-roof houses line the streets, and the large white church (which doubles as a seminary) has a great view of the countryside. Peaches and apples grow well in the fresh local climate and hills, and mountain lakes are within easy reach of a day's hike. Camping is sometimes allowed in local *haciendas;* just ask beforehand for permission to *acampar.*

With Las Cabañas de Apaneca, La Cocina de Mi Abuela and the picturesque surrounding countryside, Apaneca is ideal for a short mountain getaway. Apaneca's attractions are well-known, though, so both the "Cabins" and "Grandmother's Kitchen" could easily be filled with wealthy Salvadoran tourists on weekends.

Accommodations

Las Cabañas de Apaneca An architect owns this hotel and restaurant, and it shows. The entire complex, which houses a flower garden, is spotless and meticulously landscaped. Sturdy wood cabins straight out of the Swiss Alps, complete with bunk beds, have stunning views down the valley from individual porches. Six- and eight-person cabins are available in addition to the regular rooms. The restaurant serves traditional food under carved wood pillars. Breakfast with coffee is $2.85, while a grilled veal dinner costs $5.75. It's a great place to spend the weekend if there's space, but reservations are usually necessary a week in advance. *(Tel 479-0099; 4D $40, 1 quad $46, 7 cabins, all with private baths; 1pm checkout; restaurant Mon-Fri 11am-5pm, Sat 11am-9pm, Sun 8am-6pm)*

Food & Drink

La Cocina de Mi Abuela A national legend, La Cocina de Mi Abuela (Grandmother's Kitchen) was opened four years ago by a veterinarian and his mother. This large gourmet restaurant is a shrine to another age decorated with antique photographs, plates, railings and stained-glass windows. Thirty wooden tables are inside on a tiled floor, while a gorgeous flower garden with a fountain sits outside beside a cage full of monkeys. More tables wait outside, where the veranda is patrolled by troops of short-tempered ducks. Soups cost $3.50, full plates like lasagna $5.75. Specials include an "Indian chicken plate" and chicken soaked in *chicha*. Reservations may be necessary. *(Tel 428-0809; Sat 11-5, Sun 11-7)*

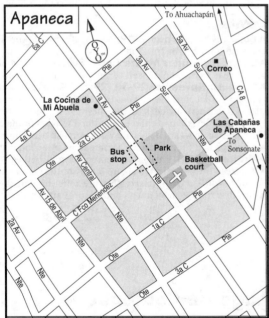

Hiking

Laguna Verde A good two-hour hike to the northeast of Apaneca, four kilometers through the forest to a lagoon. The land is privately-owned, and there are cabins in the area.

Laguna las Ninfas Another lagoon about two kilometers to the north near Cerro las Ninfas (1,756m), which is smaller than Laguna Verde and slightly closer. The forest is more spectacular than the lagoon itself.

El Congo

This town is the main transit point along the Panamerican Highway between San Salvador and Santa Ana at the turn-off for the Lago de Coatepeque and Cerro Verde. Fruit and vegetables from all over El Salvador and other Central American countries are sold here at restaurants that double as impressive produce stands.

A favorite stand is Merendero Paraíso Tropical, the last stop on the right side going toward Santa Ana. Try a fruit shake with milk and say hello to Martha Isabel Serrano, the lady who has run this place with her sons for years. She claims to have started the "fruit shake trend" back in the 1970s. *(Panamerican Highway 50km west of San Salvador and 12km east of Santa Ana)*

Cerro Grande de Apaneca   A beautiful nearby hike and climb. Head south about one kilometer to the Cantón Quezalapa to find this mountain, also known as Chichicatepec. From there it's about two hours to the peak at 1,816 meters.

Details

■ **Buses: Ahuachapán (249)**, every 15 min, 14km, 40min. **Sonsonate (249)**, every 15 min, 27km, 1hr 20min.
■ **Crafts: Artesanías Madre Tierra**, 800 meters east of Las Cabañas de Apaneca on the road to Sonsonate, sell ceramics and rough wood furniture.
■ **Festivals: November 29-30 (29)** San Andrés Apóstol. **December 24-25 (24)** Nacimiento del Niño Jesús. Features the Baile de la Garza (Dance of the Garza). The cast of characters includes three policemen, a mayor, a bride, a groom, a "rascal", an Indian and the *garza,* a child dressed in a wooden frame covered with a white sheet. Each character wears a specific wooden mask according to the character he or she represents, and they all dance accompanied by string instrumental music.
■ **Market:** Peaches are sold in September and October.
■ **Visitor's Information:** Pick up a copy of the green and black brochure *"Ecotour por la Cordillera de Apaneca"* (Nature tour through the Apaneca range) in town, which describes nearby towns and natural attractions.

Lago de Coatepeque

58km from San Salvador
20km from Santa Ana

The enormous, peaceful crater Lake of Coatepeque sits east of Cerro Verde and the Santa Ana and Izalco Volcanoes. This is where El Salvador's aristocrats come to chill out and play, either in private homes which monopolize the shoreline or at one of the two luxury hotels. The three huge mountains and the achingly blue water of the lake add up to one beautiful scene.

The road from the Panamerican Highway splits at the edge of the lake and turns to dirt. Since the road to the right is filled with private homes and doesn't have any passageways to the lake, head left to the hotels and semi-private beaches. A few *balnearios públicos* (semi-public beaches) near the Hotel Torremolino have access to the lake, and charge next to nothing for admission and parking.

If you didn't happen to bring your own jet-ski, you can still hire a boat for a tour of the lake. Find a captain at either hotel who will bring you to an isolated spot, but make sure that if he drops you off he'll return for you later. A trip all the way around the lake usually costs around $7 for a 30-minute ride. Some boats can carry up to 15 people, and large groups are much cheaper per person. A ride to Isla del Cerro costs more, but there you'll find that hot springs just beneath the surface of the lake turn the place into a stone-age hot tub.

Coatepeque is beautiful, but suffers from its popularity. The large, private houses make access to the lake almost too difficult to be worthwhile. There are places to swim for everybody else, but with crowds, buses and garbage to battle, the experience can be less than relaxing. To really enjoy Coatepeque, come during the week...or buy a house on the shore.

Accommodations

Hotel Torremolino This white colonial building offers patios, a clean pool and a large grassy area fronting the beach. The rooms are big but far from cheap. The restaurant has a great view of the lake and live Latin music on weekends. A *mojarra deshuezada* (boneless stuffed fish) runs $5-$9, and a *sopa de mariscos* is yours for $5.75. (*About 3km left of the fork in the road, the first of two hotels; tel 346-9437; 10S $23, 5T $28.75, some with AC, all with private baths; laundry; pool; restaurant 8am-8pm*)

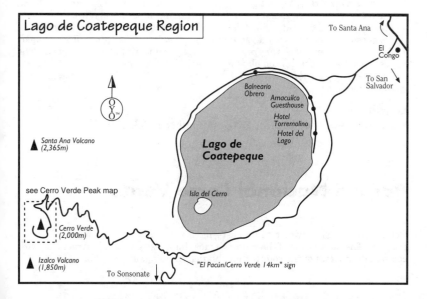

Lago de Coatepeque Region

To Santa Ana

El Congo

To San Salvador

Balneario Obrero

Amacuilco Guesthouse

Hotel Torremolino

Hotel del Lago

▲ Santa Ana Volcano (2,365m)

Lago de Coatepeque

see Cerro Verde Peak map

Isla del Cerro

▲ Cerro Verde (2,000m)

▲ Izalco Volcano (1,850m)

To Sonsonate

"El Pacún/Cerro Verde 14km" sign

> **"We play for all the candidates that arrive here. In this country it is best to be as neutral as possible and make sure you're in the good graces of whoever has power."**
>
> — Band member, on which political party his band plays for

VOICES FROM THE WAR

Hotel del Lago The 120-year-old Hotel del Lago is the oldest hotel in the country and once served as a quiet lakeside retreat for harried Salvadoran presidents. Until remodeling plans are carried out it will remain one of the most charming. Older parts of the hotel have big wooden doors and colorful tile floors. The restaurant is straight out of an old movie, with high ceilings and *merengue* music on Sunday afternoons. Try the *sorbete con merengue* (the desert, not the music) or a bowl of *sopa de cangrejos* (crab soup) for $4. Other dishes, including fresh fish, are $6-$9. *(4km from the fork in the road; tel 346-9511; 16D $23-$35, all with private bath, fans; laundry; 2 pools; restaurant 7am-9pm)*

Amacuilco Guest House Amacuilco is very well maintained but it feels weird and spooky, with an occult atmosphere and creepy decor. Also, for some strange reason, the owners only welcome foreigners here. The eating area has a floor of wooden boards that look out over the lake, where they serve meals for $1.75-$3. The pool sits next to a small grassy area and a small outdoor library. *(100 meters north of the Hotel Torremolino; 3D $14, 2 larger rooms $17.25; laundry; pool)*

Balneario Obrero A typical government-run resort with a concrete wharf and trash everywhere. To spend the night here you need permission from the Labor Ministry in San Salvador (Blvd del Ejército, tel 295-0817). If you manage to get permission (either in San Salvador or by sweet-talking the *balneario's* manager) the cabins are free, but they're not anything you'd want to pay for anyway. The restaurant serves a chicken plate for $1.50. *(Near the fork in the road, to the left; tel 346-9402; 30 cabins, all with 4 beds, private bath, table and chairs; restaurant 6am-7pm)*

Details
■ **Buses: Santa Ana (220)** via El Congo, until 6pm, 20km, 1hr.

Parque Nacionál Cerro Verde

70 km from San Salvador

Cerro Verde is El Salvador at its best—forests, mountains, volcanoes and clean, crisp air. The park is one of the country's most impressive natural attractions, with commanding views of the countryside, hiking, camping, and a comfortable hotel.

Half of the beauty of Cerro Verde is the 2,000-meter ascent of the mountain of the same name. The road up, red with volcanic soil, was finished only in 1990 after six years of effort. The project was supposed to have been completed in the early 1970s, but construction funds were repeatedly embezzled.

The first half of the climb reveals the panorama of the Lago de Coatepeque to the northeast. Soon the air grows chilly and you can see the huge Santa Ana Volcano to the north. By the time you've put on your sweater near the top of the road, the famous black cone of the Izalco Volcano comes into view, followed by the Hotel de la Montaña.

The hotel and a parking lot sit atop the thickly-forested Cerro Verde, with various hiking paths leading off in all directions. Izalco looms just off the hotel's balcony, almost close enough to touch, and views of the Lago de Coatepeque and the Santa Ana Volcano are only a short hike away. You can climb either volcano in a reasonably strenuous day hike. An orchid garden near the hotel is usually open, there's a playground with a tree house for children and a few small *comedores* sell snacks. The air is clean and cool—even cold at night—and the views are unbeatable.

Flora and Fauna

The high-altitude forests of Cerro Verde shelter more species of plants and wildlife than any other place in the country. The woods are filled with squirrels, weasels, rabbits, porcupines, moles and armadillos, and an occasional mountain lion has been known to visit. There are many species of birds at Cerro Verde as well, including toucans, 14 varieties of hummingbirds (one as light as three grams), the *guardabarranco* (known for its beautiful chirping) and *xaras,* with black heads and iridescent blue bodies and wings.

In addition to the orchids in the orchidarium, another type of high-altitude plant called the epiphyte is common to Cerro Verde. Look for plants that resemble the tops of pineapples perched on the limbs and trunks of trees. Instead of drawing nutrients from their host, epiphytes can live off of the water and organic debris that accumulate in the crevices between their leaves or draw enough moisture to survive from the clouds that roll through the forest.

Hiking & Camping

Follow an easy path through the woods from the parking lot to a lookout over the Lago de Coatepeque, about ten kilometers to the northeast, and another over the Santa Ana Volcano. Camping is allowed near the parking lot.

Santa Ana Volcano Halfway around the lookout path, another trail leads north towards the Santa Ana Volcano. Santa Ana, also known as Llamatepec, or "Father Hill," is El Salvador's largest volcano (2,365m). At the top are four small craters superimposed on a larger, older crater, and a green lagoon filled with sulfuric water. The volcano erupted three times in the early part of this century—always at the same time as Izalco—and is considered active. A moderately strenuous three-hour hike will bring you to the top. The trail passes by the Finca San Blass, a private farm where you can camp if you get permission.

Izalco Volcano Izalco is a geological oddity, one of the youngest volcanoes in the world. In 1770, a smoking hole in the middle of a farmer's field slowly began to burp out volcanic rocks. Over the next two centuries, Izalco grew continuously and spewed enough lava to be named the "Lighthouse of the Pacific" by sailors who navigated by its glow. Native tribes, on the other hand, called Izalco the "Inferno of the Spanish." The eruptions stopped in 1966—just as construction on the Hotel de la Montaña was finished.

Today, the perfectly-shaped cone is 1,900 meters high without a speck of green on its barren slopes. The trail to the top begins 200 meters down the road from the hotel, and is a difficult climb over volcanic rocks. You can reach the rim in about four hours and wave at everybody back at the hotel.

Lago de Coatepeque A ten-kilometer hike leads to Lago de Coatepeque, the blue jewel visible from the trail around the hotel. The trailhead is called El Jicote and is four kilometers up the road to Cerro Verde from its intersection with the road around the lake from El Congo. The trail leads downhill towards the lake and is easy to miss. Look for it on the right if you're heading toward the top, a little less than a kilometer around the bend from the Lago de Coatepeque viewpoint.

Accommodations

Hotel de la Montaña The Hotel de la Montaña is the only hotel on Cerro Verde, which is fine if you can afford it and don't mind a government-run hotel. Lava rocks dot the walls and paths and a friendly staff keeps the flower gardens tidy.

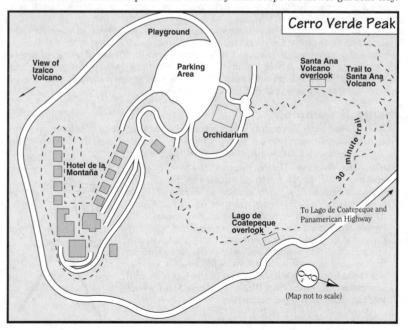

Cerro Verde Peak

Playground

Parking Area

View of Izalco Volcano

Santa Ana Volcano overlook

Trail to Santa Ana Volcano

Orchidarium

30 minute trail

Hotel de la Montaña

Lago de Coatepeque overlook

To Lago de Coatepeque and Panamerican Highway

(Map not to scale)

Ten rooms overlook the Izalco cone, and all the rooms have fireplaces which supplement the unpredictable hot water supply, although you have to ask for wood. A glass-walled restaurant serves excellent food within sight of the volcano. A full breakfast is $2 and dinner runs from $5 to $6. The hotel is very popular, and May and June are the best months to come. Reserve a week in advance for weekday stays and two weeks in advance for a weekend stay; reservations should be made through ISTU (tel 222-3241). Prices are higher on weekends and for rooms with a view of the volcano. *(20 rooms, $25/$37.50, additional bed $9.50, all with private bath; noon checkout; restaurant; cafeteria; bar)*

Details

■ **Buses:** If the bus is your only option, plan to spend the night on the mountain or to leave early. Since a connecting bus will probably be necessary, be sure not to get stuck in between. From Santa Ana, bus **348** transits El Congo and continues on to Cerro Verde. From Sonsonate or the south, it's a bit more complicated. Ask the driver of buses along the Panamerican Highway to drop you off at Puerto Negras, six kilometers past Armenia and next to a Texaco gas station. Then take a bus to El Pacún, near the "Cerro Verde 14 km" sign. Finally, hop on any bus going to the top of the mountain.

Santa Ana

Santa Ana

Pop. 240,000
63km from San Salvador

Santa Ana Then

El Salvador's second-largest city sits in the Valley of Cihuatehuacán on the northeast edge of the slopes of the Santa Ana Volcano. This temperate, fertile area has been inhabited for a long time. Pok'omáme tribes first settled here around the 5th or 6th century. Pipils arrived from the north five centuries later, absorbing some elements of the Pok'omáme culture and erasing others, including the language.

Just as the movement for independence was gaining momentum in the early 19th century, Santa Ana was beginning to prosper through its burgeoning coffee industry. When forced to choose sides in the fight for independence, many of the local gentry were content with the status quo and swore loyalty to the king of Spain.

In 1811, however, citizens of Santa Ana joined with other nearby towns to battle royal troops and called for the abolition of taxes on tobacco and *aguardiente,* a popular sugarcane liquor. On September 21, 1821, the people of Santa Ana learned, via mail, that the movement for independence had succeeded. When the good news reached the crowd that was waiting in the main plaza, celebrations erupted that lasted for days.

The 19th century was hard on the city, although the population continued to increase. In 1822, Guatemalan forces occupied Santa Ana in an effort to force El Salvador into the new Mexican empire. José Arce eventually succeeded in recap-

TO THE WEST

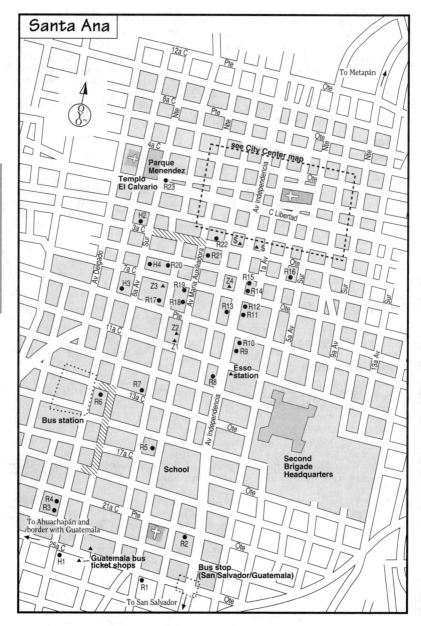

Santa Ana

To Metapán

see City Center map

Parque
Menendez

Templo
El Calvario

R23

H2

R22

R21

H4   R20

H3   Z3   Z19

R17   R18

Z2

Z1

R7

13a C

R6

Bus station

R5

17a C

School

R4
R3

To Ahuachapán and
border with Guatemala

H1

25a C

Guatemala bus
ticket shops

R2

To San Salvador

R1

Bus stop
(San Salvador/Guatemala)

Second
Brigade
Headquarters

Esso
station

R8

R9
R10

R11
R12

R13

R14
R15

R16

Z4

Av María Auxiliadora

Av Independencia

C Libertad

1a Av

Av Delgado

5a Av

9a Av

13a Av

3a Av

Centuries ago, Santa Ana was known as the "City of Priestesses." The area's early resident tried to influence nature and the spirits through *tehuas* or mystic mediators. *Tehuas* occupied an important place in pre-Columbian society. Sometimes they cast beneficial spells to help and protect people; other times they interpreted signs to predict the future.

turing the city. Revolutions were suppressed in 1837 and 1839. In 1863, Rafael Carrera, president of Guatemala, occupied Santa Ana with a force of 6,000 soldiers and used the city as a base to attack Salvadoran fortifications at Coatepeque. In spite of all this, Santa Ana continued to grow and thrive. By the turn of the century, the city counted 30,000 inhabitants.

Santa Ana wasn't terrorized with guerrilla attacks during the early part of the civil war, but it did suffer other problems. Unemployment hovered around 50 percent in the city for much of the 1980s and was as high as 70 percent in the countryside.

Wealthy plantation owners and local business owners supported ARENA and some funded death squads. In July 1981, ten employees of a circus—mostly clowns—were murdered by a local death squad.

Santa Ana Now

The *segunda ciudad* (second city) is second only in size, with open streets, lavish national theater and an abundance of stylish restaurants. Sharp green hills surround the city, with the cones of Cerro Verde and the Izalco and Santa Ana Volcanoes further to the south. It's still a coffee town, surrounded by many plantations where workers till the rich volcanic soil.

Santa Ana has retained more of its colonial heritage than most cities this size, and is therefore more pleasant than the country's choking capital. Wide, clean streets pass between old buildings in surprisingly good condition, most are under two stories high and painted in pastel colors. The low buildings leave lots of blue sky that gives the city a spacious feel. Local artisans are famous for their leather goods.

A given on any itinerary west of San Salvador, Santa Ana enjoys a cool climate and an impressively large fruit market. Come here to relax, enjoy the city and maybe even have dinner at a fancy restaurant. The hiking, camping and boating to the south are among the best in the country, and both the Lago de Coatepeque and the Guatemalan border are within easy reach. Santa Ana's architecture is unmatched anywhere else in the country, especially the cathedral and national theater. You could while away an entire afternoon admiring the colonial houses—in particular those around 4a C between 6a and 10a Av—peeking through the grillwork into the gardens and enormous courtyards.

Accommodations

Hotel Sahara The top of the line for Santa Ana. Clean but a little cramped, this place was built by ex-president José Napoleón Duarte in 1952. *(3a C Pte between 8a and 10a Av Sur; tel 447-8865; 8S $18.50, 7D $25, 3T $32, all with private bath, cable TV; laundry; restaurant 7am-9pm)*

Internacional Hotel-Inn A cramped but clean and friendly place. Ana Rivas is the pleasant owner, and she runs a tight ship. The restaurant next door is run by her sisters. You can hop a bus on its way from Ahuachapán to San Salvador right out front. *(25a C Pte and 10a Av Sur, tel 440-0810; 8S $11.50, 4D $20, 2T $28.75, all with private bath; laundry; noon checkout; restaurant)*

Hotel Libertad (City Center map) José Valmoré García, the owner, will show you to your spacious room. There's a nice view of the bell tower from the stairs, but the rest of this hotel could use a thorough scrubbing and new fixtures. You can put your own locks on the doors, which is probably a good idea. *(Next to the cathedral; tel 441-2358; 6S $8, 6D $11.50, 6T $14.25, most with private bath; laundry; noon checkout)*

Hotel Livingston The concrete rooms are run-down but at least the sheets are clean. Decent for the budget traveler. *(9a C Pte and 10a Av; tel 441-1801; 8S $4.60, 12D $13.80, all with private bath; parking; 24hr checkout)*

Hotel Roosvelt The sign is misspelled, but anyway it's a spacious, open place with old rooms. *(8a Av Sur between 5a and 7a C Pte; tel 441-1702; 2S $5.75, 1D $20, most with private bath; 24hr checkout)*

Food & Drink

Café Amigo (City Center map) One of a handful of spots around town that serves as a gathering spot for Santa Ana's recovering alcoholics. Since everyone knows each other, the café can be an interesting place to talk over coffee and cigars. *(8am-12:30pm, 3-11pm)*

Cheese Shop (City Center map) A small light-green place that sells different kinds of cheese. *(C Libertad and 4a Av Sur)*

Kiko's Pizza/Rosti Pollo Sixteen-inch pizzas for $8.25, $0.70 per topping. A chicken dinner to go will run you $6, but a quarter chicken with chips and a Coke is only $2. *(Av Independencia; 9:30am-2pm, 4-8pm)*

Ky Jau (City Center map) The best chow mein in town for $3.50. Other dishes range up to $8.50. *(C Libertad between 4a and 6a Av; 11:30am-9pm)*

Las Brasas Steakhouse (City Center map) Fourteen tables fill this clean restaurant with a grill in the middle of the dining room. A tenderloin steak costs $5.75. *(C Libertad between 4a and 6a Av Sur; 11:30am-2pm, 5-8pm)*

Los Horcones (City Center map) Hanging banana plants and bamboo columns give Los Horcones a definite jungle atmosphere true to its name (The Tree

Trunks). Food is served on clay plates at interesting wooden tables with odd-shaped benches. A delicious onion soup is $1.70, and a *carne asada* costs $2.40. Top it all off with a fruit shake for $0.80. Vegetarian dishes are also available. Eat upstairs on the terrace where there are more tables and a great view of the main plaza. *(Across from the church on 1a Av; 9:30am-10pm; tel 441-3250)*

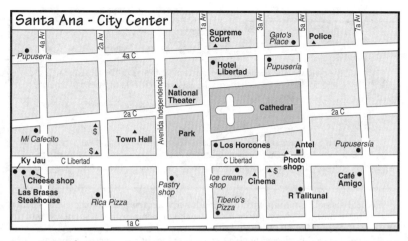

Santa Ana - City Center

Lover's Steak House An unpretentious place with a red and white exterior and Coke ads drawn on the wall. Meat, rice and salad cost $0.75. *(Av María Auxiliadora and 25a C; 11am-9pm)*

Regis Restaurant This high-quality *cafetería* has been around since 1972. Seafood plates can cost up to $10, but an economy plate with potatoes, salad and soup is yours for $2.85. Daily soup and seafood specials. *(9a C Pte and 6a Av Sur; 8am-10pm)*

Restaurant El Tucán El Tucán was born during the war when the owner and cook, Rene Lobato, decided to open a restaurant where Salvadorans could go to enjoy the food rather than just fill up or get drunk. Rene is a nice fellow willing to answer hard questions about his country. His restaurant is formal, decorated with Salvadoran paintings and leather strap chairs. The second floor has romantic lighting, hanging plants and a balcony. Main dishes are $5-$11.50, and the onion soup is excellent. *(Av Independencia and 9a C Ote; 11:30am-3pm, 5:30-10:30pm)*

Restaurant Freddy's A red tile roof and Pepsi and Coke ads make Freddy's an easy place to spot. Inside through the wooden gate is a bar and an enclosed patio with 60 tables. This spotless establishment serves $5-$8 plates and hosts musical groups on weekends, playing everything from *salsa* to ballads. *(Av María Auxiliadora between 15a and 17a C Pte; 11am-11pm)*

Restaurant Los Patios The entrance to Santa Ana's classiest restaurant is a large, semi-circular wooden door that opens into a shaded interior courtyard decorated with hanging plants, a fountain and a stone garden. This stylish, laid-back place has over 200 seats at 50 tables and golden walls. Don't be confused by all the colonial styling—they take credit cards here. Plates start at $5 and climb to $9 for a 20oz T-bone steak. *(21a C Pte between Av Independencia and María Auxiliadora; 11am-3pm, 5-10pm)*

Restaurant Talitunal (City Center map) Edwin Maldonado is a surgeon who opened Talitunal (Nahuat for "Sun and Land") after becoming a vegetarian for health reasons. He gave up traditional "chemical" medicine in—of all places—

And Wash Behind Your Ears

During the civil war, the US didn't have any combat troops in El Salvador, but it did allow some advisers to operate there. The advisers were told to live by two quick rules for the duration of their stay:

1. Don't give advice.
2. Don't get shot.

In reality, US advisers acted as they pleased. They carried guns and were frequently on the fringes of battle scenes, helping the army to coordinate its forces. If they became too closely involved in the war, though, they were recalled and immediately replaced.

---

medical school, came up with a recipe for a vegetarian hamburger and opened this little haunt eight years ago. The soybean hamburgers are chewy, but the natural bread for $0.90 can't be beat. The menu is mainly vegetarian and changes every day. Every healthy goodie you could ever desire is for sale here, including medicinal plants, honey, and natural pastas. Some not-so-healthy but delectable pastries are also very inexpensive. *(9am-7pm)*

Toto's Pizza A big modern fast-food joint with a salad bar ($2.85 per trip) and 16-inch pizzas for $8. *(11am-9pm)*

Sights

Santa Ana Cathedral (City Center map) The most famous cathedral in El Salvador was begun in 1905 in a neo-gothic style. The imposing white facade is currently undergoing restoration; inside are 13 naves decorated with images dating back to the 16th century. A high ceiling and worn wooden floor leads to a white altar. The pink and grey columns look like marble, but they're actually painted concrete.

National Theater (City Center map) Santa Ana's gorgeous wood theater was begun in 1902, and still recalls the city's heyday at the turn of the century, when coffee export taxes were earmarked for its construction. When the national theater in San Salvador burned down in 1910, all the theater companies moved to Santa Ana, to the delight of the city's art lovers. Things soon took a turn for the worse, though, and during the economic crisis of the 1930s it was used as a (gasp!) movie theater, which it remained until 1978 when serious repairs were begun. A restoration project funded by the Mexican government is currently underway, and should be completed by the end of the decade.

A set of grand wooden stairs leads to the inside of the theater, which is being refurbished but is still an impressive example of what can be done with quality woods and a whole lot of taste. Stylized tiles line a foyer with maroon wooden columns supporting a ceiling painted in pastel blue and rose. The theater itself is also maroon, with three terraces and balconies. Notice the wooden railing on the third terrace and the ceiling paintings of Mozart, Beethoven, Strauss and Tchaikovsky. Below the stage, three large basins of water create an echo that allows actors' voices to resonate.

During town festivals, the theater usually hosts art exhibitions. Performances and cultural events are also held occasionally; check with the desk for a schedule or call Yuri Ben-Iosef in San Salvador (see San Salvador).

Templo El Calvario A figure of Jesus in purple robes carrying the cross stands inside this church in Parque Menéndez. The walls are lined with detailed sculptures, and the image of Jesus on the door is repeated above the altar.

Shopping

Luís Pedro Leather Shop A small boutique with leather shoes and bags made in Santa Ana. Dress shoes run about $15, belts $18 and purses $70. Everything is high-quality. *(Av María Auxiliadora and 11a C Pte; 9am-12pm and 2:30-5pm)*

Sergio Acevedos, Bootmaker If you want a truly unique souvenir from El Salvador (and have a few extra *colones*), take home a pair of Sr. Acevedos' hand-tooled leather boots, better than anything in Texas. Sergio is a legend in Santa Ana, and if you speak Spanish, it's great to spend a few hours here chatting with him. Pick the pair of boots you like from one of the magazines he has lying around, and he and his crew will custom-make them for you using any type of leather or reptile skin they have on hand (you pick that too).

Regular leather boots start around $90, and complicated orders take up to two weeks. Sergio has been practicing his craft for 61 years, ever since he started his apprenticeship in 1933. Today he fills many orders from the US embassy. The best and only way to see his work is to arrive when other people's boots are ready and waiting to be picked up. Trust us—they're incredible. *(Av María Auxiliadora #40, between 9a and 11a C Pte, a green shop with small Coke sign; open around 8am-8pm)*

Details

■ **Domestic Buses:** Make sure you get your ticket at the correct kiosk, since there are three and each sells tickets to different destinations. **Ahuachapán (210)**, every 15 min until 5pm, 34km, 1hr 10min. **Cerro Verde (248)**, 8:40, 10:20am, 1:40, 3:20pm, 47km, 2hr. **Chalchuapa/Tazumal (218)**, every 10 min until 7pm, 13km, 40min. **Lago de Coatepeque (220)**, every 25 min until 5pm, 28km, 1hr 15min. **Metapán (235)**, every 15 min until 6:20pm, 45km, 1hr 30min. **San Cristóbal (236)** via Candelaría de la Frontera, every 15 min until 7pm, 32km, 1hr 10min. **San Salvador (201)**, every 15 min until 5:50 pm, 63km, 2hr. Direct every 7 min, 1hr 30min. **Sonsonate (216)**, every 15 min until 5:40pm, 40km, 1hr 10min.

■ **Festivals: July 18-26 (25)** Señora Santa Ana.

■ **International Buses:** Buses to Guatemala are run by five different companies originating in San Salvador. They all cost the same, but some have AC and bathrooms. Note: the Las Chinamas border crossing to Guatemala City has been closed because the bridge was destroyed in the war. When the bridge is repaired, bus routes will once again pass through Las Chinamas. San Cristóbal is currently being used as a crossing point, even

A series of strong earthquakes and chicken pox epidemics in the early 18th century wrought havoc on the population of Santa Ana. In a desperate cry for relief, the town fathers invoked the Virgen del Rosario, promising her a great festival every year in exchange for her protection. Over the years, the festival has expanded from nine to fifteen days.

though it adds an extra hour to the journey. **Guatemala City (415)**, every hour until 6pm, 4hr 30min, $4.75.

■ **Sports:** Soccer games are played in the stadium on Sundays.

Near Santa Ana

Turicentro Sihuatehuacán Six and a half kilometers east of Santa Ana you'll find three pools, including one Olympic and one kiddie-size, along with tennis courts, restaurants, picnic areas, sports fields and an outdoor theater. Admission gives you access to changing rooms and lockers. *(Catch bus 51a or 51b between 25a C Pte and 10a Av Nte, or in the Central Park in front of the cathedral; 8am-6pm; $0.75 per person; parking $0.75)*

Texistepeque

Nahuat, "Place of Snails"
Pop. 26,000
80km from San Salvador
16km from Santa Ana

Texistepeque Then

Like many early Pok'omáme cities in El Salvador, Texistepeque was taken over by the Pipils in the late 13th century. By the beginning of the 18th century, the town was still purely indigenous without a single *mestizo* family (much less any pure Spanish) in residence.

Texistepeque Now

The approach to Texistepeque from Santa Ana to the south isn't too attractive, except for the volcanic cones that jut out of the surrounding plains like huge earth pyramids. The new road has three lanes, but someone apparently forgot to decide which direction traffic in the middle lane is supposed to travel, which results in many high-stakes games of chicken. The road passes a terrible landfill on the way to the town's ramshackle dirt-road entrance that is decorated with political graffiti.

Everyone seems to know everyone else in Texistepeque. The atmosphere is very familiar—many of the restaurants aren't even marked as restaurants—but the town is anything but closed. Residents, including many who have lived in the United States, are eager to talk to the infrequent traveler who passes this way. There aren't any hotels yet, but at least one is planned for the near future. If you're looking for a place off the beaten track to meet everyday Salvadorans and hear about their lives, stop off here on your way north to the Bosque Montecristo, the Lago de Güija and the Honduran border at Anguiatú.

Food & Drink

Drive-In El Viajero Fast food in the Shell gas station at the entrance to town, with sandwiches and hot dogs for $1. *(7am-6pm)*

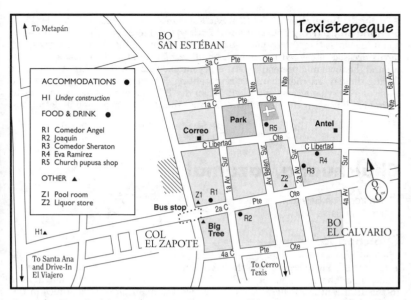

Joaquín Fast food in the $1 range. Set in a small house—you can peek inside it and the others attached to the same courtyard. *(4:30-9pm)*

Comedor Angel The owner, Coralia Cortez, will whip you up something up for breakfast, lunch or dinner—you just have to ask.

Comedor Sheraton This place has a terrace but no sign. Look for the pink door next to the blue house. *Pupusas* for $0.10, or a beef steak for $1.15. *(6-8am, 11am-8pm)*

Don Eva Ramírez A local favorite that serves pig's foot soup with yucca, pumpkin and plantain on Mondays. Other more palatable daily specials include *lomo relleno* (meat stuffed with vegetables) on Thursdays and stuffed bread with chicken on Saturdays.

Church Pupusa Shop Serves *pupusas,* milk tapioca and bread cake on weekends. Belinda and Isela Dalila, the two bubbling girls who work here, love to talk about their town.

Hiking
Cerro Texis A.k.a. Cerro Huevo, a.k.a Cerro Piedra, this hill goes by many names but you can't miss it three blocks southeast of Texistepeque.

Details
■ **Buses: Metapán (235)**, every 15 min until 7:10pm, 25km, 50min. **San Salvador (201a)**, every 2 hrs until 3:25pm, 83 km, 2hr 45min. **Santa Ana (235, 235a)**, every 20 min until 5:35pm, 16km, 40min.

■ **Festivals: December 25-27 (26)** San Estéban and the Virgen of Belén de Güija. **Semana Santa (Holy Thursday and Friday)** On Holy Monday the town presents a skit known as the "Talciguines." According to tradition, the Talciguines are seven devils dressed in colored tunics with handkerchiefs around their heads, who run around the town and pretend to beat everyone they meet with a whip. At one point during the day, another character representing Jesus shows up wearing a purple tunic and carrying a cross and a bell. When the Talciguines meet Jesus, they try to whip him, but when He shows them the cross they fall to the ground in defeat.

Chalchuapa/Tazumal

78km from San Salvador
14km from Santa Ana

Chalchuapa

Chalchuapa was the center of El Salvador's early Pok'omáme civilization. In the 15th century, Pipils moved into the area and forced the Pok'omámes to leave for Guatemala. The city is on the road to Guatemala and was repeatedly fought over in the 19th century. Federal armies occupied the main plaza three times in the 1820s, and in 1851 Guatemalan troops stormed the town.

In spite of its bloody history, Chalchuapa today isn't much to fight over. The streets are narrow and dusty, and the Church of Santiago looks completely bombed out. Sleep in Santa Ana and come here for the day.

Tazumal Ruins

The ruins of Tazumal are the most famous and best-studied ruins in El Salvador. They're won't blow you away, but the view from the top of the surrounding countryside is worth the climb.

■ **History.** The Pacific coastal belt between Tapachula, Mexico and the Río Lempa in El Salvador was the cradle of the oldest civilization in Mesoamerica. Tazumal is an ancient site which, according to estimates, has been populated for the past 3,200 years. Native tribes were living in this area as early as 1200 BC, although the earliest phases of construction didn't begin until around 500 BC.

The site changed hands more than once and was linked through trade to other civilizations throughout Central America. Ceramic remains found at Tazumal indicate a possible link with the Mexican civilization of Teotihuacán. Mayan objects have been found which date to the 7th and 10th centuries AD, and other artifacts show a Pipil influence.

Excavations carried out between 1942 and 1954 revealed two different building complexes. The older one, known as mound number one, is sometimes compared to the main mound of the ruins of San Andrés. It consists of a rectangular terraced platform 23 meters high, crowned by a pyramidal temple. The structure probably served as both a sanctuary and as an astronomical observatory, and archaeological evidence indicates that it endured as many as 14 phases of construction.

The recently-discovered mound number two, situated immediately to the west of mound number one, is similar. Though the mounds appear to be united, they are actually separate structures. Archeologists have also unearthed part of a court once used to play *tatchi,* a pre-Columbian ball game. This court, most of which is covered by the cemetery next door, is difficult to distinguish.

A small museum next to the excavation is well-organized, with many ceramics on display as well as a model of the entire site. English and Spanish captions describe both the objects and the laborious process of excavations and preservation. Cheap ceramics are sold at the entrance, but don't believe anyone who tells you they have "original" artifacts, since everything is either in a museum or covered in concrete.

A well-known stela called the "Queen of Tazumal," now in the National Museum in San Salvador, was found here. The three-meter high image bears both male and female features and has the head of an animal, probably a monkey. Many other artifacts found at Tazumal are also displayed at the National Museum, which unfortunately has been closed since the 1986 earthquake.

In spite of its reputation, the site is disappointing, especially if you've just been to Guatemala or Honduras. Although excavation is still underway, what little that has been uncovered is encased in concrete. At sunset, though, when you can still see the structure's shape but the concrete fades and the crowds are gone, the ruins take on the glow of another century. *(11a Av Sur, a 10-minute walk east of town; Tues-Sun 9-5; admission free)*

Details

■ **Buses: Ahuachapán (202, 406)**, every 7 min until 6pm, 18, 15min. **San Salvador (202, 406, 456)**, every 7 min until 6pm, 78km, 1hr 15min. **Santa Ana (210, 218, 277)**, every 15 min until 6pm, 14km, 45min.

Metapán

Nahuat, "River of Agava"
Pop. 72,700
111km from San Salvador
40km from Santa Ana

Metapán Then

Metapán, in El Salvador's northwest corner, is an ancient town that has adapted well to the 20th century. Descendants of the Maya-Chorti have inhabited the area since the 13th century. By the time the Spanish arrived in the 16th century, Pipils had come to dominate Metapán, though locals spoke a dialect that included some Maya-Chorti words. Metapán was among the first cities to follow the lead of Father Delgado as he led the fight for independence from Spain in November 1811. At the time, the people of Metapán rioted against the government, stoned the house of the Spanish mayor and threatened to lynch anyone who didn't support their cause.

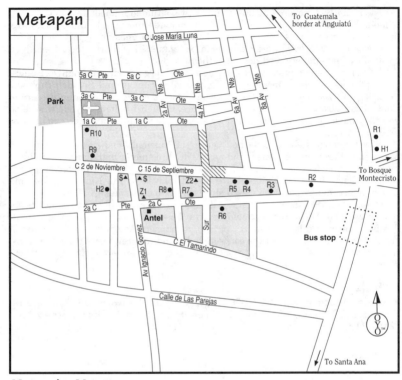

Metapán Now

Today, the second-largest city in the department of Santa Ana prospers from its mining and ranching industries. The main plaza is surrounded by tall palm trees and you'll hear music and see cowboy hats everywhere. Metapán has a few more restaurants than most cities of its size and at least one good hotel. The restaurant and the town's proximity to Bosque Montecristo, the Lago de Güija and the Honduran border make Metapán a convenient stop, either on your way out of the country or just to explore the area.

Accommodations

Hotel San José At Metapán's best hotel, carnivores will love the *Corazón de Lomito al Carbón*, 12 oz of grilled steak for $9. *(Tel 442-0556; 15S $17.25, 15D $23, all with private bath, TV, AC; restaurant 9am-9pm)*

ACCOMMODATIONS ●
H1 Hotel San José
H2 *Hospedaje Recinas*

FOOD & DRINK ●

R1 Restaurant Diamond
R2 *Ice cream shop*
R3 *Los Bocaditos*
R4 *Restaurant Milano*
R5 *Pastry store*
R6 *Multidelicias*
R7 *Pollo Kentucky*
R8 *Sorbetería El Polar*
R9 *Restaurant Rincón de Pelón*
R10 *Pastry shop*

OTHER ▲

Z1 Supermarket
Z2 Supermarket

Food & Drink

Pollo Kentucky A 3-piece meal costs $2.65. *(7:30am-9pm)*

Restaurant Milano As Italian as rural El Salvador gets, with Latin background music and pasta for $2.30. *(8am-12pm)*

Restaurant El Diamond Friendly types run this open-air restaurant next to the Hotel San José. Plates run around $4.00. *(9am-9pm)*

Multidelicias A pizzeria and pastry store with clean white tables, green chairs and a good atmosphere. Pizza costs just $5, and pastries are $0.20 or less. *(10am-9pm)*

Sorbetería El Polar Serves ice cream, breakfast or lunch (or ice cream *for* breakfast or lunch). *(7:30am-8:30pm)*

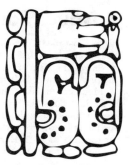

Sights

Church of San Pedro This white colonial church with beautiful red doors, which vaguely resembles a yellow doll house, dates from 1740. The organ hasn't worked for ages, though, and today is home to several bats. Also inside are images of saints who gaze down from above and stand vigil from within glass cases decorated with gold-painted wood. Below the church are catacombs which can be entered through a trap door in the floor of the main nave. People hid here during the civil war when the town was bombed.

Hiking

A number of hiking opportunities, compliments of the area's overactive geology, lie directly south of Metapán along the road to Texistepeque and Santa Ana.

Cerro Metapán Directly southwest of Metapán, this 640-meter hill overlooks the Laguna Metapán, a small companion lake to the Lago de Güija in a valley formed by ancient lava flows.

San Diego Volcano (790 m) A few kilometers south of Metapán on the shores of the Lago de Güija, San Diego has a well-formed crater at its summit.

Cerro El Desagüe (460 m) South of the San Diego Volcano, El Desagüe also overlooks the lake. It's smaller but closer to the road, near kilometer 102.

Details

■ **Buses: Anguiatú/Guatemalan border (211a)**, every 30 min, 12km, 30min. **San Salvador (201a)**, until 5:45pm, every 10 min, 111km, 4hr. **Santa Ana (235)**, every 15 min, 40km, 1hr 30min.

■ **Festivals: June 25-29 (28)** San Pedro. **October 25-November 5** Todos los Santos. **December 16-26** Virgen de Perpetuo Socorro. Fifteen masses, called *misas juradas*, are celebrated in this ten-day festival. By tradition, each mass is sponsored by a particular local family, as long as family members survive. According to legend, an ancestor of each of the families promised the Virgen that they would observe these masses in exchange for protection from cholera.

Bosque Montecristo

Almost lost in the clouds of the Central American highlands, Montecristo is one of El Salvador's last remaining regions of unspoiled wilderness beauty. The park is El Salvador's slice of the larger international park of El Trifinio, which straddles the area where El Salvador, Honduras and Guatemala converge.

Montecristo has escaped the deforestation that has ravaged so much of the rest of El Salvador's surface, and it's reassuring to see that it is so well-maintained— maybe it's because the three countries meet here and are competing for the nicest section of forest, or maybe it's just too hard to reach. Regardless, Montecristo is by far the best place in El Salvador to experience the outdoors, with unequaled hiking and camping and an endless supply of cool, fresh air.

Making the journey from Metapán to here is emerging from a night of urban bustle and commotion to a day of cool breezes and dripping trees. Montecristo is hard to get to, but well worth the effort. So worth it, in fact, that you might want to spend a night or two here exploring the gorgeous topography. If you ask the people at the gate, they may be able to supply you with firewood for the chilly nights.

Montecristo sits in the most humid area of El Salvador, a corner of the country drenched with over two meters of rainfall per year. Clouds scud through the hills and keep the humidity high even at night. It can get cold at this altitude, especially at night, so bring at least one warm layer, and preferably a waterproof one too. Within the park you'll find the Cerros Miramundo (2,394m), Brujo (2,410m) and Montecristo (2,418m). The last one gives the park its name and includes on its peak the exact point where the three countries converge, called El Trifinio.

At about 2,000 meters, the normal lowland forest gives way to the dripping *bosque nuboso* (cloud forest) for which the park is famous. Cypresses, pines and oaks, some up to 30 meters high, crowd close enough together to block out most of the sunlight in spots. Unfortunately, the lower limit of the cloud forest used to be closer to 1,800 meters, but encroaching small farms have pushed it higher in recent years. To camp in Montecristo, you need permission from the Agricultural Ministry in Soyapango. Call 342-0119 for the Ministry's phone number. You can also get a topographical map at the Instituto Geográfico in San Salvador (see San Salvador).

Animals Courting, Please Do Not Disturb

Montecristo is one of a handful of places left in Central America where it is possible to conduct ecological studies in a tropical cloud forest, with its rich but threatened abundance of plant and animal life. El Trifinio is closed from May to the end of October to allow the animals a chance to breed in peace.

Flora and Fauna

Orchids, mosses, fungi and lichens hide in the shadows, and some types of ferns tower over a meter and a half tall. If you're lucky you might spot porcupines, foxes, raccoons, white-tailed deer and even a jaguar. Beautiful butterflies are everywhere, even near the top.

> ## "Cada vez que destruyes parte de la naturaleza te destruyes a ti mismo."
> ("Every time you destroy a part of nature
> you destroy part of yourself.")
>
> — On ticket to enter Bosque Montecristo

VOICES

Los Planes

Los Planes, a recreation area within Montecristo, is one of the few public areas in the country with garbage cans that people actually use. It has a soccer field, picnic tables, bathrooms, cooking grills and camping space beneath tall cypresses. From Los Planes a number of hiking trails lead off into the wilds. At the far end of the camping area is a well-marked path that leads down to a river. A five-minute hike will bring you past an orchid garden to a small, crystal-clear waterfall.

Another path leaves from behind the soccer field. It's much less distinct, so look for signs of heavy travel. After about 50 meters through constant birdcalls and insects noises, the path becomes clearer and begins to go downhill, with natural tree-root steps. Walking another five minutes brings you to a hanging bridge. Go left at a fork in the road, then left at the next, smaller fork and uphill. Twenty meters past the barbed wire fence is a beautiful panoramic view straight out of the Sound of Music. To the right in the distance you can glimpse the Lago de Güija.

If you're up for a more serious trek you may try to tackle El Trifinio, visible four kilometers away from the soccer field. The dirt road there is open only from October to April, but it is barely passable with a 4x4. There are other well-traveled paths in the area, so if you decide to take one—and why not?—just make sure you can find your way back. Always hike prepared, too, with warm clothes, a water-proof layer, a water supply and a realistic estimate of your own limits.

Getting There

Montecristo's beauty is due in large part to its inaccessibility, so expect that getting will be difficult. No buses reach the top and you can't enter on foot. You have the choice of bringing your own car, hiring a taxi or catching a pickup from the market in Metapán ($0.60 per person) to Majadita, a village partway up the mountain. There are two pickups that make the trip each day, one in the early afternoon and another in the late afternoon.

The park's gate is five kilometers northeast of Metapán. The dirt road up turns into a rough concrete track more suitable for a 4x4 than anything else. Four kilometers inside the park is the administrative area of San José, with offices and a huge colonial house decorated with hanging baskets, orchids and wild ferns. The next stop on the road up is Majadita, and 18 kilometers inside the gate is Los Planes. Hiking to Los Planes from San José will take you more than three hours. From Majadita the hike is a little shorter. To catch a round-trip taxi from Metapán to the camping area should cost about $35, but you might be able to talk your way into a better deal. *(6am-6pm usually; $0.35 per vehicle plus $1.15 per Salvadoran, $1.70 per foreigner)*

Lago de Güija

12km from Metapán
52km from Santa Ana

Just over ten kilometers south of Metapán, the beautiful Lago de Güija straddles the border between El Salvador and Guatemala. Large and small volcanic cones, including San Diego, Igualtepeque and El Tule, dot the lake's Salvadoran shoreline.

Some ruins on the islands have yielded museum pieces that were buried during volcanic eruptions. Cerro Negro, a rough jumble of boulders used by fishermen for shelter in emergencies, is nearby.

Isla Tipa, the largest island in the lake, once had a Pipil sanctuary, called Teotipa, that was used to worship the divine couple Quetzalcoatl and Izqueye. According to legend, the sanctuary was created when the two gods appeared out of the waters of the lagoon.

You can hire a boat to visit some of the islands or you can climb one of the surrounding hills for a great panorama of the lake all the way across to Guatemala. *(Take bus 235 from Metapán towards Santa Ana and get off at the small village of Desagüe, about half an hour's walk from the lake. Ask for directions to the lake from there)*

Top: Lago Coatepeque
BL: Fruit seller, Juayúa
BR: Making balsam, Teotepeque

Top: Tesoro Beach Hotel, Costa del Sol
BL: Family, Apaneca
BR: Bike race, Santa Ana

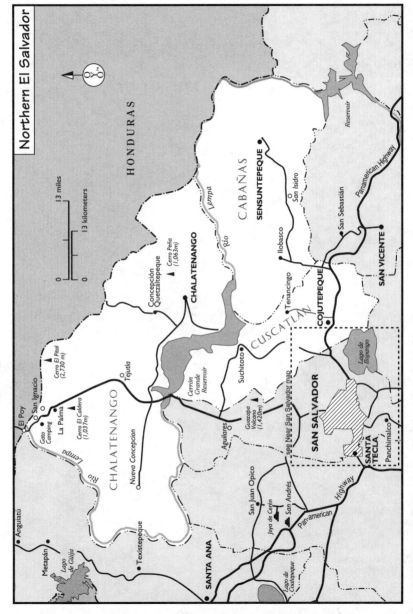

Northern El Salvador

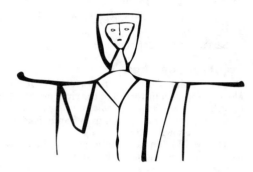

To The North

El Salvador buckles and rises as it heads north into Honduras and Guatemala. Timber is the major industry in this hilly territory near the border, while grainfields and pastures fill much of Cabañas and Cuscatlán departments. The main attractions up here are the crafts made in a handful of small towns, like La Palma's painted wood boxes, Concepción Quetzaltepeque's hammocks and Ilobasco's pottery. Other cities, like Chalatenango, Suchitoto and Sensuntepeque, are worth a visit just in themselves. In between are kilometers of secluded mountains that are perfect for time away from the city.

Like Morazán department, a combination of mountainous terrain and local poverty made northern El Salvador guerrilla territory during the civil war. Chalatenango, the second-poorest department in the country, was a base of rebel activity from the beginning of the war. The government repeatedly targeted the area during its bombing raids, causing considerable damage to many smaller villages. When soldiers arrived in town, they would hand out candy and offer rewards to villagers who turned in neighbors sympathetic to the FMLN. Painted guerrilla logos and slogans competed with army leaflets that read, "Combatant, come to the nearest barracks. Turn in your weapon. The armed forces will protect you."

It's not that easy to get around in the north. Cities are widely-spaced and buses are infrequent. The mountain roads in Chalatenango are especially bad, and the weather can get downright chilly up so high. It's beautiful country, though, and many of the small cities are worth the extra effort to get there. You can enter Honduras at El Poy in Chalatenango, north of La Palma.

■ **Emergency Police Numbers (PNC): Cabañas:** 332-2129, 332-3208, 332-3066. **Chalatenango:** 334-2483, 335-2117, 335-2435. **Cuscatlán:** 332-0359.

Cojutepeque

Nahuat, "Mountain of Turkeys"
Pop. 46,000
32km from San Salvador

Cojutepeque Then

One of the first Christians to travel through Cojutepeque, the priest Don Ravo Medina, reported in 1650 that the city's original Pipil inhabitants waded naked in the nearby rivers together "without fear of God." In the 17th century, a group of Spanish monks on a mission from San Salvador tried to remedy the situation by building the town a church.

The local Indians and European Christians, most with little or nothing in common except the land they shared, fought side-by-side during El Salvador's drive toward independence, rallying under the cry "Death to the newly-arrived Europeans!" When Spanish government forces arrived to quell the independence movement, the city's main plaza, a windmill and most of the town had already been destroyed by rebel sympathizers.

Cojutepeque's proximity to San Salvador made it known as the country's "reserve capital.". The government relocated here repeatedly, first after earthquakes which devastated the capital in 1839 and 1854, and later during periods of civil unrest.

During the civil war, rebel influence in the area created some interesting political problems. In an attempt to convince locals to support the Salvadoran government, the US government increased aid to the city, pouring thousands of dollars into the local economy. The aid often arrived in the form of food and weapons, and was sometimes used to rebuild schools and other buildings destroyed during the war. Although the FMLN objected to the source of these funds, they quickly realized that attacks on these buildings turned public sentiment against them. As a result, the rebels allowed construction to proceed, and in exchange were occasionally permitted to teach classes about leftist politics in the same buildings.

Cojutepeque Now

Cojutepeque is a bustling commercial city without much to interest the traveler besides daily Salvadoran life. The streets are filled with people selling the usual range of products and vegetables, and the few nearby sights aren't anything special. Cojutepeque has three *hospedajes,* but we don't recommend any of them.

Food & Drink

La Familiar This eatery is in a mini supermarket with a good variety of food. Sandwiches cost $1, and chicken and beef plates are in the $2 range. *(8:30am-7pm)*

La Cafeteria las Nieblas Also part of a supermarket, with a few tables. Steak with fries is $2.40. *(8am-6pm)*

Los Pichardos Restaurant and Disco Up on the second floor with a disco next door. Live music at night.

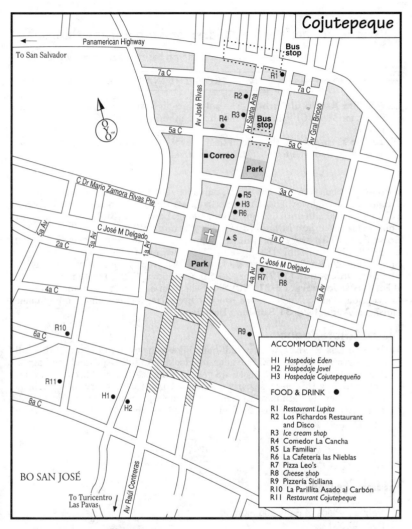

Comedor La Cancha A tiny place with five tables. Try the *encebollados*—meat cooked with onions—for $2.30. *(9am-8pm)*

Pizzeria Siciliana Not in the best part of town, but the place is small and clean. A large cheese pizza is $4, but you can load up a super size with six toppings for $7. *(9am-9pm)*

> ## "War is not healthy for children and other living things."
>
> — Slogan on baseball hat worn by guerrilla
>
> VOICES FROM THE WAR

La Parillita Asado al Carbón   The only place in town with *carne asada* (grilled meat), for $1.70. Or splurge for the shrimp in red wine sauce for $7. *(11am-3pm, 5-11pm)*

Pizza Leo's   Up here on the second floor they'll make your large ham and cheese pizza in front of you for $6. *(11:30am-2pm, 4:30-9pm)*

Details

■ **Buses:** All buses except 113 to San Salvador only take on passengers along the Panamerican Highway, about two blocks down the hill from the park. **Ilobasco (111)**, every 20 min until 5:20pm, 22km, 40min. **La Unión (304)**, every hour until 3pm, 151km, 4hr. **San Miguel (301)**, every 30 min until 6:20pm, 104km, 3hr. **San Salvador (113)**, every 5 min until 7:30pm, 32km, 1hr. **San Sebastián (110)**, every 20 min until 5pm, 18km, 40min. **San Vicente (116)**, every 10 min until 8pm, 27km, 40min. **Santa Rosa de Lima (306)**, every 40 min until 6pm, 144km, 4hr. **Sensuntepeque (112)**, every 20 min until 6pm, 48km, 1hr 40 min.

■ **Festivals: January 12-21 (20)** San Sebastián and La Inmaculada Virgen de Concepción. Vendors sell carved wood objects, modern ceramics and famous sausages. **August 28-31** San Juan Degollado.

Near Cojutepeque

Turicentro Las Pavas   An easy half-hour hike brings you to the top of this hill, the geographic center of El Salvador, overlooking Cojutepeque and the Lago de Ilopango. The air is always cooler up here and the ocean is visible on a clear day. Unfortunately, this place is poorly maintained and trash is everywhere. A shrine to the Virgen de Fátima at the summit attracts pilgrims from far away. Walk down Av Raúl Contreras to find the road to the top. *(1.2 km south of Cojutepeque)*

Suchitoto

Nahuat, "Place of Birds and Flowers"
Pop. 46,000
44km from San Salvador

Suchitoto Then

Suchitoto was one of the most densely populated pre-Columbian Pipil cities. In 1528, when repeated Indian attacks forced the nearby villa of San Salvador to temporarily relocate to Suchitoto, local tribes resisted for 15 years.

Home of the Painter

Víctor Manuel Sanabri has been painting in Suchitoto since he was a child, so it's no surprise that many of his paintings depict the town's streets and surrounding countryside. Today, much of his work—all with his characteristic signature "Shanay"—hangs in galleries in San Salvador. If he has a finished piece sitting around, though, he might be willing to part with it. Prices run between $200 and $800.

Sr. Sanabri doesn't speak any English but will be glad to show you around. His house is behind the church on 3a Av Nte, a white building with black window gratings and a large brown door with the number 8 on top and 721 on the side.

Suchitoto Now

A bustling commercial center before the civil war, Suchitoto still bears the scars of fighting—bullet holes dot buildings and other houses still lay in ruins. Now the streets are busy again but peaceful. Narrow cobblestone roads wind between the wrought iron window gratings of houses freshly painted in different pastel colors. At night, men play pool in front of Antel. Suchitoto has many side streets which are perfect for afternoon wandering. You might find yourself sitting on one of the tree-trunk benches in the park at the end of town, admiring the view out over the reservoir.

Accommodations

Hospedaje El Viajero Two cement rooms with tiny beds, and the lights don't always work. *(Rooms $2.30; laundry)*

Food & Drink

A few small *cafeterías* and *comedores* in Suchitoto serve simple plates like *carne asada* for under $2. The best are Pájaro Flor, Cafetería Stefany, Comedor El Triny, and El Trifinio.

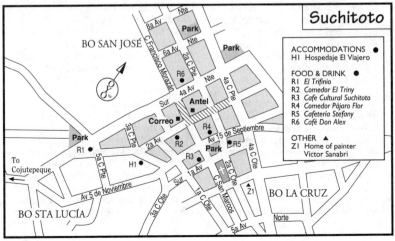

Sights

Church of Santa Lucía The original church was built in 1858 but was destroyed by fire. The current version could use a new coat of paint. Some of the buildings surrounding the church and the plaza it faces date to the 18th century.

Details

■ **Buses: San Salvador (129)**, every 30 min until 5pm, 44km, 1hr 30min.
■ **Festivals: December 6-13** Virgen de Santa Lucía and Virgen de Concepción. Candies called *colaciones,* made in the nearby Aguacayo canyon out of refined sugar, are sold.

Near Suchitoto

Cerro Grande Reservoir Suchitoto sits on the shore of this artificial lake, also known as Lago de Suchitlán, which was formed in 1976 by the construction of the Cerron Grande Dam and Hydroelectric Center. Although no tourist facilities exist on the lake, many people come here to bathe and fish near the mouths of the various rivers that empty into it. Paths down to the lake start at the north end of town. The 1½ kilometer hike takes about 20 minutes.

┤ IN THE NEWS ├

Tenancingo

This small town in a valley east of San Salvador suffered terribly during the civil war. Ongoing conflict between local peasants and property owners set the stage for the infamous 1983 bombing of Tenancingo by the Salvadoran Air Force.

After a rebel occupation of the town in September of that year, the Air Force responded by shelling Tenancingo for five hours straight. When the dust settled, 120 people—five percent of the local population—were dead and at least one-third of the town's buildings were reduced to rubble. Most of those who survived soon abandoned the town.

Three years later, the army and guerrillas declared the city a demilitarized zone, intending to allow both sides to enter the town but neither to occupy it.

The pact was eventually ignored by everyone, however, and the mayor was repeatedly threatened by the FMLN.

By the end of the 1980s, Tenancingo had calmed down and parts of the city were rebuilt and repopulated. Only a fraction of the original 6,000 inhabitants returned, though, and weeds filled the town's streets.

The road to Tenancingo, 15 kilometers off the Panamerican Highway, passes through the small town of Santa Cruz Michapa and turns from cobblestone to dirt before reaching Tenancingo. Almost a ghost town, Tenancingo is also known for a handful of local artisans who weave simple hats and bags from palm leaves. The town remains a legacy to the civil war and is a depressing but powerful place to visit.

"Careful, soldier. Minefield.
Let your officers go first."
— Guerrilla sign painted on farmhouse.

During a ceremony in Suchitoto in January 1994, government officials detonated what was supposed to be the last land mine in El Salvador. The northern provinces saw heavy fighting during the war, and many *quita-pies*, or "foot removers," were left scattered throughout the countryside even after the peace accords were signed.

Thousands of soldiers and civilians, especially farmers and children, lost limbs or their lives from stepping on mines both during and after the war. During the war, fields often lay untilled because farmers feared hidden mines.

The mines were used primarily by the guerrillas, and to devastating effect. Even though official figures claimed that only 42 percent of the army's causalities were caused by mines hidden along rural paths, in fields and in the beds of small rivers, others estimate that the army suffered as

many as 80 percent of its casualties this way.

Rebel mines were often made out of cans or bottles, powered by flashlight batteries and filled with just enough plastic explosives and metal fragments to take off a limb. The impact of the mines was as much psychological as it was physical, since most of the explosions only maimed victims without killing them. To other soldiers, a crippled comrade was seen as worse off than a dead one.

The army responded to the threat of mines by dividing into smaller tactical units and by distributing posters showing gruesome photographs of children who had been maimed by the explosives. In time, the FMLN stopped using the mines to keep from losing popular support. Toward the end of the war, the rebels switched to command-detonated mines instead, which could target soldiers more effectively.

Ilobasco

Pop. 71,500
54km from San Salvador
27km from Sensuntepeque

Ilobasco Then

The mountain village of Ilobasco, like the rest of Cabañas department, was originally occupied by the Lencas. Pipil tribes moved in toward the end of the 15th century, absorbing the culture of the Lencas and renaming the town Hilotaxca, which means "place of *elote* [soft corn] tortillas."

The population of Ilobasco remained almost completely indigenous until well into the 18th century, when the town was relocated under strange circumstances. It seems that Ilobasco was originally located northwest of its present location in an area now known as Sitio Viejo ("Old Place"). One day an icon of San Miguel, patron saint of the town, disappeared from its shrine in the church and was discovered sit-

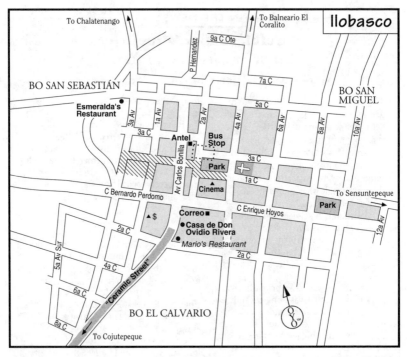

ting on a stump six kilometers away. The priest of the town, who probably felt that a new church was in order anyway, persuaded the entire town that this event was a sign from God and that the town should be moved. Before long, everyone agreed and a new town was constructed near where the stump stood.

Ilobasco Now

The road to Ilobasco winds uphill past buses belching diesel fumes and women carrying baskets of mangos on their heads. The town's meandering cobblestone streets follow the gentle slopes of the surrounding hills.

Ilobasco is well-known for its artisans, who produce painted ceramics. The tradition dates back to the 1940s, when a few families began to sculpt plain figurines out of fine-grained clay. A talented local artist soon gained national recognition for his painted ceramics, and other local artists copied the technique.

Today, Ilobasco's ceramics are one of a handful of the most distinct Salvadoran crafts. Painted mugs, jars, plates, vases and Nativity figurines are for sale in the town. Also, look for the *sorpresas*, or "surprises," which conceal tiny, detailed scenes inside a clay shell. Some *sorpresas* are real surprises, and conceal a sexual scene inside a painted egg or house.

Accommodations

Casa de Don Ovidio Rivera This small house, next door to the Funerales Vida Eterna (Eternal Life Funeral Home), is probably the closest you'll ever come to staying in a funeral home while you're still alive. The rooms are small and grimy, but many plants decorate the pink patio and make the courtyard a pleasant place to meet (living) locals. The Casa doubles as a *pensión* and may be full of boarders. Sheets are $0.60 extra and water is only available on Monday and Friday. (*$2.30 per night with common bath*)

Food & Drink

Esmeralda's Restaurant The owner, Neris Berrios, spent his 20s in the US before returning to open this place. He plays good tapes and occasionally brings in a big-screen TV to show videos. The banana *licuado* is good but watery, so if you want a thick one ask them to make it only with milk. All the food is cooked in vegetable oil (your arteries will thank you), and full meals start at $2.30.

Sights

Iglesia de Ilobasco This colonial church, white inside and out, sits next to a small garden with a cave housing the famous icon of the Virgin.

Details

■ **Buses: San Salvador (111)**, every 15 min until 5pm, 54km, 1hr 40min.
■ **Festivals: January 27-28** Romería del Señor de las Misericordias. **May 10** Virgen de los Desamparados (Virgin of the Helpless or Abandoned). **May 13** La Fruta. Held in the Iglesia de Ilobasco in honor of town's patron saint. **September 26-29 (28)** San Miguel.

Near Ilobasco

Balneario El Coralito Señora López owns this private man-made pool, which is surrounded by a few benches and tables. There are changing rooms nearby and food is sold on the weekends—pack a lunch during the week. To get there, take 4a Ave Nte to its end, go right one block and then left on the road that leads to the cantón Las Huertas, where the *balneario* is situated. The one and a half-kilometer trip should take you under half an hour on foot. (*Admission $0.80 per person*)

Sensuntepeque

Pop. 64,000
80km from San Salvador

Sensuntepeque Then

Pipil Indians overran this pre-Columbian Lenca village in the 1400s. A century later, Sensuntepeque was turned into an evangelical village by the Dominican friars of San Salvador, who erected a church in honor of Santa Barbara.

By the beginning of the 19th century, the city's residents rose up in support of Salvadoran independence and clashed with federal troops in the main plaza. The insurgents were quickly outmanned and defeated; men were thrown in jail and women were each given 25 lashes in public.

Sensuntepeque Now

The capital of Cabañas department is worth a visit if only for its ambiance. The road to the city rises and falls in the hills and valleys of the surrounding countryside, and streets are filled with people walking or waiting for buses and pickups. Sensuntepeque doesn't have any hotels or fancy restaurants, but it does have a large, thriving market. There's also an excellent view of the town and the main church from 6a Av.

The city makes up for its lack of facilities with a subtle but definitely positive vibe and a slight tinge of lawlessness. The heavy hand of the military isn't so palpable here, so Sensuntepeque feels less oppressive than other cities in the north. That, along with the fantastic market, is enough reason to drop by.

Food & Drink

Aquarius Restaurant The staff in this restaurant—really only a glorified *comedor*—are friendly and will recommend the *bistec encebollado* (beef with onions)

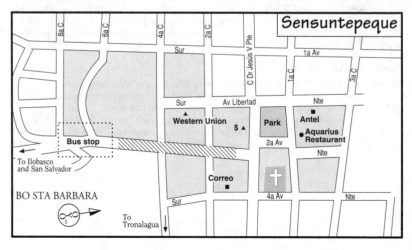

with salad, potatoes and *tortillas* for $2.85. Hamburgers and chicken sandwiches are only $0.75. There isn't any sign outside, so look for the building with the red and white painted walls. *(8am-5pm)*

Sights

Iglesia de Santa Barbara   This simple church covers an entire block. Look for the image of the town's patron saint holding a miniature church, a palm leaf and a sword.

Details

■ **Buses: San Salvador (112)**, every 15 min until 4:45pm, 80km, 2hr.
■ **Festivals: November 24-December 5 (December 4)** Santa Barbara.

Near Sensuntepeque

Tronalagua   A popular swimming spot with the locals, this reservoir is owned by ANDA (the Salvadoran water company) and serves as a big public pool. Tronalagua sits out in the woods with good views of the nearby mountains and rock formations. Small kiosks sell snacks and Cokes. To get here take 4a C Ote out of town and turn right at a fork in the road onto a second rocky road which you follow for three kilometers more. The walk should take 30-45 minutes.

Chalatenango

Nahuat, "Valley of Water and Sand"
70km from San Salvador

Chalatenango Then

The largest city in the northern region of El Salvador, Chalatenango began as a pre-Columbian Lenca village that was eventually absorbed by the Pipils. During the civil war, the army and guerrillas each struggled for control of the city, and battles raged in the streets. An FMLN stronghold throughout much of the early part of the war, Chalatenango was later occupied by government forces who turned the city into a virtual fortress and built the huge military garrison.

As a pivotal city in El Salvador's hotly-contested northern region, all funds allotted to run the city were diverted to the military. For most of the 1980s, 310 police officers had to share only nine cars and each car was allotted three gallons of gas per day.

Even with the garrison in place, the rebels didn't give up; they attacked Chalatenango in early 1989 in an effort to disrupt local elections. At one point in 1990, the guerrillas advanced to within one block of the military garrison.

During the 1994 presidential elections, the ruling ARENA party was supported in the city of Chalatenango while the FMLN was more popular in the countryside. The government tried too hard to change the vote, though, and the FMLN later uncovered the names of 17 long-deceased "supporters" of ARENA on the voting lists.

> "We are under the protection of God. It is probably better.
> We don't understand the politics of either side."
>
> — Villager, on Salvadoran politics

─────┤ VOICES FROM THE WAR ├─────

Chalatenango Now

Today the former military fortress is a comfortable city filled with typically Salvadoran one-story buildings with red tile roofs. Tall green mountains surround Chalatenango, providing a backdrop for a view of the Lago de Suchitlán, the artificial reservoir formed by the Cerro Grande hydroelectric project to the west.

The war has left its mark on the city and its buildings, many of which still bear bullet holes. Signs of recovery are apparent in the handful of furniture and appliance stores, which don't get much business from the soldiers who continue to walk the streets.

Many people in Chalatenango have lighter skin, hair and eyes than most Salvadorans and are descended from the Spanish who settled in the area in the 16th century. You'll see women wearing shorts and men sporting cowboy hats brought in from Cojutepeque and Tenancingo. The cowboy hats, bullet holes and shaded porch shop fronts, held up by large wooden banisters, make the city feel like a town straight out of the old frontier. Watch yourself around the garrison across from the main church, though, or you might get a *real* taste of the Wild West.

Accommodations

Pensión La Inez A dark, run-down place with big simple rooms that you can lock yourself. All the rooms share three concrete bathrooms that could use a scrubbing. No restaurant here, but they'll make you food if you ask—plates run about $1.75. *(Pink door across the street from Antel; tel 335-2085; 7 rooms, $2.85 per bed; laundry; 24hr checkout)*

Food & Drink

Restaurant El Paraíso Great, tacky velvet chairs and friendly waiters add to the ambiance at El Paraíso, the fanciest place in town. The owner lived in the US for five years, which explains the American movies they show from time to time. *Lomo de auja* (grilled meat with rice and salad) costs $2.50, but seafood dishes go for about twice that. *(11am-11pm)*

Restaurant Carmary If El Paraíso is the fanciest, then Carmary is the most pleasant. There's no menu in this clean, well-run place, so just ask for what you want. Breakfast is $0.70, and during the afternoon try one of their *panes con pollo*, a small chicken sandwich, for $0.35. *(Mon-Sat 7-10am, 11:30am-2pm, 2:30-5pm)*

Cafetín Tío Juan A modest little place for a bite, popular with bus drivers and passengers. Plates run around $1.15. *(7am-9pm)*

Sights

Iglesia de Chalatenango This colonial church was built in the 18th century and has undergone repeated repairs after earthquakes. The exterior has an interesting shape and the clock hands on the bell tower are missing.

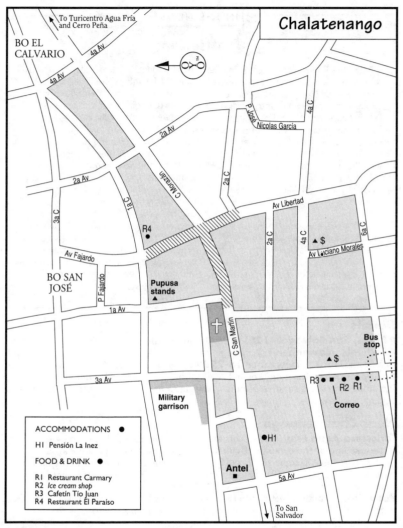

Hiking

Cerro La Peña A three-hour hike up "Crag Mountain" brings you to a view over much of Chalatenango department, including the capital. Santa Ana is barely visible in the distance. A clear path up the hill leaves from the Agua Fría *turicentro*. Ask for directions there or in town. The path is popular and well-known among the townspeople—almost everyone seems to have been there at least once.

IN THE NEWS

Traffic Jam

Few Salvadorans owned cars during the civil war, and for many years it was downright odd to see an automobile chugging past horses along country roads or keeping pace with a bus. The military had its own cars (most courtesy of the US), as did some mayors and landowners.

The capital has always been choked with the shiny sedans of the wealthy. Most Salvadorans, though, found little time to worry about automobiles, and contented themselves with buses, horses and walking.

Salvadorans working in the US and returning to their country with new wealth have added a fleet of cars to the country's highways. In towns where no more than a handful of vehicles plied the streets for decades, 100 or more now compete for room. Some Salvadorans return from the US with their own cars, which they navigate through Central America back to their own small village. In 1992 alone, more than 20,000 cars were brought into El Salvador. Others prefer to send cash to parents and relatives, who make the purchase in El Salvador.

But proud new car owners are confronted with another problem. The quality of roads in some parts of the country, especially near small villages, is so poor that horses are often faster than cars. After all, many of the country's roads were designed for four-legged travel. As a result, although an increasingly large percentage of Salvadorans have cars, many still prefer to hop a bus to get where they're going.

Details

■ **Buses: San Salvador (125)**, every 10 min until 4:45pm, 70km, 2hr 20min
■ **Festivals: November 1-2** Feria de los Santos (All Saint's Day Fair). **June 24** San Juan Bautista. **December 18-25 (24)** Nacimiento del Niño Jesús.
■ **Shopping:** The town market sells everything a cowboy/girl could possibly want, including spurs and saddles. Hammocks from Concepción Quetzaltepeque are also sold on the streets.

Near Chalatenango

Turicentro Agua Fría These pools are filled by the river which can be seen from the far end of the complex. Evidently chlorine isn't very popular around here; the untreated Olympic-sized pool has a slightly greenish cast, and the baby pool looks a little yellow. *(Three blocks from town on C Principal; $0.57 per person or car; cafetería)*

Poza Viva Ask for directions to these deep natural pools on the River Tamalasco in the direction of the cemetery to the east. *(1 km from town)*

Concepción Quetzaltepeque

Pop. 8,500
69km from San Salvador
12km from Chalatenango

Concepción Quetzaltepeque Then

Lencas were the first inhabitants of Quetzaltepeque ("Mountain of Quetzalcoatl"), as the town was called before the arrival of the Spanish). Over time the town has been influenced by the Chorti, Pipil and Ulúa tribes.

This area was claimed by the FMLN in the early 1980s. In fact, the guerrillas "celebrated" Christmas in 1984 with an attack on Concepción Quetzaltepeque, breaking a year-end truce.

Concepción Quetzaltepeque Now

The northern Salvadoran foothills surround "Quetzalte," as the town is also known, near Chalatenango and the Cerron Grande Reservoir. The road there is rocky but passable, flanked by odd-shaped hills and cornfields. Concepción Quetzaltepeque is a small, unassuming town known for its high-quality handmade hammocks. The streets are quiet; children hum soap operas themes and cowboys ride horses out in the fields.

Inside, however, entire families are busy weaving the hammocks for which the town is famous. These hammocks have been woven by generation after generation, and their quality and price vary widely depending upon the materials used and the ability of the weaver. Generally, the thicker the hammock, the better the quality.

The best nylon hammocks are made out of the same nylon used in fishing nets, usually imported Korean or Taiwanese twine. A cheaper type of nylon used comes from Honduras. A good, thick nylon hammock sells for $57.50 in San Salvador, but only costs about $30 here.

Cotton hammocks, which are harder to find but softer and prettier, can be custom-sewn with any words you want. A thin, narrow cotton hammock will cost around $8 ($14 in San Salvador), while thicker, wider cotton hammocks with wooden frames cost up to $30. Hammocks made of a natural fiber called *mezcal* are also available, but the material is a little rough.

Most weavers leave their doors wide open and are happy to invite you into their homes; just ask first. The house of José Ernesto Silva is a good place to stop by, chat and see weaving firsthand. His nylon hammocks are beautifully detailed, with carved handles.

The six children of María Teodora Sanches de Pérez, between six and 23 years old, help her weave *mezcal* hammocks. Each hammock takes one person about half a day to make. In the Pérez household, and in many others, you can see the entire process: first the fiber is finger-combed, then strung, dyed and woven. A well-made, narrow *mezcal* hammock costs about $4.

The Cooperativa Inmaculada Concepción has been selling hammocks for about three years and recently filled orders for European and American mail-order companies. A first-rate, cotton hammock that sells in the US for $125 costs about $30 here. Their nylon hammocks are well-made but not especially decorative, and their natural-fiber hammocks are just passable.

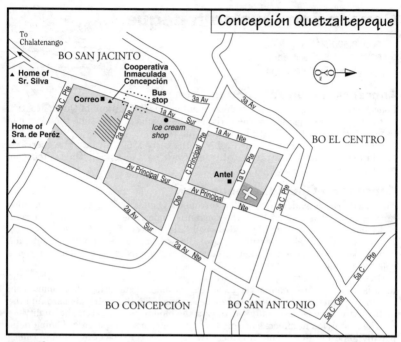

Concepción Quetzaltepeque

Details

■ **Buses: Chalatenango (300b)**, every 30 min until 4pm, 12km, 30min. **San Salvador (126)**, 5am, 69km, 2hr 20min.
■ **Festivals: January 19-20 (19)** San Sebastián Mártir. **December 6-8 (7)** Virgen de Concepción. You can see pictures of this festival on the wall of the Cooperativa Inmaculada Concepción.

La Palma

Pop. 14,400
82km from San Salvador

La Palma Then

The tiny village of La Palma sits eight kilometers south of the Honduran border, just off the main road north from San Salvador. In the early 1980s the army tried to organize a civilian defense militia in La Palma to protect the town from guerrilla attacks. Few people joined, though, because until that point the town had not been attacked and people feared that a militia would just invite problems.

In 1984, President Duarte met here with rebel leaders at the Iglesia Dulce Nombre de María in an attempt to end the civil war. The peace talks were held under tight security and with high hopes among supporters of both sides. In the end, Duarte and guerrilla leaders reached an impasse that ultimately undermined Duarte's ability to govern and contributed to the escalation of the war.

La Palma Now

At first glance, La Palma seems an unimpressive mountain hamlet. People ride horses and donkeys down the streets, past a church painted by Fernando Llort. Llort's influence on La Palma doesn't stop there, though. The artisans of La Palma labor in 110 different shops to produce the painted ceramics, leather, wood, seeds and cloth goods for which the town is famous.

Over 200,000 of these pieces are made each month, painted in the wide-eyed, colorful style popularized by Llort. You can peek behind some of the gift shops to view the artists at work . Ask politely, though; since this town is more isolated than other craft villages, the artists may be a little bit uncomfortable at first, especially if you can't speak Spanish. La Palma is a little out of the way, but the craft shops, hiking trails and the Hotel La Palma make the town a worthwhile stop, either on the way to the northern border or for a day's side trip from the capital.

Accommodations

Hotel La Palma All the facilities in this comfortable hotel are brand new, since it was destroyed during the war and reopened only in early 1994. It's obvious that the owner, Salvador Zapada, went to great lengths to find new furniture and to make this out-of-the-way hotel look good. The hotel has wooden ceilings and a ceramic shop sits by the entrance.

> **"As far as the investigation of the deaths of the four nuns and the two lawyers, we ask the congressmen, Mr. Reagan and the American public: Where are the human rights of more than 30,000 Salvadorans dead in a sterile and fratricidal struggle? Or is it that the lives of six people are more valuable, just because they are Americans?"**
>
> — *El Diario de Hoy* advertisement, on US Congressional opposition to fund Salvadoran army because of its human rights abuses, 1982

VOICES FROM THE WAR

TO THE NORTH

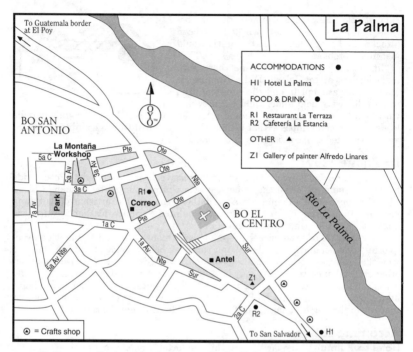

Paths near the hotel lead down to the La Palma River. Sr. Zapada will help you plan an all-day group excursion into the nearby mountains for about $35 for five people. *(Tel 335-9012; S $11.50/$17.25 on weekends, T $17.25/$23, all with private baths; laundry; 24hr checkout; restaurant 7am-9pm)*

Food & Drink

Restaurant La Terraza Go through a garage and up a spiral staircase to find this rooftop restaurant, the fanciest place to eat in town with interesting artwork on the walls. Most dishes are $1.70-$2. *(9am-9pm)*

Cafetería La Estancia A friendly restaurant with a visitors' book to browse through. Crafts and local artwork decorate the walls, and dishes are around $2.50. *(8:30am-8pm)*

Sights

Gallery of Alfredo Linares The gallery sells high-quality paintings of typical La Palma scenes by Sr. Linares, who studied in Italy and is now a local legend. Prices for originals run from $10-$600. Reprints are around $13 and colorful postcards cost $1. *(9am-12pm, 1-5pm)*

Hiking & Camping

Cerro El Pital (2,750m) Cloud forests wait on top of this hill, on the Salvadoran side of the border to the northeast. Ask in San Ignacio, four kilometers north of La Palma, for directions to the dirt road that leads toward the mountain.

Gato Camping This little campground is in the middle of nowhere, a few kilometers north of La Palma on the road to San Ignacio and the border. It's set up like a summer camp, with a volleyball court, lots of wooden signs and trailheads leading into the nearby countryside. If you want to go hiking, plan ahead and buy a map from the Instituto Geográfico Nacional in San Salvador (see San Salvador). Otherwise, you may get lost since even the owner doesn't seem to know the trails very well. Bring food for your stay here. *(86.5km north of San Salvador, about 10km north of La Palma; open every day, $1.70 per person)*

Details

■ **Buses: El Poy (119)**, every 30 min until 4pm, 11km, 30min. **San Salvador (119)** every 30 min until 4pm, 82km, 3hr.
■ **Festivals: February 10-18 (17)** Dulce Nombre de María.

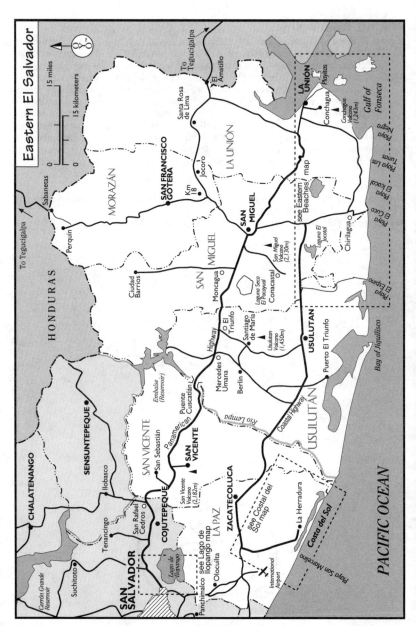

Eastern El Salvador

To The East

Past the Lempa River, El Salvador's terrain quickly becomes rougher and wilder. Although this region saw the hottest fighting of the civil war, it remains beautiful. It's a little less user-friendly than the west, but offers some hidden gems to travelers willing to do a little exploring. Eastern El Salvador runs from the rolling hills of Morazán and northern La Unión department, through the hot plains of central La Unión and San Miguel, over the volcanic coastal mountain range and down into the Pacific. Many of El Salvador's exports are grown on the rich coffee, sugar and cotton plantations in San Vicente department, while Usulután's fertile valleys produce cotton, coffee and fruit.

San Miguel is the busy commercial hub of the east, and the port city of La Unión sits on the sweaty shore of the Gulf of Fonseca, just around the corner from outstanding beaches. San Francisco Gotera and Perquín are nestled in the damp mountains to the northeast. Whether you feel like climbing a volcano or lazing away the afternoon on an island in the Gulf of Fonseca, you can find it in the east. Have an unforgettable meal at La Pema in Santa Rosa de Lima, learn about the history of the rebel movement at the FMLN museum in Perquín or stroll down the best beach in the country at El Espino. Take your pick.

The San Vicente region has always been one of the most prosperous parts of El Salvador. Add this to the underdevelopment and poverty of the rest of the east and you have a recipe for turmoil. As a result, the northeast became a guerrilla stronghold during the civil war and saw intense and frequent battles. FMLN guerrillas stationed on the Usulután Volcano launched raids on government troops in the city of Usulután. The department's economic importance led US advisors to say that the war "would be won or lost in Usulután."

Peasant migration away from the region emptied much of San Vicente department and bloated refugee camps in the capital. When US aid was funneled to rebel-controlled towns in the department, the FMLN allowed schools to reopen—

provided that teachers would step aside for one class period each day and allow a rebel instructor to "teach" the students.

Of 20 mayors in San Miguel department in 1985, two were kidnapped, two killed, four resigned and eight went to work in the capital. Morazán, the center of rebel operations and the location of many FMLN training camps and arms factories, had it the worst. This "zone of subversive persistence," as the government called it, was razed, bombed and depopulated until few of the people left there trusted anyone else.

In spite of the turmoil that the east has recently endured, it is still one of the most interesting and surprisingly welcoming regions of the country to visit. Things are much safer now and the guns-in-your-face checkpoints are long gone. Since the east is hot and dry in the center, muggy near La Unión and dripping to the north, come prepared for almost any weather.

Cities are more spread out than they are in other regions, which makes it harder to get where you want to go. Buses eventually reach even the farthest towns, though, over some of the worst roads in the country. You often have to switch buses at intersections to get to out-of-the-way cities like San Francisco Gotera.

The Panamerican Highway links San Vicente to San Salvador and Usulután, running onward to the Honduran border at El Amatillo. Cross into Honduras there or at Sabanetas, the soon-to-be-opened border crossing north of Perquín. Or hop a boat across the Gulf of Fonseca to Honduras or Nicaragua—just make sure your papers are in order.

■ **Emergency Police Numbers (PNC): La Paz department:** 334-0444, 334-1324, 334-1301. **La Unión department:** 664-0084, 664-4046, 664-4187. **Morazán department:** 664-2072, 664-2007. **San Miguel department:** 661-4728, 661-1455, 661-1677. **San Vicente department:** 333-0432, 333-0880. **Santa Rosa de Lima:** 664-2072, 664-2007. **Usulután department:** 662-1337, 662-1333.

Costa del Sol

54km from San Salvador

Sun-soaked and wave-stroked, this 15-kilometer stretch of sand in the center of El Salvador's Pacific coast is one of the country's most famous and popular beach destinations. As a result, everything here tends to be more expensive—many parts of the "Coast of the Sun" are crowded with mansions, imported cars and expensive hotels. If you have the cash to spare, splurge and treat yourself to a luxury hotel. With a little legwork, though, you can leave the development behind and spend the day on your own special slice of empty sand, with warm waves and palm trees thrown in for free.

Olocuilta

Olocuilta, 16 kilometers from San Salvador along the highway to the airport, is known throughout the country for *pupusas* made of rice rather than corn. *Pupusa* stands line the parking lot on the edge of town, and are often filled with Salvadorans stopping by to take some home. Rice *pupusas* taste a bit lighter than ones made from corn, but they're still fried in lard. A popular place to buy them is the Pupusería Marinero Martínez, owned by friendly Sra. Angelia Marinero.

■ **Buses:** Ask where the buses stop; they stop on the highway below, under the bridge or in the parking lot. All of these buses also return to San Salvador (every few minutes until 8:30pm, 16km, 30min). **Costa del Sol (495)**, every hour until 5pm, 37km, 2hr 20min. **Usulután (302)**, every 30 min until 6pm, 80km, 2hr 30min. **Zacatecoluca (133)**, every 15 min until 8:30pm, 25km, 1hr.

There aren't any cheap hotels on the Costa del Sol. Since many parts of the beach and the small towns nearby are on the dirty side, you should only come here for the day if you don't want to spend loads of money. Camping out isn't easy since there aren't many deserted stretches of coast with shade like there are in other parts of the country. The road to Costa del Sol branches off the road to La Herradura, 11 kilometers south of the Coastal Highway. A few buses from San Salvador run along the coast.

■ **Buses: San Salvador (133, 495)**, every 30 min until 4:30pm, 54km.

Playa San Marcelino

Large waves caress two kilometers of this so-so beach at the beginning of the Costa del Sol. Facing the ocean, the best beaches are to the left; to the right is the mouth of the polluted Jiboa River. Local fishermen launch their boats to go fishing in the late afternoon, usually around 5pm. If you're around when they leave, you can try to talk your way into a short ride into the waves—forget about amusement parks, this is the real thing. It's also interesting to watch the fishermen unload their catch in the early morning and late evening. There's also a *turicentro* here with entrances to the beach and the estuary on opposite sides of the road, but it's not very clean.

Accommodations

Kennymar On the beach, the Kennymar has three simple rooms next to a seafood restaurant. The ocean is your shower. *(3 rooms $6, $11.50 plus deposit for fan and TV)*

Costa del Sol Club A plush place two blocks from the beach with sports facilities, pools, miniature golf, a Jacuzzi and a disco. The club's beach area hides another pool, a restaurant and gazebos. One night with food costs about $115, and reservations are necessary through Condominios Cuscatlán in San Salvador (25a Av Sur and 4a C Pte; tel 222-6764, 222-8249). *(Tel 334-0630; 32D, 24 quads, 2 suites; laundry; pool; restaurant)*

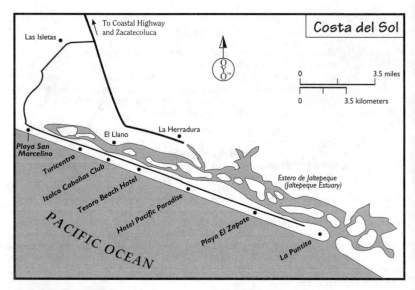

Izalco Cabaña Club Actually a hotel, the Izalco Cabaña Club has clean but run-down and overpriced facilities. Somebody should set that poor monkey free, too. An attached restaurant serves seafood soup for $5.75 and fish plates for $4.50-$6. *(Next to turicentro; tel 323-6764; 13S $60, 17D $77 in back, $86 by beach, all with private bath, AC, huts $23; laundry; 11am checkout; restaurant 6am-9pm)*

Playa Los Blancos

The trashy entrance to the public part of Playa Los Blancos is crammed with *come-dores* that give way to empty expanses of sand and shallow waves. The best part of the beach is near the Tesoro Beach Hotel, where it's as wide and flat as a foot-ball field. This is about as good as El Salvador's "popular" beaches get—which is pretty good.

Accommodations

Tesoro Beach Hotel If you can afford it, this is the classiest hotel on the Coast. The tiled-floor rooms have all the amenities, including hot (albeit brackish) water, and many look directly out over the ocean. When the place is full, which occurs less and less often lately, the indoor restaurant is open. Otherwise, eat outside by the ring-shaped pool, have a drink at the bar or wander off into the distance on the seemingly endless beach out front. Bands play outside on week-ends. *(Tel 334-0600; 120 rooms $171 and up, all with TV, AC, hot water; laun-dry; 2pm checkout; pool; 2 restaurants; parking)*

Hotel Pacific Paradise The wallpaper looks older than anyone who works here and the walls out front are covered with as much duct tape as paint, but the El Zapote beach out front is beautiful. Gazebos are free for guests on weekdays, otherwise they cost $6. Hammocks are $2 per day. One trip to the weekend buffet at the restaurant will run you $9.75. *(6S $57, 4 bungalows $98, all with private bath, TV, AC; laundry; 4pm checkout; restaurant 7-9am, 12-3pm, 7-9pm)*

La Herradura

60km from San Salvador

This small fishing town, with nets under repair at every turn, isn't too impressive at first glance. La Herradura's saving graces are fresh seafood for sale on the pier and the tranquil Jaltepeque Estuary, where green trees overlook muddy waters branching out in every direction towards the Pacific Ocean. A number of outdoor kiosks on the pier sell raw clam cocktails and chicken plates for $2.75-$3.50. If your tastes run to sushi instead, raw fish is also available to go.

Even better than the fish, though, is hopping a boat to explore the estuary and nearby islands. Prices will be outrageous (over $20) if you're not ready to bargain. The cheapest way to go is with locals, who use the boats as transport to outlying points. Boats are designed to hold at least ten people, so that's one way to split costs. Be sure that the boatman understands how long you want to be out on the water, where you want to go, and that the price includes a return trip (*ida y vuelta*), or you may find yourself playing Robinson Crusoe. Prices for locals are under $1.50 each way, so you can see how much a little bargaining can save you. The most visited islands are: La Tasajera (25km, 30min), La Calzada (10km, 20min) and Isla Colorada (35km, 1hr).

■ **Buses: Costa del Sol (495, 193, 193b, 193e)**, 20km, 30min. **San Salvador (495)**, every 15 min until 6:00pm, 60km, 2hr. **San Vicente (193, 193e)**, 5:30, 6, 8, 9am, 12, 1:15, 3:15, 3:45pm, 66km, 2hr 15min. **Zacatecoluca (193b)**, 5, 9, 10:40am, 12, 3, 4:40pm, 42km, 1hr 35min.

"One is big, strong and blond. The other is short, weak and dark. The people always support the short, dark one."

— Guerrilla, using Mao Zedong parable to explain why the people would support the rebel movement

VOICES FROM THE WAR

TO THE EAST

Usulután

Nahuat, "City of the Ocelots"
Pop. 79,000
112km from San Salvador

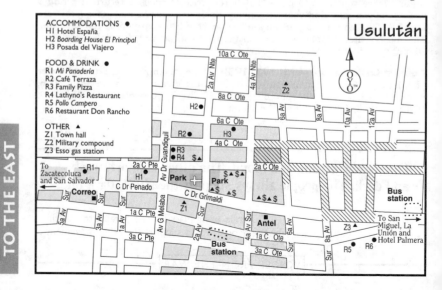

Usulután Then

Usulután's original Lenca inhabitants were pushed aside in the 15th century by immigrating Pipil tribes. In 1529, the Usulutecos battled Spanish forces under the command of Diego de Rojas. Although Rojas was captured, the native armies were only able to hold off his forces for a short while. Usulután was sacked and burned by English pirates near the end of the next century, and in the early 19th century El Salvador's first coffee bush was planted nearby.

During the civil war, guerrillas repeatedly attacked the military garrison in the center of town, and houses were occasionally damaged in street fighting. A 1988 attack on the garrison was timed to coincide with a meeting of Central American foreign ministers, who were trying to implement a regional peace plan engineered by Costa Rican President and Nobel Prize winner Oscar Arias.

Usulután Now

The capital of Usulután department sits off the Coastal Highway at the foot of the coastal mountains, to the south of the volcano of the same name. A colorful pastel cemetery at the western entrance gives way to a city that bustles with business all day long. Usulután isn't large, but it has the feel of a big city. Shops line streets that bristle with signs and are packed with constantly-moving crowds of people. Vendors sell huge baskets of shrimp in a thriving central market. The camouflaged tower at 8a C and 8a Av is a sobering reminder of the city's recent history and is worth a look.

There are plenty of places to eat in Usulután and a few good hotels. It's a good place to stop on your way along the coast to the east and it makes a decent jumping-off point for the Costa del Sol, Bay of Jiquilísco and beaches further east.

Accommodations

Hotel España This old place is fairly well-maintained but time has still taken its toll. A grand entrance with a world map, old wood furniture and high ceilings give it a relaxed, tired atmosphere. A *plato del día* at the restaurant usually includes chicken and rice, and costs $2.50. *(Tel 662-0358; 4S $7, 2D $9.20, 2T $11.50, all with private bath, fan; laundry; 3pm checkout; restaurant)*

Posada del Viajero Modest rooms surround a small courtyard in this cozy place that is larger than it looks. *(Tel 662-0217; 20D $4.60 with shared bath, $7 with private bath, all with fan; 24hr checkout)*

Hotel Palmera A compromise—the best hotel in Usulután is also outside of town. Clean and a good value. A taxi there should cost about $1.70 and a plate in the attached restaurant costs $2.85. *(2.5km east of Usulután on Coastal Highway, take bus 89 from next to Pollo Campestre, get dropped off at the Universidad Gerardo Barrios next to hotel; tel 662-0161; 12S $6 with fan, 29S $8.75 with AC, 4D $15; all with private bath; laundry; pool; noon checkout; restaurant)*

Food & Drink

Restaurant Don Rancho Half cafeteria-style, half *à la carte*, and overhead fans to keep you cool. A buffet lunch in the leafy patio runs around $2.30, and a shrimp plate is $5. Enter through the small parking lot. *(11am-8pm)*

Lathyno's Restaurant One of the classier places in town with light music, an open courtyard with a fountain and...tablecloths! Seafood and pasta plates run $4.50-$8, with weekly specials. *(10am-10pm)*

Family Pizza This pleasant, clean joint serves juice, beer and pizza only. A large cheese pizza costs $5.75, but you can enjoy a personal cheese pizza for $2.85. *(11am-9pm)*

Café Terraza Popular with students, with lots of tables and bright colors. School kids gossip and sip Cokes in a friendly atmosphere (in spite of the red and green-checkered floor). A *pollo empanizado* with fries and salad goes for $2.85. *(9am-9pm)*

Sights

Río El Molino This river and man-made pool saw some action during the war, but is still worth the short walk from the main plaza. *(½km southwest of Usulután)*

Laguna Palo Galán A public lagoon and pool, but the Río El Molino is better. *(Take urban bus "Palo Galán" towards the Hotel Palmera, 15min)*

The Hammock Maker

Marroquín Aguilar Cruz is a wizened old fisherman who lives on the outskirts of Puerto El Triunfo. You might spot him outside his house twisting nylon on an old machine for the finely-woven hammocks he weaves. He learned his craft from Mexican seamen he worked with for 22 years. His hammocks are very soft and fine, take two weeks to make and require eleven pounds of nylon each. A medium-sized one will run you upwards of $100. *(4a C Ote and Av Jorge Guirola/1a Av, at the north end of town across from the huge tree)*

Details

■ **Buses: Berlín (349)**, every 20 min until 4pm, 22km, 1hr 15min. **Jucuarán (358)**, 4 buses until 4pm, 40km, 2hr. **Playa El Espino (351)**, 5, 7am, 2pm, 33km, 2hr. **Puerto El Triunfo (363)**, every 15 min until 5:30pm, 8km, 30min. **San Miguel (301, 335, 373)**, every 10 min until 5:30pm, 65km, 1hr 40min. 335 is an express bus via the Panamerican Highway. **San Salvador (302)**, every 10 min until 4:15pm, 112km, 2hr 30min. **San Vicente (417)**, every hour until 2:30pm, 78km, 2hr 30min. **Santiago de María (349)**, every 20 min until 4pm, 22km, 1hr 15min. **Zacatecoluca (171)**, every 90 min until 2:30pm, 55km, 1hr 20min.
■ **Festivals: November 18-25 (24)** Santa Caterina de Alejandra.

Puerto El Triunfo

Pop. 14,200
107km from San Salvador
20km from Usulután

Puerto El Triunfo Now

The road south to Puerto El Triunfo from the Coastal Highway almost peters out in the dusty town of Jiquilísco. At the south end of town, the road grudgingly becomes paved again and continues to the port.

El Triunfo is a clean and quiet fishing village with a small, shady central market. The dock isn't so pleasant, though, and the water seems to turn into a sea of mud in the distance. Fishing boats of all sizes are tied up side by side at the dock. If you make it here, you'll want to grab a bite of seafood and take a boat ride out into the bay. At best, Puerto El Triunfo is a day trip from Usulután.

Boat Trips

Renting one of the small, colorful fishing boats with an outboard motor from the dock to explore the bay and islands is a pleasant way to spend a day. The best islands to visit are Isla San Juan, Isla La Parilla, Isla Coral de Mula and Isla de Menéndez. Isla Coral de Mula is the only one with regular passenger service ($0.60 one way). For any of the others, you have to rent a boat yourself.

It's easiest (and cheapest) to rent a boat for a whole day, rather than by the hour. Make sure the boatman understands how many hours you intend to be out and what destinations you want to see, and expect to pay about $17.25 for the whole day. Isla La Parilla has a place to buy beverages, but otherwise you'd better carry your own food and drinks.

Details
■ **Buses: San Miguel (377)**, every 40 min until 8:30am, 11am, 3pm, 75km, 2hr 40 min. **San Salvador (185)**, every 30 min until 7am, 2:20pm, 107km, 2hr 30min. **Usulután (363, 366a)**, every 10 min until 5:30pm, 20km, 50min.
■ **Festivals: May 1-2 (1)** Día de La Cruz. **May 10-13 (12)** Virgen de Fátima.

Berlín

Pop. 37,000
109km from San Salvador
35km from Usulután

Berlín Then
This traditional coffee-growing city was built in 1885 in the fertile Valle Agua Caliente (Hot Water Valley) overlooking the Lempa River. Farms around Berlín grow much of the country's coffee. Because the FMLN established many camps on the slopes of the nearby Tecapa Volcano, Berlín was fiercely-contested up to the very end of the civil war. Guerrillas warned local coffee pickers against going to work in the fields in an effort to destabilize the country's coffee-dependent economy.

Seven hundred guerrillas seized Berlín in 1983 after local government forces were diverted to fight another battle in a remote part of the country. The Salvadoran Air Force proceeded to strafe the city plaza with US-supplied jets, and reduced an eight-block section of the town to rubble. Even though the army retook Berlín in three days, the guerrillas considered the battle a victory. Enormous coffee warehouses were set ablaze as the guerrillas retreated.

Berlín received more US economic aid than any other rural Salvadoran city and was often called a "US propaganda village." When guerrilla forces took control of as many as 25 percent of El Salvador's cities in the early 1980s, the US diverted military aid money to reconstruct schools and hospitals that had been damaged by

And I'll Need That By Tomorrow
During their temporary "liberation" of Berlín, guerrillas looted the bank, pharmacies and stores. Soon the biggest spending spree in the city's history was underway. FMLN commanders ordered hundreds of pairs of shoes and new uniforms, tailored quickly enough so that they would be ready before the army could retake the city.

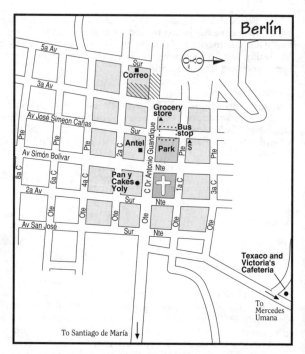

the war and to plant crops in fields long abandoned by war-ravaged farmers. Some schools in Berlín still bear the name of the US congressman, Clarence Long, who initiated the program.

Berlín Now

One of the best things about Berlín is the road there, which slowly winds and twists its way upward from Mercedes Umana into the mountains. Make sure to sit on the right hand side to see the hills folding down into the Lempa river valley, which lies on one side of the far-off department of San Vicente. Also on the right, the Tronador geyser shoots off steam periodically. The air cools as the road climbs until it arrives at the Texaco station at the entrance to Berlín. Berlín is dirty and still bears the scars of fighting. Many of the buildings, especially the church bell tower, are peppered with bullet holes. There are a couple of good places to eat and some hiking paths in the hills around the city, but otherwise there isn't much to Berlín.

Top Left: San Vicente Volcano
Top Right: View from Parque Balboa
Bottom Left: *Frijoles* for sale, Chalatenango
Bottom Right: Henequen field

Top Left:	Hammock maker, Puerto El Triunfo
Top Right:	Street vendor selling yarn puppets, Santa Ana
Bottom Left:	Gatekeeper, Playa Icacal
Bottom Right:	*Campesino,* San Juan Opico

Food & Drink

Victoria's Cafetería An outdoor restaurant with the nicest bathroom you're likely to find in these mountains. Ten big plastic lawn tables, plenty of chairs and a big Coke refrigerator are set inside. A meat dish with rice, salad, tomato and onions is $2.85. *(Next to the Texaco; 6am-10pm)*

Pan y Cakes Yoly A clean, friendly fast-food joint with red and white benches. Often frequented by mothers and their children, so no alcohol is sold here. Bread is three for $0.11, cakes cost $0.25 and a large pepperoni pizza is $7. Try the *volteado de piña* (upside-down pineapple cake) for $0.50. *(8am-10pm)*

Details

■ **Buses:** Mercedes Umana sits at the intersection of the road to Berlín and the Panamerican Highway, so many buses to cities along the highway can be caught there. Buses that pass by Mercedes Umana include **301** (San Salvador-San Miguel), **304** (San Salvador-La Unión), **306** (San Salvador-Santa Rose de Lima) and **309** (San Salvador-Santiago de María). **Mercedes Umana (304)**, every 45 min until 5pm, 8km, 30min. **San Salvador (303)**, 4 buses between 4:30am and 1pm, 109km, 3hr. **Usulután (369)**, every 2 hrs until 3:30pm, 35km, 90min.

■ **Festivals: March 15-20 (18)** San José. Tricycle and motorcycle races (separately, of course), theatrical presentations and musical concerts. **December 11-12 (11)** Virgen de Guadalupe. During the Procession of the Indians, participants wearing Indian costumes parade accompanied by band music and firecrackers. **December 24-25** Nacimiento del Niño Díos. Images of San José and the Virgin are brought to each house in search of donations. Songs and fireworks on the 24th are followed by a Misa de Gallo (Rooster's Mass) late at night.

Near Berlín

Cerro Pelón The two to three-hour hike up this hill to the east of Berlín offers a good view of the city and the beautiful hills and mountains of the coastal range from 1,400 meters up. The hike is about five kilometers each way.

"Cuidado con el ciclísta, podría ser su hermano".

("Be careful of the cyclist, he could be your brother.")

As you travel around El Salvador, you'll notice a series of road signs with personal messages imploring drivers to watch out for cyclists alongside the road. These precautionary signs are the brainchild of one Dr. Ayalla, known throughout the country for his efforts to make the roads safer for everyone. Shocked by how many Salvadoran cyclists were being hit by cars, Ayalla secured permission from the government to erect signs throughout the country with messages designed to remind motorists of the danger. "La familia del ciclísta le agradese." ("The cyclist's family thanks you.")

Santiago de María

Pop. 23,500
118km from San Salvador

Santiago de María
Usulután

Santiago de María Then

The first of the many successful coffee plantations around Santiago de María was owned by General Gerardo Barrios. An earthquake and the eruption of Cerro El Tigre to the east in 1878 caused part of the mountain to collapse and buried more than a dozen peasants in their homes on the skirt of the volcano.

During the 1980s, local coffee owners ignored rebel threats and refused to raise worker wages from $3 to $4.50, as required by law. Rebels occupied the town in 1983 long enough to harvest a crop's worth of coffee. The FMLN also attacked an enormous coffee storage compound in the area owned by then-president Cristiani in order to draw attention to their struggle.

Santiago de María Now

The second-largest town in Usulután department is surrounded by mountains and is enveloped in clouds which roll up and down its steep streets. Kids in their school uniforms crowd the clean central park during their mid-day lunch break and head out to the cinema at night for movies. The surrounding countryside is spectacular, and you can go for a mountain hike in just about any direction out of town.

The Man Who Makes Boots

If you'd like a great souvenir from Santiago de María, ask for directions to the house of López, *el hombre que hace botas*. Inside his house, which has no sign out front but doubles as a workshop, Don Ramón can make you a simple pair of handmade leather boots for about $40.

After you choose from the many types of leather and reptile skin he has lying around, Don Ramón will trace your foot measurements on a sketch pad and tell you to come back to pick them up in about a week, depending on how busy he is.Or, if you're staying in San Salvador, he can call you when they're ready. If your Spanish is pretty good, you can even arrange to pick them up at San Salvador's Eastern Bus Terminal from the driver of the 1pm bus from Santiago de María (you pay the driver).

Accommodations

Hotel Villahermosa Looks like someone's living room turned inside out, with plants, music and couches. Clean, spacious rooms and bathrooms are complemented by a friendly atmosphere. The restaurant serves fast food for $1.75-$3.50 a plate, and a beer is $0.70. *(Tel 660-0146; 5S/D $5.75/$9.20, 2T $13.80, all with private bath, fan; 24hr checkout; parking; restaurant 7:30am-6pm)*

Hospedaje El Quetzal The owner complains he's had no business since the Villahermosa opened next door. No surprise.

Food and Drink

Restaurant El Único This simple *cafetín* overlooking the park occasionally offers movies on the VCR. *Camarones empanizado*, a shrimp dish, costs $2.85. *(8:30am-10pm)*

Carnes y Maríscos Tony Bad screechy music and tacky beer posters, but all in all this is a comfortable place to kick back for lunch. Try the fried, breaded shrimp—you eat the whole thing, eyes and all. Delicious. *(9am-midnight)*

Details

■ **Buses: Berlín (322, 348, 348a)**, every hour until 5pm, 30km, 40min. The bus that passes Mercedes Umana instead of Alegría takes 1hr 30min instead. **San Miguel (322, 335)**, every 30 min until 3pm, 24km, 1hr 15min. **San Salvador (302)**, every 30 min until 8am, 1:15pm, 2:40pm, 118km, 2hr 30min. **Usulután (302, 357, 362, 370)**, every 15 min until 5pm, 14km, 1hr.
■ **Festivals: February 19-25 (24)** Santiago Apóstol.

ACCOMMODATIONS ●
H1 Hospedaje El Quetzal
H2 Hotel Villahermosa

FOOD & DRINK ●
R1 *Pastelería*
R2 Restaurant El Único
R3 Carnes y Maríscos Tony

OTHER ▲
Z1 Basketball court
Z2 Cinema
Z3 Monument
Z4 Shell gas station

Hiking

Cerro El Tigre A few kilometers to the east of town, this monster is the most impressive climb within easy distance. A hike to the summit leads you 1,500 meters up through coffee plantations. There's a great view of Santiago de María and the entire valley from the top.

TO THE EAST

You need at least a day to get up and back. Go prepared since the path isn't too clear, even though the mountain itself is visible from the town.

Cerro Oromantique This smaller hill is less than a kilometer directly south of Santiago de María. A few hours' hike brings you to the top, for a view of the town and the much larger mountains in every other direction.

Laguna de Alegría On the road to Alegría, west of Santiago de María, sits a crater lake in the volcano of the same name. It gives off sulphur fumes that are said to be medicinal—they may be good for you, but they make the place too smelly for swimming. The hike and the view are both great, though. If you take the bus to Alegría, ask the driver to let you off near the volcano (*cerca del volcán*).

San Vicente

San Vicente

Pop. 73,000
58km from San Salvador

San Vicente Then

San Vicente was founded in 1635, when 50 Spanish families gathered under a shady tree on the banks of the Río Acahuapán to create a new town that would be safe from the increasingly hostile Indian population nearby. The town was named after San Vicente Abad, a famous Spanish martyr.

Aquino's Folly

In 1831, rebel forces under indigenous leader Anastasio Aquino spread out from Santiago Nonualco, and eventually gained control of the entire coastal region between the Comalapa and Lempa rivers. The town of San Vicente sent two forces to subdue the rebels, but both were defeated. Aquino advanced towards San Vicente and, in 1833, occupied the town's central plaza.

When Aquino's troops took San Vicente, they sacked the town and robbed the Church of Pilar of much of its valuable jewel collection. Drunk with alcohol and success, Aquino crowned himself "Emperor of the Nonualcos" with the Crown of San José, still on display in the Iglesia del Pilar.

As he prepared to return home, Aquino abducted Lucilla Marín, a beautiful young local woman, and left with her in hasty retreat. Marín's uncle Escolástico chased after Aquino with an army of 150 Vicenteños, determined to rescue his niece and to teach Aquino a lesson. Escolástico caught up with Aquino in Santiago Nonualco, soon defeated him and freed Lucilla. As both sides counted their losses, Escolástico captured Aquino and returned with him to San Vicente, where the rebel leader was tried and executed.

San Vicente emerged as a seat of power in the 19th century. During the brief existence of the Central American Federation in the 1830s, San Vicente served as El Salvador's capital for a few years. The town has suffered through many serious earthquakes, including an especially destructive one in the 1930s. During the civil war the area endured heavy fighting as FMLN troops moved south through the region and battled with the army. A strong army presence settled over the town, with a huge military compound at its center.

San Vicente Now

The capital of San Vicente department is nestled in the Jiboa Valley, one of the most beautiful valleys in El Salvador, at the foot of the San Vicente Volcano. Rolling hills and fields of sugar cane surround San Vicente, which in spite of its rocky history is one of the most pleasant, relaxed cities in the country. From the Panamerican Highway to the west you can get a spectacular view of the city, with its white church, clock tower and

In 1774, a mudslide near the peak of the San Vicente Volcano released a raging torrent of water down its side. San Vicente itself was spared only because the hill of San Antonio, which sits between the town and the volcano, diverted the water around San Vicente into two streams. The gully carved by the torrent can still be seen as a scar down the side of the volcano.

TO THE EAST

Bones in the Plaza

On his way to church one day in the late 18th century, a visiting curate noticed human bones scattered around San Vicente's main plaza. When he inquired, the clergyman learned that certain people in the area practiced a strange ritual; they exhumed dead bodies to obtain particular bones, which they used in a magic ritual that they believed made them impossible to capture or confine. Those covered by the spell were even supposed to be able to escape effortlessly from jail. The rest of the bones were simply discarded in the plaza.

---

the twin peaks of the volcano in the background. A plantation owned by former President Cristiani is visible on the slopes of the volcano.

Women stand at the entrance to San Vicente selling red, white and black beans by the pound. The city is an archetypal colonial town with cobblestone streets and a prominent clock tower that overlooks the central plaza. The volcano is reachable in a day's hike and you can cool off in the nearby Apastepeque *turicentro*. This calm, quiet city has a number of quality restaurants, making it a good place to stop off the Panamerican Highway as you head east.

Accommodations

Hotel Villas Españolas Built in a traditional Spanish style but modern on the inside. Rooms all have TV and well-kept private baths. Singles and doubles are the same size. *(11S $8.50, 4D $11.50, all with private bath, TV; noon checkout)*

Casa de Huéspedes El Turista An old but clean and friendly place, and a good second choice if the Villas Españolas are full. *(18S/D $7, all with fan, most with private bath, hammock, TV; noon checkout)*

Hotel Orquídeas Inn Clean and simple. The five downstairs rooms have private baths that are tidy but smell a little funny. They'll cook you some food in their own kitchen if you ask politely; plates are around $3. *(Tel 633-0900; 18S $5.75, 6D $7.50, T $10.35; laundry; 24hr checkout)*

Hotel Central Park Although it isn't as nice as the Villas Españolas, the Hotel Central Park is still a good value. It's also a good place to meet people in town. *(Tel 633-0383; 9S $6.25, $7.50 with TV, $11.50 with AC and phone, 9D $9.75/$11/$14, all with private bath; laundry; restaurant 6:30pm-9pm)*

Food & Drink

Restaurant Casa Blanca Very comfortable setting in a pleasant hanging garden with trees and a clean little pool. A grilled steak with potato and salad goes for $4.60. Other dishes range from $2.85 to $8. *(11am-9pm)*

Comedor Rivoly Like no other *comedor* in town, the Rivoly is a spic and span cafeteria with plenty of orange and white tables and chairs. Plates are in the $2 range. *(7am-7pm)*

Chentino's Pizza These friendly guys have their act together; they've been here for two years and have another shop in San Miguel. Come here for pizza and natural fruit shakes—nectar of the gods. A large plain is $5.75 (piled high for $7) and shakes are under $1. *(10am-9:30pm)*

Sights

Iglesia del Pilar The church was ordered built in 1762 by
Francisco de Quintanilla. He died in Guatemala, but his son
completed the construction. Today this beautiful church,
which survived Aquino's ransacking, is decorated with
benches, an altar made of dark wood and intricate designs
on white walls.

Details

■ **Buses:** There are two bus stations in San Vicente. **Station #1: Costa del Sol
(193)**, 5:30, 6am, 12, 1:15pm, 55km, 2hr 30min. **Ilobasco (530)**, 7, 11:30am,
4:30pm, 33km, 1hr. **San Salvador (116)**, every 20 min until 6:30pm, 58km, 1hr
30min. **Usulután (417)**, 5, 6:15, 7, 8, 11:30am, 63km, 2hr 15min. **Zacatecoluca
(117)**, every 15 min until 6pm, 23km, 50min. **Station #2: Amapulapa Turicentro (176)**, every hour until 6pm, 9km, 1hr. **Apastepeque (156)**, every 15 min
until 6pm, 12km, 1hr. **San Sebastián (176a)**, 7am, 2pm, 20km, 1hr.

■ **Festivals:** Crafts made in the penitentiary of San Vicente, including wooden
toys, decorations and stringed instruments, are sold during the town's festivals.
January 1-30 (5) Romería del Señor de Esquipulas. A masquerade ridicules local
figures during this pilgrimage, and processions wind through town on January 14
and 30. **October 1-15 (14)** Nuestra Señora del Rosario. **October 16-November
16** La Feria de Los Santos. Originally centered around the indigo trade, this fair
has become the most popular *fiesta* in San Vicente. It's a more commercial festival
than some, with many different products brought in from neighboring towns for
sale. **December 15-31 (26)** San Vicente. **December 24-25 (24)** Nacimiento del
Niño Jesús. A group of young people called Los Pastores dress as shepherds—complete with robes, hats and shepherd's hook—and visit the church and various
houses as they sing songs about the birth of Christ.

The Legend of Pilar

According to a traditional story, a couple named José Marino and Manuela Arce lived
together in San Vicente in the middle of the 18th century. One night Arce, crazy
with jealousy over her husband's constant philanderings, plotted to kill him. When she
approached, murder in her eyes and knife in her hand, a framed image of the Virgin of
Pilar on the wall of the room began to shake violently. Arce fled in terror.

The Virgin's warning wasn't sufficient to hold off Arce's fury for long, though, and
soon she went after her husband again. But once again, just before she attacked, the
picture shook wildly and Arce fled in fear. After this happened a third time, Arce
became convinced that a higher spirit was involved and, trembling with remorse, she
gave up her plot to kill her husband.

Marino, meanwhile, began construction on a small chapel on the western side of
the plaza of Pilar where he planned to house the lifesaving image of the Virgin.
Although Marino died without completing the chapel, the site was set aside as a tribute
to the Virgin of Pilar. It was later replaced by the larger Church of Pilar which stands
there today.

Near San Vicente

San Vicente Volcano "Chichontepec," the Nahuat name for this huge dormant volcano, translates loosely as "Mountain of Two Breasts." A flat peak and a cone-shaped peak each rise to about 2,200 meters, with a depression in between that used to be a crater. The volcano hasn't erupted recently, but hot springs at its base known as Los Infernillos make you wonder if it really is dead, or just sleeping.

The climb to the top follows a long, steep trail that starts just past the Amapulapa *turicentro*. If you walk the whole 14 kilometers from San Miguel, it should take you at least six hours each way. It's quicker and easier, though, to catch a ride around the base of the volcano to the north first, to the small town of Guadalupe. From there it's about five kilometers to the top, or a two-hour hike.

Los Infernillos (The Little Hells) These natural hot springs, in the sugar fields on the southern side of the base of Chichontepec, are bathed in strong sulfuric fumes and smoke. For years, people with health problems came here to be cured by the water. During the war the area was mined by the FMLN so few people showed up. Now that the area has been de-mined life is returning to normal.

Turicentro Apastepeque Relive summer-camp memories at this crater lake, the smallest *turicentro* in the country but one of the cleanest and most pleasant. A section of the lake is separated for use by families, which is probably best since it plunges to over 100 meters deep in the middle. Be careful swimming out alone—there aren't any lifeguards. String up your hammock between a couple of shady trees and hang out. Take bus 156 or 156a from San Vicente and ask the driver to let you off at the sign for the *turicentro*. From there it's about a kilometer and a half to the lake. *(8am-5pm; $0.60 per person and car)*

Turicentro Amapulapa A good place to relax if you can ignore the trash. The largest of the four pools has a small waterfall but looks a little grimy. A statue of San Cristóbal, the patron saint of motorists, gazes down on everything. A few huts serve food and drinks for reasonable prices. Take bus 176 from San Vicente or catch a pickup. *(8am-6pm; $0.60 per person and car, cabins $3.50)*

San Sebastián

Pop. 23,500
49km from San Salvador
15km from San Vicente

San Sebastián Then

In September 1988, ten peasants near San Sebastián were killed by government troops, continuing a pattern of rural massacres that had become common through the early part of the war. Information about the case was both shocking and predictable. Ballistics evidence showed that all been shot at close range. Witnesses described how army troops had surrounded their hamlet, herded residents into a school and separated a group of "rebel collaborators." As the accused were being led away for questioning, they were gunned down at close range.

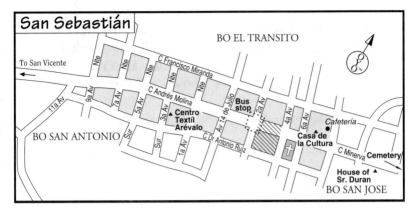

The army had a different story to tell. After first claiming that the peasants were guerrillas killed in combat, the army changed its account to say that they had been caught in the crossfire of a guerrilla ambush. The guerrillas, they said, had returned later and shot up the bodies at close range to make the army look guilty.

At first, the army's claim of rebel cross fire was accepted and the case appeared closed. It was reopened, however, when US Vice President Dan Quayle visited El Salvador and threatened to withhold the $1.5 million that El Salvador was receiving daily unless the military demonstrated a commitment to improving human rights. Quayle declared that the incident at San Sebastián would be a test case.

With the US pressing the military for results, the media reported that a high army figure would soon be jailed. US officials were quick to portray the reports as a sign that the army had reversed course and would now answer to Salvadoran law.

Just as quickly, though, events took another turn. In 1990, charges against 11 of the 12 army officers indicted in the San Sebastián massacre were suddenly dropped. US policy makers and Ambassador Walker, who had personally encouraged progress in the case, were stunned and embarrassed. Nonetheless, US military aid continued.

During a soccer game near San Sebastián towards the end of the war, rebel troops surrounded the field and herded 200 people, including players and food vendors, off into the hills. Within ten days, everyone had escaped or been freed from the rebel camp, returning with tales of endless propaganda speeches and lousy food. Players, still wearing only their thin soccer uniforms, complained that they had almost frozen. In the end, the operation turned into a public relations nightmare for the FMLN, and soccer games in the area were suspended indefinitely.

San Sebastián Now

The road to San Sebastián passes through the quiet town of Santo Domingo. Recently paved, it's a pleasant detour past small farms, swaying cornfields and wandering cows. Although most of San Sebastián itself is downright drab, some scenes are almost painfully picturesque, with yards of brilliantly-colored yarn left to dry outside red-tiled houses.

> "How long will I serve? I would say I will serve until I get my letter of warning from the FMLN. Some people say you have to die for democracy, but they aren't here. Those are just the words of people who are not threatened."
>
> —Village mayor, discussing FMLN warning to mayors to resign or die

VOICES FROM THE WAR

The town is famous for its weavings which, sadly, are falling behind the times. The ancient art of making the weavings has survived, but ever since synthetic materials were introduced and cheap Asian imports arrived, the final products have become nothing you'll want to send home.

Nonetheless, the technique is interesting. Weavers use foot pedals to manipulate pairs of sticks to create the designs. More complex designs must be planned in advance. The larger the weaving, the more pairs of sticks are needed. The town's artisans are usually delighted to show you how everything works, and they may even let you pass the shuttle a few times.

Crafts

Casa de la Cultura This is a good place to appreciate the painstaking labor that goes into each weaving. A few looms inside surround a pretty little enclosed garden. Knock if they look closed. *(8am-4pm)*

House of José Carmen Durán Sr. Durán employs a full brigade of weavers who labor away on some ancient looms inside this combination funeral home/weaving studio. Locals buy blankets here and resell them in San Salvador. *(Look for the "Funeraria Durán" sign two and a half blocks from the market, right next to the cemetery)*

Centro Textil Arévalo The machines inside this blue shop, home of Inéz Arévalo, are more complex—notice the design cards above the looms that automatically produce patterns.

Details

■ **Buses: San Salvador (110)**, every 30 min until 4:20pm, 49km, 1hr 30min. **San Vicente (176)**, 6:30am, 1:30pm, 15km, 1hr.

■ **Festivals: January 23-28 (27)** San Sebastián Mártir. **December 11-12 (11)** Virgen de Guadalupe. **December 24-25 (24)** Nacimiento del Niño Díos.

IN THE NEWS

Troubled Bridge Over Water

The bridge that carried the Panamerican Highway over the Río Lempa, called Puente Cuscatlán, was once a symbol of Salvadoran pride and hard work. The FMLN blew it up during the war, though, and today only the end pieces remain.

The Panamerican Highway passes around volcanoes as it winds east from San Vicente, and eventually the view opens onto a 180-degree cornfield-filled panorama overlooking the river and Usulután department. Along the highway leading down to the river are kids and ladies selling fresh fish, which they hold out to passing cars.

These days all traffic passes over two rickety temporary bridges 100 meters upriver from the original bridge. As you cross you can see the 15th of September Dam to the north. It's interesting that the only political graffiti on the old bridge is for the FMLN.

San Miguel

Pop. 192,000
138km from San Salvador

San Miguel Then

Barely seven years after the Spanish founded the city in 1530, San Miguel was almost wiped out by an indigenous insurrection that shook many parts of Central America. The native population, enraged by their treatment at the hands of the Spanish, seized San Miguel and other cities.

When the city government came under attack, it sent out a desperate call for help to the capital which soon dispatched reinforcements. As churches in San Salvador rang their bells in support of the Spanish in San Miguel and government troops rushed to the city, the insurrection grew more fierce. Troops battled for six months before the rebellion was eventually suppressed.

Toward the end of the 17th century, English pirates appeared off the coast and sacked undefended indigenous villages along the shore. When San Miguel and San Salvador prepared their armies for a full-scale invasion, the pirates decided to flee rather than fight. As they fled back to their ships, they left behind an image of the Virgin Mary in the port of Amapala. Soon the icon, which came to be known as "The Miraculous Patron," was brought to San Miguel where an elaborate procession was held in honor of all who survived.

During the early years of the civil war, the army stationed some of its best forces near the city in an attempt to neutralize the guerrillas next door in the department of Morazán and on the slopes of the San Miguel Volcano. From the volcano, rebel troops periodically launched raids on the city's electrical installations and were able to black out eastern El Salvador. The Deliro Bridge, five kilometers to the south, was repeatedly attacked by the FMLN in an attempt to knock out transit between San Miguel and the capital.

TO THE EAST

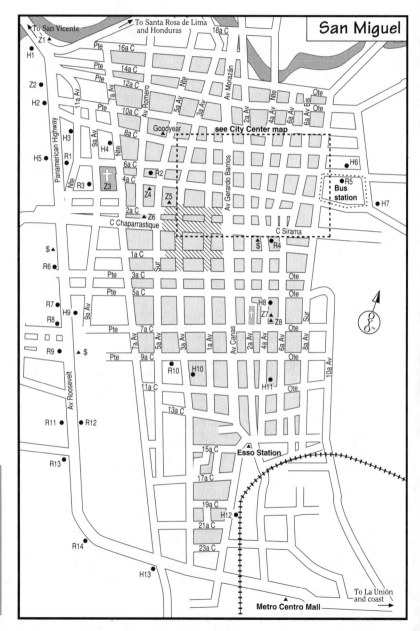

San Miguel Now

El Salvador's eastern hub sprawls alongside the Panamerican Highway on its way toward La Unión, in the shadow of the San Miguel Volcano. The sticky heat can't suppress this bustling commercial center where streets are practically bursting with business and trade.

Some of the richest coffee fields in El Salvador lie on the slopes of the enormous volcano which overlooks the city. San Miguel is the country's center for the production of cotton and henequen, a natural fiber used to make bags, ropes and hammocks.

San Miguel is a place to enjoy crowds, eat well, visit a thriving market and watch a soccer game, but it's not a place to relax. Prices are higher here than in the west and the sun beats down on the low-lying countryside without mercy. The market is a crazy clutter of wooden tables where you can browse through heaps of inexpensive plastic watches, hand-hammered pots, imitation jewelry, live lizards and hand-rolled cigars.

Accommodations

Hotel Caleta This reasonably clean hotel with small rooms around a little courtyard seems to be a favorite of local mosquitoes, so BRING REPELLENT. *(Tel 661-3233; 35D $4.90 with fan and common bath, $7.60 with fan and private bath, $12.65 with AC and private bath; laundry; 2pm checkout)*

Hotel Central A study in contrasts: big rooms with fresh sheets but the bathrooms stink and facilities are falling apart. There isn't a restaurant here, but they'll cook something up for you for about $1.40 if you ask. *(Tel 661-3141; 14 rooms $4.00 per person with fan, $5.75 with private bath, $8.60 with AC and private bath; 24hr checkout)*

Hotel Trópico Inn This dated hotel, once the only quality stop in San Miguel, suffered repeated guerrillas attacks during the late 1980s. In 1989, a celebration during the Miss San Miguel pageant was interrupted by a guerrilla assault on the city. The Salvadoran vice president was attending the ceremonies, conveniently enough, and became trapped. The next day he was evacuated by helicopter.

The chaos has taken its toll on the building and now the nicest part of the Trópico Inn is the first five meters inside the entrance. The rooms are small, dark and old, old, old. Singles and doubles are exactly the same, just with different size beds. El Mandarin, just down the road, is the better choice by far. *(Tel 661-0774; 63 rooms, S $33.35, D $40.50, all with private baths, hot water, TV, phones and AC; laundry; restaurant 6:30am to 11pm)*

TO THE EAST

> **"In one of the most bizarre incidents of the war, the FMLN occupied a cattle farm in eastern San Miguel department and, using machine guns and grenades, killed 204 milk cows."**
>
> — News report, 1987

VOICES FROM THE WAR

Hotel del Centro (City Center map) A respectable father-and-son establishment with a friendly staff and very clean rooms. Lunch at the restaurant costs about $4.00. *(Tel 661-6913; 14S $10.00 with fan, 13S $14.00 with AC, 1D $21.25 with AC, all have private baths, TV; noon checkout; restaurant 6am-9pm)*

Casa de Huéspedes El Viajero Reasonably clean, though a little run-down. Small rooms with a courtyard that serves as a parking lot. *(12 rooms $4.60 with shared bath, 8 rooms $5.75 with private bath; 24hr checkout; parking)*

Hotel Panamericano (City Center map) A large hotel with grungy rooms, all of which are singles, but they'll add more beds if you want (for free), so bring your friends! *(24 rooms $4.60, $5.75 with fan, $9.80 with AC, all with private bath)*

Hotel Oasis Many vendors and traveling doctors stay in this spacious yet simple hotel during the week. The rooms are clean, but the bathrooms don't sparkle. The cafeteria will cook up whatever they have on hand for about $4. *(Tel 661-2126; 7S $8.60, 15D $15.00, all with private baths; cafeteria)*

Hotel China House This clean hotel has hammocks in the center of a courtyard attached to a restaurant that serves Chinese, American and Salvadoran plates from $2.85 to $3.50. The China House Combination for $3.45 includes chop suey, chicken, salad, potatoes and fried rice. Jaime Quan, the very personable owner, speaks English. His grandfather came to San Miguel and opened China House after emigrating to Mexico from Canton, China. *(Tel 669-5029; 6S $11.50, 13D $17.25, all with private baths, AC; laundry; noon checkout; parking)*

Mini-Hotel Novel A little concrete compound with no windows but a small central area where people hang out and talk. *(Next to bus station; tel 661-4206; 4S $4.00, 3D $4.60; laundry; 24hr checkout)*

Hotel El Mandarín San Miguel's nicest hotel isn't inexpensive, but it's new and well-managed, on par with a rural Holiday Inn back home. The restaurant serves Chinese food for $3.50 to $8 a dish, including a great big bowl of wonton soup for $3.50. The owner, a Chinese immigrant who has lived in El Salvador his entire life, ran a Chinese restaurant in town for many years. *(Tel 669-6969; 32 rooms, S $28.75, D $34.50, all with private baths, AC, cable TV; laundry; pool; parking; 2pm checkout; restaurant)*

Hotel La Terminal A clean, pleasant enough place that will soon add 12 more rooms. The ones they have now are comfy, but a little cramped with a bed, couch and chair all squeezed in. Plenty of parking space, though. *(Across from bus station; 12 rooms, D $12.65, T $17.25, all with TV, AC, private bath; 24hr checkout; parking; cafetín)*

Food & Drink

Family Pizza (City Center map) Try a 12-inch pizza for $5.75 at this popular after-school hangout with pastel walls and hanging plants. *(7am-7pm)*

Comedor Buen Gusto (City Center map) A little dive specializing in enormous oysters; just look for the ladies hammering away outside. Twelve small oysters go for $2.30, and a dozen big ones are $4.60. It's not open every day...just depends on how the fishing goes

Baty Carnitas Restaurant (City Center map) Take a seat inside this swanky place at one of the white tables under a good strong fan. Plates of chicken and shrimp are $4.60 and up. *(9am-8pm)*

Pastelería Lorena (City Center map) Plenty of space inside to enjoy Lorena's wide variety of pastries. Pastries and bread start at $0.10, and juices are $0.70. *(8am-6pm)*

Pastelería Francesa (City Center map) The selection here isn't as big as Lorena's next door, but Francesa has AC. *(Next to Lorena's; 8am-5:30pm)*

Pupusería Las Gemelas On a good weekend they'll sell 1,000 *pupusas* here. Good news: they cook them in margarine, not lard. There's no sign outside, so look for the green plastic sun shade over the door of a red and white house. *(Weds-Sun 4:30-9pm)*

Restaurant Gran Tejano (City Center map) Dark inside and decorated like a ranch, with wooden tables and animal hides on the wall. Kind of smells like a ranch, too. Main dishes cost $5.75-$9.20. *(11:30am-9pm)*

Restaurant La Ronda This friendly joint is a good place for a drink. An $0.80 beer comes with little meat, chicken or shrimp appetizers, or *bocas*, which would otherwise cost $0.30. A *plato típico mixto* is $3.70. *(10am-10pm)*

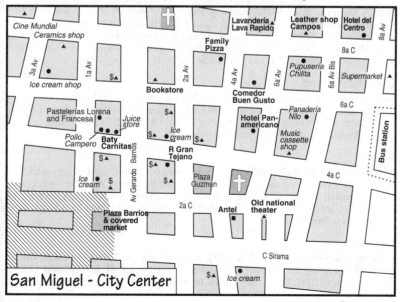

San Miguel - City Center

Abracadabra, Royal Flush

Judging by the comments of an 18th century traveler who passed through the city, San Miguel has seen its share of action. In his diary, the traveler noted how the city was set in the panoramic foothills of the San Miguel Volcano and how the Spanish, *mestizo* and indigenous populations generally lived together peacefully.

But, he added, San Miguel was "a hell of dissidence and gangs" where "the dominant vice is gambling." "This vice is so extreme," he continued, "that gamblers steal everything from their wives, even their dresses, and leave them naked as the day they were born just to be able to play."

Apparently, some gamblers even resorted to witchcraft. The traveler wrote that gamblers would first grind human bones into a powder, use the powder to form a candle and burn the candle wherever they played. The magic smoke that was released made everyone sleepy and was supposed to help the gambler win more easily.

Restaurant La Pradera This white open-air building, set off from the road, has been run by a father and son for the past three years. Dishes are on the expensive side; a plate of shrimp costs $9.50. *(11:30am-9:30pm)*

Pupusería Los Gorritos *Pupusas* here run $0.23 and are made with vegetable oil. *(Across from Pollo Campero; 4-9pm)*

Restaurant La Pampa Argentina If you've got a big hole to fill and a little money to burn, try one of La Pampa's two specialities: a *churrasco* (14 ounces of grilled meat) for $8 or the *pamperito mixto* (meat with shrimp) for $9.75. Both come with soup, salad, garlic bread and a baked potato. *(12-2:30pm, 6-10pm)*

Willy's Comida a la Vista/Tacos y Pupusas "Vicky" One place with two names; in the morning, this small clean cafeteria is Willy's and in the evening his wife Vicky takes over. He sells chicken and rice for $1.15, while she'll whip you up a taco for $1.40. Willy lived in New York and met Vicky, who also runs a local bakery, when he returned to El Salvador. *(7am-4pm, 4-9pm)*

Entertainment

Disco El Alazán Looks like an enormous high school dance hall packed with plastic tables. The restaurant here serves small dishes, like *tortas,* for around $2.30. At night, the cover is $1.15-$1.70, plus another $1.50 when a live band is playing. *(Restaurant 5pm-5am, disco 9pm-5am)*

Sights

Iglesia Capilla Medalla Milagrosa A hospital compound used to surround this beautiful little white church that was designed by French nuns who worked in the hospital. The hospital is now gone and the church windows display some of the finest stained glass in El Salvador. The church is enclosed by a black steel gate and a forest of trees.

Details

■ **Buses: Ciudad Barrios (316, 317)**, every 20 min until 2:30pm, 48km, 2hr. **El Cuco (320)**, every 30 min until 5pm, 40km, 1hr 30min. **El Tamarindo (385)**, every hour until 3pm, 75km, 2hr 15min. **La Unión (324)**, every 10 min until 6pm,

Pupusa vendor, Olocuilta

Two boys at sunset, Playa San Marcelino

42km, 1hr 20min. **Moncagua (90)**, every 10 min until 5:30pm, 13km, 40min. **Perquín (332)**, every 1-2 hr until 12:40pm, 85km, 2hr 30min. **Puerto El Triunfo (377)**, every 30 min until 5pm, 67km, 2hr 15min. **San Francisco Gotera (328, 332, 337, 386)**, every 15 min until 6:10pm, 35km, 50min. **San Salvador (301)**, every 15 min until 6pm, 138km, 3hrs. **San Vicente (301)**, every 15 min until 4:30pm, 96km, 2hrs. **Santa Rosa de Lima (306)**, every 10 min until 5:30pm, 49km, 1hr. **Usulután (373)**, every 10 min until 5:40pm, 60km, 1hr 30min. **Zacatecoluca (301a)**, every 90 min until 12:30pm, 60km, 2hr 45min.

■ **Festivals: November 14-30 (20, 21)** Nuestra Señora de la Paz. Hot-air balloons, go-kart, bicycle and motorcycle races. **Late November** Carnival Noviembrino. A well-known carnival that attracts visitors from all over.

■ **Laundry: Lavandería Lava Rápido** One of the few do-it-yourself laundromats in the country. $1.15 per load for eight pieces, $1.40 to dry, no ironing. *(8am-5pm)*

■ **Shopping: Leather Shop Campos** A leather store selling souvenirs made of cow, snake and lizard hide. Wallets are $2.30, belts $3.45 and saddles $13.80. *(8am-5pm)*

Near San Miguel

San Miguel Volcano This granddaddy of a mountain, largely isolated from the rest of the Chinameca range, juts 2,140 meters out of the southern coastal plain. The volcano looks especially impressive from the Coastal Highway, and as you drive away in any direction it remains visible for kilometers.

Chaparrastique, as it is traditionally known, is good for a serious climb. Be careful, though, since it occasionally comes to life—it last erupted in 1976. The climb to the top winds through some enormous coffee plantations. In fact, you're not likely to see much on the way up except coffee plantations, bushes and pickers. If that sounds interesting, and you can handle sulphur fumes at the top, then you'll get a world-class view down into the crater. A dirt road leads to the top. Bring your own food and drink.

You can either drive or catch a couple buses to get to the mountain *pueblito* of Conacastal. From there, there's a path that leads to the top of the volcano. If you're going by bus, catch one that's heading to San Vicente and asked to be dropped off six kilometers west of San Miguel on the road to the left that leads toward San Jorge. At that point, the Laguna Seca (Dry Lagoon) El Pacayual is to the right and the San Miguel Volcano is to the left. From the intersection, get a lift up into the mountains and hop off at Antel in tiny Conacastal. The entrance to the Finca Miracielo is pretty clear—there's a red door with two white pillars and a sign outside that reads, "Recibidero Prieto." If you're coming by car, be out by 6pm or they'll lock you in. Sr. Ricardo Men holds the gate keys, so you'll want to speak with him before leaving your car behind.

Laguna El Jocotal Get a taste of the rough beginnings of Salvadoran ecotourism at this unofficial bird sanctuary/wetlands preserve. Unfortunately, things still have a ways to go. Women wash clothing and men fish at the lagoon. The area is rich with wildlife, but passing through the small village and crossing the muddy estuary to reach it isn't the most inviting prospect. You have to take a boat out into the lagoon to truly appreciate the surroundings. A

Jocoro

This small town in the southern foothills of Morazán department 22 kilometers from San Miguel saw a lot of fighting during the war. Today, it's a quiet, pretty stop-off on the road between San Miguel and Santa Rosa de Lima. There aren't any hotels or restaurants in Jocoro, but there's some good hiking in the hills just to the south.

one-hour ride with one of the local fishermen should run about $2. A slightly longer trip will allow you to visit one of the four islands in the lagoon; La Monca is the best.

Look for the turnoff for the Cantón Borabollón off the Coastal Highway between San Miguel and Usulután, near a light blue church at km 132. Bus drivers should know where it is. The concrete road leads away from the San Miguel Volcano towards the cantón. The government was supposed to pave this road to increase tourism, but it looks like they ran out of steam after the first 80 or so meters—from there on in it's all mud. The lagoon is about one kilometer from the small cluster of houses that comprise the cantón. Notice that the walls and building foundations are built with rock from the San Miguel Volcano.

Eastern Beaches

Some of El Salvador's best beaches are located between Usulután and La Unión along the Coastal Highway. Set against the coastal mountain range, a few have clean, white sand and are hundreds of meters wide.

Playa El Espino

Playa El Espino is, hands down, both the best beach in the country and the most difficult to get to. But rest assured, the rocky approach over mountains and through small rivers is worth enduring. El Salvador's coastal Shangri-La is a beach connoisseur's dream that will make you want to ride a horse naked down the sand, like in some B-movie dream sequence.

The beach is big enough for a boardwalk, two Club Meds and crowds of thousands, but it's absolutely silent, clean and devoid of gaudy houses. The lazy Pacific waves lap the sand in slow motion, while the beach itself (like any good beach) is lined with palm trees and continues out of sight in either direction. A few *comedores* are near the end of the road, and serve seafood dishes for about $3. Come here to get away from absolutely everything: walk for hours, swing in a hammock, pretend you're a million kilometers from anywhere. You won't be disappointed.

If you're driving, turn off the Coastal Highway at the sign for Playa El Espino and Jucuarán 11 kilometers east of Usulután. After a short detour over a steel bridge, follow the incredibly rutted road up and over the mountains. Hold on to the dashboard and stay right at the large tree near the turn-off for Jucuarán at the top of the mountains. After you pass over the crest of the mountains, the ocean never looked so welcoming.

Details
■ **Buses: Usulután (351)**, 5, 7am, 2pm, 33km, 2hr.

Playa El Cuco
The road to El Cuco twists its way up and over the coastal mountain range, with a great view of the San Miguel Volcano to the right. The beach itself—once you get away from the little town at the end of the road—is another one of El Salvador's hidden coastal gems. Wide, white sand stretches off into the distance, and everything is yours during the week. The gorgeous vista is completed by palm trees, red tile roofs and mountains in the distance.

Most of the area is privately-owned, and consequently some hotels may want to charge you to enter the beach through their property. Get off somewhere along the dirt road that runs parallel to the beach, think inconspicuous thoughts, cross over quietly and you can probably get in for free. Or just ask permission to enter through someone's private lot. You can catch a ride on a pickup running up and down the road along the beach, and shower in one of the local shops for next to nothing. The town is filled with little *comedores* that sell seafood plates for $2.85-$5.75.

Accommodations
Hotel Leones Marinos A large, walled-in coconut grove. The rooms are large and have hammocks but the beds have no mattresses and the bathrooms are old and run-down. Go to El Cuco to eat. *(150m from El Cuco; 14S $11.50, 6D $17.25, all with private bath; 24hr checkout)*

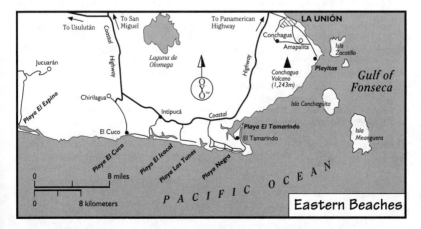

> **"It is always the same. The army comes and goes. The guerrillas come and go. We hide under our beds."**
>
> —Villager, on life during the war
>
> VOICES FROM THE WAR

Hospedaje Rico Mar The price for these little concrete huts with no windows fluctuates inexplicably for essentially the same rooms. Bring your own sheets. *(10S $2.85-$5.75 with shared baths; 24hr checkout)*

Hospedaje Buenos Aires You'll know this place by its red door, green walls and tile patio. They'll ask $5.75 for a night in a stark concrete room but try to bargain; you might be surprised. Day rates are slightly lower. *(Next to Rico Mar; 12S $5.75 with shared baths)*

Hospedaje Vásquez Very basic—the owner won't give a price but don't pay more than $3 to stay in this simple little concrete shack. *(10S)*

Ospedaje Arriasa Yes, the name is spelled correctly, but no, it's not a nice place to stay. The rooms have packed dirt floors, shower water comes from a well and the bathroom is a hole in the ground. *(8 rooms $1.15)*

El Tropi-Club Cabañas The club has a grassy area flanked by palm trees good for relaxing, but it's just a little too expensive. The rooms, with two beds, thatched roofs, brick floors and big fans are clean but not much for the price. A restaurant operates on weekends, serving up shrimp dishes and the like for $5.75-$8, but they might cook you something during the week if you ask. *(Near the Hotel Cuco Lindo; 12 cabins $18/$25/$32 for the day/overnight/24hrs, all with private bath, fans, 3 suites $38/$50/$63.50, all with private bath, AC; laundry; restaurant)*

La Tortuga Trailer Park and Bungalows Set back in a pleasant coconut grove with small, white adobe cabins, this place is a real surprise and is seldom full. The cabins are clean and have modern bathrooms, but bring your own sheets and food. The beach is quiet and often deserted. You might have to knock on the brown door to get the gatekeeper to let you in. *(about 2km from El Cuco; cabins $15 for 2 people, $20 for 3 people, all with private bath, kitchens; 24hr checkout)*

Hotel Cuco Lindo A collection of grubby white beach huts that looks like a little ghost town. Rooms are very simple, the bathrooms OK, but the whole place is awfully old for the price they're asking; go to Tortuga instead. Bus 320 to San Miguel comes by here at 6, 11am and 5pm. *(1km from El Cuco along road parallel to the beach, go left when you hit El Cuco and continue straight; S $7 with shared bath, sleeping mat, 11 cabins $18.50 with 2 beds and fan, $28.75 with AC, large bed and sleeping mat; 24hr checkout)*

Details

■ **Buses: San Miguel (320)**, every 90 min until 4pm, 37km, 90min.

IN THE NEWS

Intipuca

At first glance, the unassuming little town of Intipuca near Playa Icacal in La Unión seems like any other seaside village. Spend some time there, though, and you'll notice that the streets are a little cleaner, the pastel colors a little brighter and the iron gates a little newer in Intipuca than in most towns, and for good reason. Intipuca receives more money from relatives in the US than any other town its size in El Salvador—more, even, than many large cities. Fifteen thousand Intipuqueños live in Washington DC and its suburbs, and send nearly $100,000 back to Intipuca per month.

Such a huge cash flow has had interesting consequences. Five courier services bring packages and letters to this town with a population of just 12,500. More phones calls are made from Intipuca to the US than from almost any other city in the country. During holidays, the national airline offers special deals to residents of Intipuca.

Playa El Icacal

The clean shores of Icacal stretch for 13 kilometers from end to end, with a great combination of unspoiled beauty and relatively easy access. The soft, white sand is more than 100 meters wide at low tide, and the ocean is only knee-deep even far from the beach. Locals say that this is the safest beach along the estuary that connects to Playa El Cuco. There aren't any places to spend the night, just plenty of palm trees waiting for a hammock. Some places along the road sell sodas, but come prepared with food and drink anyway.

The beach seems wide enough to land a plane on, and it is; during the war, guerrilla contraband and arms were brought in here at night by boat and plane from Nicaragua. Every once in a while a Cessna still lands here.

Getting There

The turnoff from the Coastal Highway is 25 kilometers west of La Unión, across the street from a rock with a green PCN fish painted on it. Acres of spiky, grey-green *maguey* (henequen) cover the surrounding fields. The shady dirt track is barely passable by regular car. Four kilometers in, you might have to bribe the old gatekeeper with a few *colones* to let you enter this "private" stretch of beach.

Details
■ **Buses: San Miguel (385)**, 6, 7:30am, 4pm, 39km, 1hr 30min.

Playa Las Tunas

Playa Las Tunas, 24 kilometers west of La Unión, is a typical Salvadoran beach town; there's trash everywhere, and boom boxes and old concrete *comedores* line the ocean. It's a great beach if you feel like hanging out and drinking beer, but go next door to Icacal if open sand is your thing.

Las Tunas does have a few good places to eat, and when you arrive kids run up to you offering seafood cocktails. You may want to grab a bite here and sleep somewhere else. The turn-off to the beach is across the street from the pink and white-striped church, about 24 kilometers west of La Unión. There are some simple concrete rooms available in town for $5.75 a night.

Food & Drink
Restaurant Blanquita Waves break up against this restaurant set off the beach on a pile of rocks—sit too near the edge and you'll get doused. Under the open roof you'll find concrete benches and tables, a few hammocks and a rowdy beach crowd drinking beer in the afternoon. Clams and oysters cost from $3.50 to $4.60, depending on the size. *(7am-5pm)*

Details
■ **Buses: La Unión (383)**, every 15 min until 5:30pm, 24km, 1hr. **San Miguel (385)** 8am, 5:30pm, 47km, 2hr 30min.

Playa Negra
Playa Negra has a few decent, expensive hotels, but otherwise it's a narrower version of Las Tunas, with fewer rocks and even more trash.

Accommodations
Hotel Playa Negra Clean, comfy, spacious and pricey, with a leafy terrace and cloudy pool. An open-air restaurant serves "international food" and looks out over the beach. Seafood dishes in the 24-hour restaurant are $7, but you can get a cocktail for $3.50. *(Road to El Tamarindo, km8; 10 rooms, $35 with 1 bed, $46 with 3 beds, all with private bath, AC; free laundry; pool; 24hr checkout; restaurant open 24 hours)*

Torola Cabaña Club The same people who run the Izalco Cabaña Club in La Paz run this place, which has a stylish new interior and comfortable wicker chairs. Rooms are decent and classy in a simple way, but like its sister hotel it's overpriced. The pool down below has an entrance onto the beach, and there's a view out over the beach from the expensive restaurant on the pier. *(Tel 664-4516; 6S $85 with beach view, 6D $62, 8T $69, all with private bath; laundry; 2pm checkout; restaurant)*

Hotel Mar y Tierra The concrete rooms around a dirt courtyard are Spartan but clean. The prices aren't so Spartan, though, unless you fit ten people to a room, which they allow. The prices double for 24 hours, and you can get a seafood plate at the restaurant for $3.50. *(10S $11.50 for 12 hours, all with private baths, fan; restaurant)*

Food & Drink
Restaurant La Mariscada Serves seafood and other dishes outside on a sandy front lawn under multicolored umbrellas. The owner is a Salvadoran who recently returned from San Francisco to open this restaurant. Seafood plates are $4-$7, and the tasty *sopa de consommé* is $4.60. *(7am-10pm)*

El Tamarindo

This dusty fishing town at the end of the road south of La Unión isn't worth a trip all the way out here just in itself. But a few small openings to the water outside of town lead to cleaner and quieter sections of beach with a great panorama of the nearby volcanoes and islands. El Tamarindo doesn't feel as exotic as Espino or Icacal, but these hidden spots are more easily accessible and more pleasant than any other beaches nearby.

To find a good part of El Tamarindo beach, stop about one kilometer before the town at the first or second dirt road after La Mariscada. From there, take a side passage to the beach past one of the big, well-maintained houses. Even though it's lined with houses and boats, the beach is quiet on weekends; the volcanoes and gently curving shore can almost convince you you're on a tropical island. The bodies of land visible in the bay, from left to right, are the Conchagua Volcano near Usulután, the islands of Conchagüita and Meanguera, and the northwest edge of Nicaragua.

Details

■ **Buses: La Unión (383)**, every 90 min until 5:20pm, 44km, 1hr 30min. **San Miguel (385)**, every hour until 4:30pm, 55km, 2hr 30min.

La Unión

Pop. 62,000
183km from San Salvador

La Unión Then

La Unión became eastern El Salvador's largest port near the end of the 17th century, replacing the older port of Amapala to the south near Playa El Tamarindo. La Unión was repeatedly attacked by Spanish forces during battles for Central American independence. In 1856, troops from El Salvador and Guatemala set sail from here to battle William Walker in Nicaragua. In the last two centuries the city has been repeatedly jolted by earthquakes, though none have hit since the late 1940s.

La Unión Now

Just before it reaches La Unión, the Panamerican Highway heads off to the north for the Honduran border at El Amatillo, and the Coastal Highway heads south and west for the eastern beaches. The port city of La Unión is set along the western shore of the Bay of La Unión off of the Gulf of Fonseca, bordered on the south by mountains that fold and slip quietly into the sea. The city has gone downhill since the port closed about ten years ago, but rumor has it that the Japanese government plans to reopen the port in the near future.

TO THE EAST

The city itself is run-down and dirty, but a few good, inexpensive places to stay and the beaches nearby make it a worthwhile stop in the east. Use La Unión as a base to explore some of the better beaches to the south by day, and relax at Gallo's Restaurant at night.

Accommodations

Hotel Portobello La Unión The best hotel deal in La Unión is three stories tall with a parking area, large rooms, clean showers and hammocks in every room. The owner Luís opened the hotel in 1994, and he and his family will help you out around town. He also has some interesting stories to tell about his life in this war-ravaged region, and his rocky road from selling cattle to opening a hotel. *(Tel 664-4113; 20 rooms, S $4.60, D $5.75, $10 with AC, all with private bath; laundry; 24hr checkout; parking; cafeteria)*

Hotel San Francisco Large metal doors off the street mark the entrance to this old but passable hotel. *(Tel 664-4159; 17S $5.75 with fan, 13D $11.50 with AC, all with private bath; 24hr checkout; parking)*

Hospedaje Anexo Santa Marta The graffiti on the doors add to the run-down, homey feel of this place. A central courtyard with trees and plants looks like someone's overgrown backyard. The entrance is on 7a Av Nte. *(Tel 674-4238; 9S $3.50, 2D $5.75, all with private bath, fan; 24hr checkout)*

Casa de Huéspedes El Dorado Alicia is the nice lady who runs this pleasant place, and she loves to talk with guests. The rooms are clean and all have hammocks. *(Tel 664-4724; 10S/D $4, $4.60 with private bath; 24hr checkout)*

Hotel Centroamericano Located in a fenced-in yard with the look and feel of a military compound. A big, dated lobby and old bathrooms complete the picture. *(Tel 664-4029; 8S $5.75 with shared bath, 4S $7 with private bath, 8D $9.25 with private bath and AC; noon checkout; parking)*

Food and Drink

Pastelería y Baty Jugos Claudita The pizza at this combination pizza shop/*cafetería* is doughy, but the *licuados* slide down nicely. Large pizza $6, or $1.50 per piece. *(Mon-Sat 7am-9pm)*

Gallo's Restaurant This classy restaurant is a great deal and one of La Unión's saving graces, with the tastiest food south of Santa Rosa de Lima's La Pema. Waitresses serve steaming plates of real Mexican food that sizzle for a minute after they're set down in front of you. Plates of corn *tortillas*, *burritos*, *tacos* and *enchiladas* cost $3.50-$5.75.

If you approach La Unión at the right time, the view can be downright spectacular. Try to take the Panamerican Highway east from San Miguel late in the afternoon. You'll leave the San Miguel Volcano behind as the road climbs over the coastal mountain range. Suddenly, the Conchagua Volcano and the Gulf of Fonseca come into view ahead with the city of La Unión in between, as the entire panorama is lit up by the sun setting over Honduras. Sit on the left of the bus for the best view.

Owner Alex Gallo worked in a Mexican restaurant in Washington DC for 14 years and then returned to El Salvador to open his own. He wanted to keep prices low so locals could enjoy his restaurant too. There was a problem with the

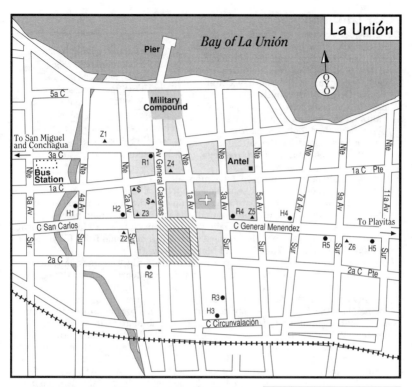

quality of local *tortillas,* so he buys his Mexican-style *tortillas* directly from San Salvador. *(8am-midnight)*

Details

■ **Buses:** To get to the Honduran border at El Amatillo, you must first go to Santa Rosa de Lima. **Conchagua (382)**, every 20 min until 6pm, 4km, 20min. **El Tamarindo (383)**, every 20 min until 5:30pm, 30km, 1hr 30min. **Playitas (418)**, every 30 min until 5pm, 13km, 1hr. **San Miguel (324)**, every 8 min until 5:50pm, 42km, 1hr 20min. **San Salvador (304)**, every 30 min until 2pm, 183km, 4hr. **Santa Rosa de Lima (342)**, every 15 min until 5:50pm, 48km, 1hr 30min.

■ **Festivals: December 3-31 (7)** Virgen de Concepción.

ACCOMMODATIONS ●

H1 Hotel Portobello La Unión
H2 Casa de Huéspedes El Dorado
H3 Hotel Centroamericano
H4 Hospedaje Anexo Santa Marta
H5 Hotel San Francisco

FOOD & DRINK ●

R1 *Cafetín El Marinero*
R2 *Pollo Rico*
R3 *Gallo's Restaurant*
R4 *Pastelería y Baty Jugos Claudita*
R5 *Snack bar*

OTHER ▲

Z1 Office of Immigration
Z2 Basketball Court
Z3 Police Station
Z4 Music Hall
Z5 Video Arcade
Z6 Hospital

Near La Unión

Conchagua Volcano Of all the volcanoes in El Salvador, few have such a choice location; from the top you can see all the islands of the Gulf of Fonseca, Honduras to the east, Nicaragua to the southeast and the Pacific Ocean to the south. The four-hour hike to the peak from the village of Amapalita on the road to Playitas passes coffee plantations and only takes three hours coming back. Head for the antenna at the top of the mountain. *(Take the bus to Playitas and get off at Amapalita)*

> Some of La Unión's inhabitants are descended from English pirates who raped and pillaged their way through indigenous populations in the 17th century. Their distinctive light hair, fair skin and blue eyes serve as a reminder of what El Salvador has endured over the centuries.

Playitas Eight kilometers from La Unión, Playitas is a 100-meter black sand beach in front of a fishing village. This is the real thing: wooden fishing boats are rolled up onto the beach on logs, and in the afternoon fishermen repair their nets in the fading light. Some places in town serve drinks and fresh fish. The islands of Conchagüita and Meanguera loom just off the beach. Around the corner to the left (not visible from Playitas) are the smaller islands of Zacatillo and Martín Pérez.

The *pueblito* of Playitas isn't the most inviting place to hang out, and the beach itself doesn't justify a trip. A boat ride to a nearby island, though, is a great way to spend a solitary day or two hiking and camping.

Tiny Zacatillo and Martín Pérez are practically near enough to swim to; the former has the Playa Carey on its southern end. Conchagüita is 15 minutes away by boat, and a day trip there should cost no more than $17.25. You'll be quoted $23 for a ride to the clean, black sand beaches of Meanguera, farthest away and the largest Salvadoran island in the Gulf, but a little haggling will work wonders. The ride takes a little over half an hour. Offer half payment up front and the rest when you're picked up (as the song says, "Don't pay the ferryman/ 'til he gets you to the other side…"). Both of the larger islands have *pueblos* where you can buy drinks. Finding some fresh fish for lunch should be easy, but bring food and water anyway. Boats usually leave early in the morning. *(Take C General Menéndez out of La Unión to the east past the naval base, or bus 418)*

Conchagua

Potón, "Flying Jaguar"
Pop. 32,500
5km from La Unión

La Union
Conchagua

Conchagua Then

The original inhabitants of Conchagua lived on the islands of the Gulf of Fonseca, just offshore from La Unión. The name Conchagua originally belonged to one of the Lenca towns on the island of Conchagüita.

In the late 17th century, English pirates raided the islands and pillaged the towns, leaving the indigenous populations with little or nothing. When the towns-people decided to emigrate to the mainland, they petitioned the Spanish king for land and were granted a site on the edge of the Conchagua Volcano. Ten years after founding the new Conchagua, villagers began construction of the church that still survives (with a few new coats of paint).

Conchagua Now

This small town is nestled partway up the slopes of the 1,245-meter Conchagua Volcano to the south of La Unión. The church is well-maintained and local choirs sometimes perform inside.

Conchagua is charming for what it doesn't have: heat, trash, traffic and crowds. It's a place to come after a day at the beach to breathe in some cool mountain air, sit in on a church service and talk to residents around the *pupusa* stands about their relatives in the US. If you come early enough, you might even be able to join a game of basketball.

If you're driving, take the Panamerican Highway out of La Unión and turn left 20 meters before the Esso gas station, across the road from the cemetery. Soon you'll pass railroad tracks and the cobblestone road becomes paved for the rest of the four kilometers to Conchagua. If you stay until the early evening after the last bus leaves (and you should), you can catch a taxi back to La Unión from here for about $1.25. A ride in the other direction, though, costs about $3.

Sights

Iglesia Colonial de Conchagua This pretty, cream-colored church is decorated with light blue trim. The church was first built in 1693 and still has its original facade. Images inside date back to the 17th century.

Hiking

La Glorieta If the views from Conchagua aren't enough, the lookout called La Glorieta offers a view out over the city of La Unión, the Gulf of Fonseca and its islands and all the way to Honduras across the Gulf. Start on the opposite side of the church and continue uphill on foot for about half an hour.

TO THE EAST

Details
- **Buses:** The bus stop is next to the church. **La Unión (382)**, every 20 min until 6:20pm, 5km, 20min.
- **Festivals: January 18-21 (19)** San Sebastián. **July 24-25 (24)** Santiago Apóstol.

Santa Rosa de Lima

Pop. 37,500
176km from San Salvador
44km from La Unión

Santa Rosa de Lima Then

Manuel Días, a rich Spaniard from Peru, bought land in northeastern El Salvador in 1743 and erected an enormous *hacienda* which he named Santa Rosa de Lima in honor of Peru's patron saint. In the 19th-century, a traveler described the town as a "pretty and progressive city with stone streets."

In 1983, El Salvador's eastern border trade with Honduras almost collapsed when rebel troops blew up six bridges connecting the two countries, including the bridge at the El Amatillo border crossing just east of Santa Rosa de Lima. Honduran troops opened fire on the guerrillas but were unable to stop the destruction, which the FMLN claimed was in response to a speech by President Reagan calling for a renewed battle against them.

Santa Rosa de Lima Now

The second largest city in La Unión is surrounded by the low mountains that fill northern La Unión and Morazán departments and run to the border with Honduras. Santa Rosa de Lima is a dusty place with lots of buildings under construction, and it suffers occasional power and water shortages. The L-shaped church seems almost too large for the town, but the interior is clean and well-kept and has a fresh coat of paint. Santa Rosa de Lima is best known as the home of La Pema, one of El Salvador's most famous (and unpretentious) restaurants, which justifies a trip to the city all by itself.

Accommodations

Hotel El Recreo Best lounge area in town, complete with couches and chairs. *(Tel 664-2126; 10S 5D $4.60 per person, all with shared bath, fan; 11am checkout; free laundry; parking)*

"It's a lie. There are plenty of bombs."

— Peasant, responding to government claim that the
Salvadoran air force never bombs civilian targets

VOICES FROM THE WAR

TO THE EAST

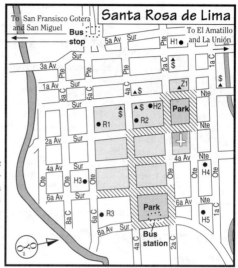

ACCOMMODATIONS ●
H1 *Hotel Florida*
H2 *Hospedaje La Esperanza*
H3 *Hospedaje Mundial*
H4 *Hotel El Recréo*
H5 *Hotel El Tejano*

FOOD & DRINK ●
R1 *Comedor*
R2 *La Pema*
R3 *Comedor*

OTHER ▲
Z1 *El Presidio*
Z2 *Biblioteca Municipal*

Hospedaje Mundial Basic rooms are passable on a budget if you bring your own sheets. *(18 rooms $2 with fan and shared bath; 24hr checkout)*

Food & Drink

La Pema Truly a Salvadoran national culinary treasure, La Pema is famous from Ahuachapán to Zacatecoluca. La Pema may not be easy to find but it's worth the hype, as many ambassadors and other foreign dignitaries can attest. All of the tables in this simple restaurant are usually full, with everybody busy enjoying one of the two dishes they serve. Mariachi bands serenade you as you dig into a steaming bowl of *mariscada,* a rich cream-based soup overflowing with enough seafood to sink a trawler, for $7. *Carne de res* is also available for the same price, and don't miss the *ensalada de frutas,* a huge mug of apples, mangos, oranges and grapes for only $0.60. Tasty *pupusas* filled with a special cheese are included with every meal.

Eufemia de Lazo has been cooking everything herself since the early 1970s to make sure the quality is up to her exacting standards. She hasn't expanded to other restaurants because she wants to be able to keep tabs on quality. Her daughter, however, will soon open a restaurant in San Miguel. *(Unmarked red and white building next to BanCo on 4a C; Tues-Sun 9:30am-4pm)*

Details

■ **Buses:** To go to San Francisco Gotera, hop a bus towards San Miguel and ask the driver to drop you off at *"la diez y ocho"* (bus stop #18), which will put you on the road to Gotera. From there catch any bus north. **El Amatillo (330, 336, 342, 346)**, every 13 min until 5:30pm, 30km, 1hr 30min. **La Unión (342, 343, 344)**, every 10 min until 5:45pm, 44km, 1hr 30min. **San Miguel (306, 330)**, every 10 min, 40km, 1hr. **San Salvador (306)**, every 30 min until 2:20pm, 176km, 4hr
■ **Festivals: August 22-31 (30)** Santa Rosa. Includes famous rodeos.

| IN THE NEWS |

Neighbor Friction

The Salvadoran government suspected Nicaragua of shipping arms to the FMLN throughout the war, but lacked hard evidence for a long time. The army suspected that rebels brought the equipment overland on the backs of donkeys or with boats through the Gulf of Fonseca. Finally, when a Nicaraguan aircraft crashed in El Salvador in the late 1980s and was found to be filled with missiles intended for the rebels, the Salvadoran government suspended relations with Nicaragua.

Daniel Ortega, Nicaragua's president at the time, responded that, "as a Nicaraguan, I feel proud that this murderous government has cut relations with us." After the Ortega government was defeated in subsequent elections and four Nicaraguan officers were arrested for smuggling supplies and weapons to the FMLN, the two countries eventually reestablished relations.

San Francisco Gotera
(Gotera)

Potón, "High Hill"
Pop. 17,000
197km from San Salvador

San Francisco Gotera

San Francisco Gotera Then

The ruins of ancient San Francisco Gotera are now no more than two rectangular buildings set atop the Cerro de Corobán, four kilometers to the northeast of the town's present location. It is uncertain when the town relocated, but the townsfolk were probably motivated by the difficulty of finding drinking water nearby and the strong mountain winds, which made fires difficult to control.

A visitor to the new and improved Gotera in 1811 noted that its indigenous inhabitants spoke a unique dialect of the Lenca Potón language, incomprehensible even to other native speakers. The Goterans, on the other hand, could understand other Potón speakers without a problem.

During the civil war, Gotera had the misfortune to serve as a military stronghold smack in the center of a guerrilla-dominated department. At one point in 1981, urban gun battles left the city's streets filled with bodies.

For most of the war, though, life in the city remained at least superficially normal. San Francisco Gotera was one of the few places in the region that had a consistent supply of electricity. Soldiers filled the streets and the army occupied the central plaza, which didn't leave much room for locals to socialize. Although life in Gotera during the war was difficult, it was simply unbearable in many other towns in the province. The capital became a center of refuge for up to 15,000 people who left towns north of the Río Torola in the early and mid 1980s.

San Francisco Gotera Now

San Francisco Gotera hugs the hills of central Morazán, which give it one of the more beautiful settings in the eastern part of the country. Barefoot children play soccer up and down the city's gently rolling streets.

On the west side of town is a ridiculous legacy to the town's recent history: a huge camouflaged military compound with the bold logo *Bienvenido al DM-4 / No Hay Misión Imposible* (Welcome to DM-4/No Mission Is Impossible). The garrison sits right next to a beautiful colonial church, like a child's clubhouse next to a wedding cake. History buffs might find some of the town's graffiti interesting, including some in support of the LP-28, an early leftist group. In spite of its past, San Francisco Gotera has an indefinable good "feel" to it.

ACCOMMODATIONS ●
H1 Hospedaje San Fransisco

FOOD & DRINK ●
R1 Comedor Melita
R2 Restaurant El Bonanza
R3 *Cafetín*
R4 *Super McPollo*
R5 *Cafetería Candy*
R6 Café Plaza
R7 *Comedor*
R8 *Cafetería Yaneth*

OTHER ▲
Z1 Police Station
Z2 Casa de la Cultura
Z3 Cine Morazán
Z4 Military Compound
Z5 Photo Shop

Accommodations

Hospedaje San Francisco A relaxed place with a small courtyard around a garden. Rooms are clean with hanging light bulbs, hammocks and tile roofs. *(Tel 664-0066; 18 rooms, S $3.50, D $5.75, T $7, all with shared bath, $8.50 with private bath; noon checkout)*

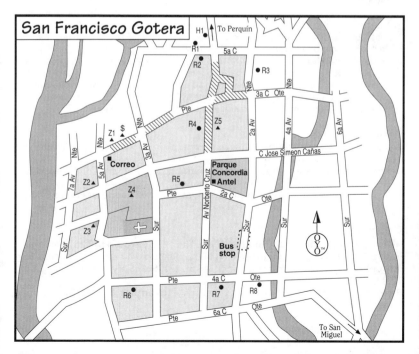

San Francisco Gotera

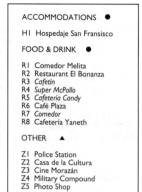

TO THE EAST

Food & Drink

Restaurant El Bonanza   In this big, plain joint you can eat upstairs on the open-air terrace, where music is occasionally played at night. The prices for seafood are steep, though, and the food is greasy. Chicken and beef dishes run $3.50-$4.50, hamburgers $1. *(9am-10pm)*

Comedor Melita   Across the street from Bonanza, with cheaper food. *(Mon-Sat 6:30am-7:30pm, Sun 6:30am-1pm)*

Café Plaza   Set back in a little courtyard with Salvadoran crafts on the walls. Good for a leisurely hamburger and a dish of ice cream. *(6:30am-10pm)*

Cafetería Yaneth   Grab a coffee and pastry here in the morning, or fast food throughout the rest of the day. Sweetbreads are inexpensive, and a cheeseburger goes for $1.50 with fries. *(6am-9pm)*

Entertainment

Cine Morazán   This surprisingly nice, modern movie theater faces the military compound and church. Movies are $1.

Sights

Iglesia de San Francisco Gotera   This beautiful yellow and white colonial church, built in 1888, is surrounded by chicken wire and spiked fences less than ten feet from the military compound. The church is usually locked, but you can get in through a side door to see the interesting tile mosaic in the shape of a huge sun above the altar. At one point during the war, the army was going to tear down this church because it blocked their view of the town from the barracks next door. Fortunately, they didn't.

Parque Concordia   A small park with a few concrete gazebos sits on top of a hill in the center of the city. From here you can see the entire town below and the surrounding hills that meander off into the distance like a herd of green camels. Climb the wall behind the bust of Francisco Morazán for the best view, but be careful of the drop on the other side. At night, the park isn't safe.

Hiking

Ask at the Casa de la Cultura—they're very helpful and will point you in the right direction for hiking in the area.

Cerro Corobán   A foot trail up this mountain near the *pueblo* of Lolotiquillo (northeast of San Francisco Gotera) has great views all the way to La Unión. The seven-kilometer hike up should take about three hours, less coming down. *(Take bus 337 to Lolotiquillo, head east)*

Details

▪ **Buses: Lolotiquillo (337)**, until 12:10pm, 7km, 1hr. **Perquín (332a)**, every hour until 2:50pm, 33km, 1hr 30min. Goes on to the Honduran border at Sabanetas. **San Miguel (328)**, every 10 min until 6pm, 40km, 1hr. **San Salvador (305)**, 5, 6am, 12pm, 170km, 3hr 30min.

▪ **Festivals: October 1-5 (4)** San Francisco. **November 8-14 (13)** Virgen de Candelaría.

Near San Francisco Gotera

"Kilometer 18" Bus Stop Many people switch buses here at the intersection of
the road between San Miguel and Santa Rosa de Lima and the road north to
Gotera. Buses pass here heading for Perquín, Gotera, San Miguel, Santa Rosa
de Lima and the Honduran border at El Amatillo and Sabanetas.

IN THE NEWS

WFMLN: Guerrilla Radio

Hidden deep in underground bunkers,
working with sadly substandard equipment and always on the move to escape
detection by the army, the FMLN's Radio
Venceremos shared the hardships that
many of its listeners had to endure during
the civil war. Through it all, Radio
Venceremos kept the country informed,
connected and entertained.

Radio Venceremos ("We Will Over-
come"), whose broadcasts could be heard
throughout the country, was the guerrillas'
most powerful political and ideological
weapon. The station, along with a handful
of other clandestine rebel stations, competed with government broadcasts for
audience and credibility. But the rebel disc
jockeys had more in mind than just advertising revenue, and they mixed news and
songs with military reports and political
opinions.

Radio Venceremos broadcasted continually despite repeated government bombing runs and jamming attempts. Sound
rooms were dug into the hillsides, camouflaged and reinforced with concrete. Disc
jockeys (including one named Elvis) used
repeater stations—boxes placed throughout the country to rebroadcast the signal
even further—to reach FMLN troops and
anybody else who would listen, especially
the rural poor.With a team of three to 15
people, the station broadcasted every day at
6pm on FM and shortwave, usually from its
bunker but sometimes in the field under
fire from government troops. Broadcasts

were made on three frequencies simultane-
ously, and disc jockeys instructed listeners
to switch from one to the other if the program was jammed.

When the peace accords were signed in
1992, the first song Radio Venceremos
broadcasted was John Lennon's "Give
Peace a Chance." Soon, Radio Venceremos
became a legitimate station and moved
into new headquarters in a middle-class
neighborhood in San Salvador, 200 kilometers from the northern mountains that
were its home for so long. The cheap
sound mixer, car battery and old auto
antenna that once carried the station's signal were replaced with state-of-the-art
equipment.

Under the new slogan "Venceremos:
Revolutionizing Radio to Unite El Salvador," Radio Venceremos has changed its
tune somewhat. Commercials now cost
money and even the government occasionally buys a spot on the FMLN airwaves. The
station has assumed a moderate political
stance and now interviews people it once
railed against, such as Salvadoran generals
and US ambassadors. Incredibly, the station
recently denounced both striking hospital
workers and Peru's Shining Path guerrilla
movement, once natural allies of the
FMLN. As a result, some Salvadorans
believe that Radio Venceremos, with its
new, pop-heavy play schedule and shift
toward the political center, has begun to
betray its original audience.

Perquín

Potón, "On the Road of Coals"
Pop. 5,400
203km from San Salvador
33km from San Francisco Gotera

Perquín Then

If the FMLN had a capital, the northern city of Perquín was it. The city's location was strategically important; Morazán is one of the poorest departments in the country, so residents were more likely to sympathize with the revolutionaries. Also, Perquín sits near an important intersection of three roads that link northern and southern Morazán.

When the army moved through Perquín, rebels retreated into the hills and waited. Government forces never stayed very long in Perquín, since troop deployments into northern Morazán required so many soldiers and because of the constant threat of guerrilla ambushes. Radio Venceremos, the radio station of the FMLN, remained undetected in its hidden underground bunkers near here for the duration of the war.

Once-prosperous Perquín was abandoned by almost everyone except rebel sympathizers during the war, leaving many buildings empty toward the end of the 1980s. By that time, many residents had acquired the ability to identify an airplane by the roar of its engines and could tell where a bomb would drop by the angle of an airplane's flight.

Perquín Now

The road from San Francisco Gotera goes up into steep mountains, past slopes filled with henequen, farms with lava rock fences and evergreen trees in the distance. Halfway there you cross a creaky wooden one-lane bridge over the Río Torola. Keep your eyes peeled for the occasional waterfall and the FMLN graffiti

Perquín is at the end of the road, although at that point it is an exaggeration to call the final few kilometers of the route to Perquín "paved" (or even a road). Though another road heads north to the Honduran border, traveling to Perquín still makes you feel like you're reaching the end of something, as if you could turn around and see the entire country spread out below you.

In the town, mountains reach of a pine-tree landscape in the distance as the sun rises and falls behind cone-shaped peaks. Perquín's climate is cool due to its altitude, and its rocky streets are unbelievably steep. It's difficult getting around in a pick-up truck, and almost impossible in a regular car.

> ### "The newly formed Ronald Reagan Battalion swept north-eastern Morazán department in a stepped-up effort to rout leftist rebels..."
> — UPI report, 1984

VOICES FROM THE WAR

Unidentifiable remains of buildings, destroyed by repeated bombings, stand on the main plaza. The outside of the church has a large mural of Archbishop Romero. The FMLN museum, right outside of town, makes the long, tough trip here worthwhile if you've already made it as far as San Miguel. Just start out early and time the buses right.

Accommodations

Hospedaje El Gigante The only place to stay in town is really just a warehouse partitioned into separate rooms with bunk beds and thin mattresses; you'll think you're in the army. The *comedor* serves a *plato típico* for $1.20. *(Take a right 200m south of town, go down a short dirt road; 15 rooms hold 4 people each, $2.85 per person, shared bathrooms, laundry; 24hr checkout; comedor)*

Food & Drink

Comedor PADECOMSM This rough-looking, simple joint overlooking the plaza is popular with locals. Food is served on picnic tables under naked hanging bulbs. There's no menu, so the selection just depends on what they have from day to day. Most plates are $1.15-$2.20, and chicken soup is $0.80. *(6am-8pm)*

FMLN Museum

This sobering museum is the place to come face-to-face with the guerrillas and learn one version of the civil war. Numerous exhibits are housed in a series of simple concrete buildings laid out along a dirt road just north of town. The little museum yard is filled with lime trees, rose bushes, a mammoth bomb crater and the remains of military jets and rusted artillery.

The idea for the museum came from Martín Vigil, a wizened, sharp ex-guerrilla who will give you an unforgettable tour (in Spanish) when he's around. Sr. Vigil scoured the country for museum pieces, photos and memories. Six ex-guerrillas work along with Sr. Vigil and give tours daily. No smoking or picture-taking is allowed inside, and a small gift shop sells T-shirts and posters.

■ **Building 1: Sala de los Héroes y Mártires** (Room of the Heroes and Martyrs). These photographs provide some background on the famous and not-so-famous who influenced the cause of the FMLN, including Martí, Sandino, Miguel Mármol (a survivor of *La Matanza* and founder of the Salvadoran Communist Party), the victims of El Mozote, assassinated human rights workers and those killed at Romero's funeral. Museum curators traveled to many small *pueblos* to visit the families of those killed and to collect these relics. On the outside back wall are German posters supporting the FMLN.

IN THE NEWS

El Mozote

A few crumbling adobe buildings scarred with bullet holes are all that's left of this small town in northern Morazán department. Yet tourists still brave the road up here to snap pictures under the disinterested gaze of a handful of National Police stationed nearby. Ask a tourist or policeman why people come, and they'll tell you why: this quiet spot was the site of one of the worst massacres in Latin American history.

The Salvadoran Army's 800-member Atlacatl Battalion, fresh from training in the US, arrived near El Mozote in December 1981 under the command of the notorious Domingo Monterrosa. The soldiers left the area three days later. Soon after, a chilling story emerged: the battalion had killed as many as 1,000 people in El Mozote and nearby villages and had left the victims, mostly women and children, jumbled together in mass graves or simply buried under the ruins of houses that the soldiers had set on fire before leaving.

The story was told by Rufina Amaya, the sole survivor of El Mozote, who was found lost and hysterical in the woods near her village six days after the army moved out. Later, Amaya described how the soldiers had arrived in El Mozote on the night of December 11 and ordered everyone inside their homes. The next morning they ordered the villagers outside and led them off in groups to be killed—first the men, then the women, then the children. Although some soldiers were initially hesitant to carry out their instructions, they eventually followed orders and systematically proceeded to execute everyone in the town.

As soldiers prepared to kill Amaya and a group of other women, she knelt to pray as the others struggled. In the midst of the commotion, Amaya managed to crawl away into the woods. She hid near enough to the town that she could still hear the killings, which went on for hours.

When the press first published Amaya's account and evidence was collected that supported her claims, the Salvadoran government said nothing. For years, government investigations made little progress, and in time the incident became a symbol of how the Salvadoran military operated outside the law, even under the worst circumstances.

The US government, after an investigation by its embassy, claimed that no evidence pointed to a systematic massacre. Behind the scenes, the Reagan administration worked to ease Congressional concerns and to continue military aid.

El Mozote was finally investigated in the early 1990s under pressure from the Salvadoran Truth Commission. In late 1992, the first skeletons were exhumed, followed by hundreds more. Dozens of bodies were found grouped inside buildings where soldiers had shot them from the doorways.

Today, El Mozote is enveloped in a quiet, eerie light during the late afternoon. A few families have moved back into town, but most buildings remain deserted. In the clearing stands a metal sculpture of a family—father, mother, son and daughter—holding hands in silhouette. On the front is an inscription: "They did not die. They are with us, with you and with all humanity."

■ **El Mozote Memorial.** A symbolic grave in memory of victims of the massacre at El Mozote.

■ **Grave of Alvaro Rodriguez Cifuentes Carmona.** Carmona was a Chilean Special Forces soldier who came to El Salvador in the early 1980s to help train the guerrillas. He was killed in Usulután in 1982 when his mortar misfired, and his remains were eventually laid to rest here.

■ **Model Guerrilla Camp.** This mock-up of a temporary guerrilla camp shows the amazingly crude conditions the rebels lived under while in the field. The simpler huts were used until 1981, when plastic huts replaced them. Rebels walked one foot in front of the other to disguise their tracks as they entered and exited campsites.

■ **Bomb Crater.** A 500-pound bomb fell here in 1981. Next to the crater is a disarmed example of this type of bomb, which explodes only after entering the ground, leaving holes the size of houses and hurling shrapnel up to 100 meters.

■ **Building 2, Room 1: Causas Que Originaron la Guerra** (Origins of the War). This room presents the cases of those who suffered under military rule. Your guide will explain that they were helpless to change the circumstances of their misery in any way except through violent struggle. Inside are displays of people who suffered and were repressed for complaining, others who organized resistance to the government, US troops deployed in El Salvador and Salvadoran government leaders. There's a seat from an airplane that was shot down by the FMLN, an unintentionally ironic quote from ex-president Reagan ("The time has come for the United States to take the initiative in other parts of the world.") and an intense photo of a man with a pistol looking out onto the Plaza Barrios from the Metropolitan Cathedral in San Salvador.

■ **Room 2: Países Solidarnos con la Lucha Revolucionaria** (Countries in Solidarity with the Revolutionary Struggle). The FMLN considered these countries friendly to their revolution and claimed that all except Nicaragua provided only non-combative aid (although Cuba and the USSR funneled arms through Nicaragua).

■ **Room 3: Vida de Campamientos** (Camp Life). This display of arms used during the war includes guns confiscated from government troops and homemade rebel bombs. Notice the detonator and instructions for assembling it. On the wall are attack plans used in 1983 to destroy the once-grand Cuscatlán Bridge and energy plants. The FMLN motto ("Resist, Grow, Advance") is displayed proudly on the wall, above uniforms captured from government troops. (The "END" label stands for the Salvadoran National Democratic Army.) The far wall has maps showing areas that were controlled by the FMLN.

■ **Room 4: Armas Convencionales** (Conventional Armaments). The surface-to-air missile launcher and guns used in war were disabled in accordance with the 1992 peace accord. Notice that the metal on the guns is sliced through the trigger area and that the larger armaments, including a 120mm gun, are disabled at other points.

Behind the building are the remains of helicopters shot down by the FMLN, including one that carried Domingo Monterrosa, the notorious commander of the Atlacatl Battalion, to his death. The destruction of Monterrosa's helicopter was a major triumph for the guerrillas.

DOMINGO MONTERROSA (1942-1984)

Controversial to the End

Lieutenant Colonel Domingo Monterrosa led a notable but controversial military career. He commanded the Salvadoran army's third brigade, served as the army's top field commander and was considered by the US government to be a "model officer." The FMLN, meanwhile, considered him the "biggest war criminal" of the civil war.

Monterrosa was a key figure in changing the image of the army in the eyes of both Salvadorans and the international community. He tried to show how the army had nothing to hide by opening its barracks to the press and allowing reporters to travel with him during military operations. He also headed a campaign to generate public support for the military by holding town meetings and giving gifts of grain or medical services to local peasants.

The FMLN, on the other hand, regarded Monterrosa as its most effective enemy, responsible for turning the momentum of the war against them. He was known as a heartless killer, and was credited with leading aggressive counterinsurgency drives such as the massacre at El Mozote in Morazán. Even as his forces committed these atrocities,

Monterrosa still managed to win some support by pressing local communities to contribute to civic action projects.

Monterrosa was killed in 1984 when his helicopter crashed. The resulting embroglio caused as much controversy as his military career had, and each side put forth its own version of the event. The FMLN took credit for the crash, claiming that it had planted a bomb in a confiscated radio transmitter. Though much evidence suggested that the helicopter had been bombed, US investigators on the scene were unable to confirm that an explosive device had been used. The political center suggested that Monterrosa had been targeted in an internal army dispute. Right-wing military officers, meanwhile, blamed President Duarte for the assassination since Monterrosa had opposed Duarte's upcoming talks with the rebels.

Monterrosa's funeral was attended by the US ambassador, President Duarte and the entire military command, marking the event as the country's first state funeral in years. When Duarte called for three days of mourning in honor of Monterrosa, the guerrillas responded by declaring three days of celebration in the areas under their control.

■ **Building 3, Room 1: Vida de la Radio Venceremos Durante la Guerra** (Life of Radio Venceremos During the War). On the green table to the right are pieces of a radio transmitter similar to the one used to blow up General Monterrosa's helicopter. The generator was used to power the radio during the war. The drawings on the wall were created in 1983 by Salvadoran schoolchildren in exile in Honduras.

On the middle table are hand-held transmitters and recorders used by Radio Venceremos reporters to report from all parts of the country. Guerrilla reporters amazed listeners with their ability to roam to even the most tightly controlled parts of El Salvador and report on events under the nose of the military. The Casio lap-top computers were used to keep track of the number of lives and armaments gained and lost in battles. On the wall to the left are photos of underground tunnels used to hide radio transmitters, protecting them from detection and making it possible to broadcast throughout the country.

■ **Room 2: Centro de Memoria Historica**. The green antenna was used to transmit radio signals from northern Morazán.
■ **Room 3: Cabina de Transmisión de la Radio Venceremos** (Radio Venceremos Transmitting Room). This mockup of Radio Venceremos' transmission room shows how the original room used cardboard egg holders to minimize noise. Notice the FM and AM transmission signals painted in red. *(Take 3a C Pte out of town to the west; Tues-Sun 9am-12pm, 1-5pm; $0.60 for Salvadorans, $1.15 for foreigners, $0.25 for children and ex-combatants)*

Details
■ **Buses: Sabanetas (332a)**, every hour until 2:50pm, 15km, 30min. **San Francisco Gotera (332a)**, every hour until 2:50pm, 90km, 2hr.
■ **Festivals: January 21-22** San Sebastián. **August 13-15 (14)** Virgen del Tránsito.

Ciudad Barrios

Pop. 27,000
159km from San Salvador
37km from San Miguel

Ciudad Barrios Then
The original Potón name for this town was Cacahuatique, meaning "Hill of the Cocoa Gardens," but it was changed in 1913 in memory of a prominent local coffee farmer. Although this small northern town was the army's strongest outpost in the northern part of San Miguel during the civil war, the city suffered repeated street battles. The nearby coffee cooperative was occasionally the focus of guerrilla attacks.

Guerrillas positioned themselves on the slopes of Cerro Cacahuatique, five kilometers to the east, and launched periodic raids on the town. When the FMLN became entrenched in Ciudad Barrios, the government sent in paratroopers and chased the guerrillas back into the hills with helicopters.

In 1982, rebel troops burned down all the public buildings in Ciudad Barrios. In November of the following year, a force of 500 guerrillas occupied the town, forced 87 government soldiers to surrender, and executed all of them.

Ciudad Barrios Now
The road to Ciudad Barrios from the Panamerican Highway passes through Moncagua and Chapeltique. The 15-kilometer drive heads up a beautiful

Geofredo Romero is a good person to know in Ciudad Barrios. After ten years in the US, Geofredo came back to his childhood home and discovered that Ciudad Barrios needed him. Now he teaches English in an academy for poor local students. He welcomes visitors to drop by with any questions about the area, or just to chat. Ask for him in town or call him at 665-9003.

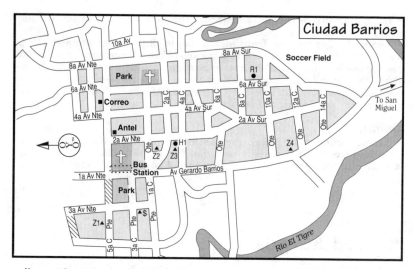

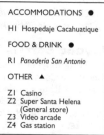

ACCOMMODATIONS ●

H1 Hospedaje Cacahuatique

FOOD & DRINK ●

R1 *Panadería San Antonio*

OTHER ▲

Z1 Casino
Z2 Super Santa Helena
      (General store)
Z3 Video arcade
Z4 Gas station

valley with steep green hills rising on either side. Streams cascade down the hillside to the left and run under the road. The fields to either side look too steep to stand in, let alone cultivate, but cultivated they are. Sit on the right of the bus if you can bear being so close to the steep drop-off.

The road emerges from the high end of the valley into the lush, rolling hills of northern San Miguel as it reaches Ciudad Barrios. In the city, kids on horseback ride up and down steep cobblestone roads which leave first-floor windows suddenly three meters above the street. Many residents work in the coffee plantations just outside of town. The huge Iglesia Roma looks like a warehouse complete with corrugated metal roof. A bust out front commemorates Archbishop Romero, who was born in Ciudad Barrios.

If you're really looking to get away from it all, Ciudad Barrios is a good escape. Come here to enjoy the cool mountain air and to talk with the residents—that is, if you can get past the curious stares. There aren't many tourists who make it this far off the beaten track, so you'll really feel like a visitor here. There's some good hiking in the nearby mountains; ask around for details.

Accommodations

Hospedaje Cacahuatique Lucky for you the only place in town is well-kept. Clean rooms and…(drum roll)…hot showers! To find it, head for the din of the arcade next door. *(Tel 665-9160; 3S $8.50, 3D $13.35, all with private baths, hot showers; laundry; noon checkout; cafetín)*

Details
■ **Buses: San Miguel (316, 317),** every 10 min until 4:30pm, 48km, 2hr.
■ **Festivals: January 10-11** Señor de la Roma. **June 26-29 (28)** San Pedro.
February 6-14 (13) Jesús del Rescate. **March 19** San José. **December 11-12
(11)** Virgen de Guadalupe Features the Procession of the Virgin, with people in
indigenous dress accompanied by band music and fireworks.

Index

PUCHASING INFORMATION

On Your Own travel guidebooks are sold around the world. If you local bookstore doesn't carry our guides, please write us for information on ordering by mail. If you would like to order copies for your bookstore or library, please contact us for a list of wholesalers and distributors in your area.

On Your Own Publications
PO Box 5411
Charlottesville, VA 22905 USA
tel: (804) 979-0050
email: jjb9e@uva.pcmail.virginia.edu